SUDDEN TRAUMA!

When Life Will Never Be the Same Again.

SUDDEN TRAUMA!

When Life Will Never Be the Same Again.

Revolutionary Principles for Healing
Emotional Wounds

Featuring real-life accounts of trauma recovery
from the files of Pioneer Clinical Traumatologist
Barry M. Richards

By F. Ross Woolley, Ph.D.
Susan Woolley, BSN, RNC, MPH
with Darla Isackson

GoldMind Publications
www.suddentrauma.com

Sudden Trauma!
When Life Will Never Be the Same Again
Revolutionary Principles for Healing Emotional Wounds
© 2000 F. Ross Woolley, Barry M. Richards

GoldMind Publications
3760 So. Highland Drive, Suite 500
Salt Lake City, UT 84106

Library of Congress Cataloging-in Publication Data
Woolley, F. Ross
Sudden trauma! : when life will never be the same again : revolutionary principles for healing emotional wounds / by F. Ross Woolley, Susan Woolley, with Darla Isackson.
p. cm.
Includes bibliographical references and index.
1. Post-traumatic stress disorder—Prevention. 2. Psychic trauma—Case studies. 3. Crisis intervention (Psychiatry) I. Woolley, Susan, 1940– II. Isackson, Darla, 1943– III. Title.

RC552.P67 W7 2000
616.85'21–dc21   00-020511

ISBN 0-9678150-0-2

Printed in the United States of America
10   9   8   7   6   5   4   3   2   1
GoldMind Publications
Salt Lake City, Utah

What Professionals Are Saying About
Sudden Trauma! When Life Will Never Be the Same Again:

Sudden Trauma may be a godsend to survivors of trauma who will at last be understood. And for the caregiver, there is now a place to turn for help.

> *John C. Nelson, M.D.*
> *Member, Board of Trustees*
> *American Medical Association*

I was deeply touched by this tremendously helpful book for trauma survivors. The clear approach for healing truly stands apart from the rest.

> *Stephen R. Covey, Ph.D.*
> *Author of* The 7 Habits
> of Highly Successful People

If this book had been available 20 years ago, I personally would have avoided years of pain. At the same time my profession would have better understood that journalists too are not immune from PTSD.

> *Chris Cramer, President*
> CNN INTERNATIONAL

This truly inspiring book with its real-life accounts of individuals overcoming seemingly insurmountable challenges, can help us to see our lives in a different, clearer, more objective perspective. It can give us the tools to face our experiences with spiritual renewal, appreciation, and strength to weather the adversity that is an inevitable part of life.

> *Al Katz, M.D., MPH*
> *Professor of Public Health*
> *Epidemiologist*

What a great opportunity for me to be guided through my trauma via clinical traumatology, of which I give my full endorsement. The positive directions in the book *Sudden Trauma* could foster the ability of survivors to thrive, and enhance their resiliency when traumatic experiences shatter their lives.

> *Stephanie G. Anderson, R.N. B.S.N.*

After my accident I was severely physically damaged, and with all the surrounding controversy I was left emotionally traumatized. It was like being lost in a dense fog. Clinical traumatology, as described in *Sudden Trauma*, acted as a beacon to guide me out of the fog and into the clear navigable situation which has allowed me to make healthy decisions. That "beacon" was so clear and strong that I want to be a part of the process: to be a worker of the lighthouse to help guide others out of the post-traumatic fog.

Robert A Zamelis, M.D.
Emergency Care Physician

The extensive experience that is detailed in this book, *Sudden Trauma*, is saying something very important. Through its numerous vignettes the book vividly depicts the impact of trauma and clearly describes an effective way to respond quickly to its impact. I highly recommend this book as a source of hope and information to those who are interested in or have been affected by trauma.

Daniel Rapp, M.D.
Neuro Psychiatrist

In twenty-plus years of claims management experience I've never seen anything work so consistently well as clinical traumatology with its precise health care directions. *Sudden Trauma* could make a world of difference to those who read it.

Scott Kelly,
Risk Management Claims Manager
Intermountain Health Care, Inc.

Sudden Trauma, which includes the unique experiences of trauma survivors, is most helpful. It is a rich resource book of specific principles for all who have experienced trauma as well as for those who are working with or caring for them.

Eugene Gibbons, DSW
Founding Dean
BYU Graduate School of Social Work

Contents

Acknowledgments

We express deep appreciation to the survivors who have shared their experiences in this book. They have patiently answered questions, offered feedback, and cooperated in every way to make the book as accurate as possible.

Leading the list of others who have worked to help get the book completed, polished, and promoted is Debbie Bake, whose enthusiasm and tireless proofreading have made a real difference. We appreciate the ongoing encouragement of colleagues, including Kimberly Dickinson, Daneen Booth, Marianne and Merlin Baker, Lee Glines, Joe Bennowitz, Steve Pohlman, Carolyn Williams, Britanny Bown, Kevin Bezzant, and Gordon Hansen.

Clearly, the writings of James Allen have made a singular difference on the emphasis given to this work, along with the more contemporary enlightenment from authors of the books mentioned in the preferred reading list. The review and endorsement of the manuscript by Chris Cramer and Stephen R. Covey is of inestimable value, as is also the incredible design and brilliant book cover artwork by James Fedor. We also appreciate the cooperation and help of Chris Cramer's secretary, Leslie Coppess, and Stephen R. Covey's secretary, Patti Pallat.

And finally, it is important to mention that the counsel of John Wesley's mother characterized the overall objective of this work. She said, **"Avoid whatever weakens your reason, impairs the tenderness of your conscience, obscures your sense of God, takes off your relish for spiritual things . . . [Or] increases the authority of the body over the mind."** As this book goes forward, it is our hope that the limitations of this effort for promoting health and well-being will be brought to our attention so that the work can be steadily improved. It is our desire to develop and pass on increasingly effective ways to heal the emotional wounds suffered by survivors of trauma.

Preface
F. Ross Woolley

SUDDEN TRAUMA! When Life Will Never Be the Same Again was written for survivors of trauma and those who love them and care for them. The insights given resound with common sense, yet *Sudden Trauma* is not a traditional self-help book. Instead, it is a resource of timely information and a guide to assist individuals to find the additional help they may need. It is my desire that this work will encourage those who are struggling.

The decision to participate as an author of *Sudden Trauma* was driven by a continuing belief that much of the negative emotional impact from traumatic events can be prevented with *timely and appropriate* intervention. As a behavioral scientist and epidemiologist (epidemiology is a science dealing with the origin, spread, and prevention of disease and health-related problems) my training and professional experience have led me to conclude that trauma affects far more people than is commonly believed. Interestingly, some people appear to be almost immune to the emotional or nonphysical consequences of trauma while others, even though physically unscathed, may develop signs and symptoms of severe emotional disturbance. If left untreated or undertreated, up to one-third of those exposed to traumatic events will develop Post-Traumatic Stress Disorder (PTSD). Previously thought to be the exclusive province of soldiers who experienced combat, battle fatigue, or shell shock, PTSD is now recognized as a problem that may affect individuals who experience *any* traumatic event. Those who have not had firsthand traumatic experiences such as those graphically described in this book may find the disruptions to people's lives that occur from such emotional wounding hard to believe. Terrifying nightmares, flashbacks, panic attacks, memory loss, sexual dysfunctions, and personality changes are but a few of the more overt symptoms of PTSD.

Unfortunately, my wife Susan and I gained our experience with PTSD firsthand. The facts surrounding the stalking, murder, and hostage siege that occurred at the Alta View Hospital's Women's Center on September 20–21, 1991, in suburban Salt Lake City, are widely known. Susan was one of the hostages. There were numerous press accounts, appearances by victims on nationally televised talk shows, and a made-for-TV movie entitled *Deliver Them from Evil* featuring Teri Garr (playing Susan) and Harry Hamlin. For those not familiar with our story, I present a brief summary below as an example of how emotional wounding can occur even when little or no physical injury occurs:

Richard Worthington, a mentally deranged father of ten, broke into the hospital seeking retribution from a doctor who had performed a tubal ligation on his wife two years earlier. His anger seemed to have been triggered by the fact that his wife signed the consent for the procedure without his permission. At the beginning of his rampage at the hospital he forced Susan and another nurse, Karla Roth, at the point of a 12-gauge shotgun into a dark parking lot. While Susan stood helplessly by, he shot and killed Karla with a .357 magnum revolver. Then he took Susan, another nurse, two infants from the nursery, a laboring mother, her husband, and her sister hostage.

For the next eighteen hours he continually threatened the hostages with the guns and with a bomb that had the explosive power of forty sticks of dynamite. Periodically he fired shots to intimidate and frighten the hostages as well as those who waited on the outside. Four hours into the siege, my wife attended the mother as she gave birth on the floor of the office in which Worthington had barricaded himself and the hostages.

During this time the families of the hostages were kept in an abandoned fire station located about 150 yards away from the hospital. Ostensibly the reason for keeping the families sequestered was to prevent them from being intruded upon by the media. However, there were police officers located at the entrances who were told to keep the families there unless they were leaving the area altogether. In effect the families were being held as "emotional hostages" not only by the acts of the gunman but also by law enforcement and other authorities.

Through the efforts of hostage negotiators, and to a large degree the persuasion of Susan and the other hostages, Worthington finally surrendered and gave himself up to a SWAT team stationed outside the barricaded office suite in the Women's Center. Although there had been only one visible "injury," the murder of Karla Roth, the nature and extent of the emotional injuries suffered by the hostages, as well as those who were closely touched by the event, have proven to be profound. The number of people whose lives were forever changed by the events of those two days is hard to calculate; conservatively, the figure could run in the hundreds.

In the weeks and months that followed the incident, Susan and I groped for solutions to problems that seemed to be escalating out of control. The first few days were almost surreal as we tried to reconcile what was happening. We met with others in a large group session conducted by a Critical Incident Stress Debriefing (CISD) team the day after the siege. Some of those who had been invited to attend said they "didn't really know why they were there," indicating that they could deal with the situation *just fine* on their own. Others broke down and sobbed as they tried to recount the horror of having been a hostage or having a baby or loved one held for eighteen hours not knowing from moment to moment whether they would survive the madness. Some who had worked in vain to try and resuscitate the murdered nurse in the emergency room were devastated by their inability to help one of their own. From the outset it was clear that many were going through a personal hell that others did not understand.

In the coming days and months there were some natural alliances formed among those who felt they needed help. The CISD people made it clear that they were only available for a few days and beyond that, people should seek their own counselors. We joined a small discussion group led by social workers from the hospital. From the outset, however, they stated that the magnitude and duration of the problem were beyond their scope.

Susan and I were contacted by a friend who had been the director of the Division of Mental Health in Hawaii and with whom we had become acquainted when we lived in Hawaii in 1990. His question to me was not the expected "How are you?" Rather, it was "Are you getting the help you need?" My reply was, "I don't know. There are people trying to help, but I really have the sense that they don't know what to do with us." He put us in touch with Dr. Frank Ochberg, an eminent psychiatrist at Michigan State University, a pioneer in the treatment of PTSD. Frank made two trips to Utah in the next few months, paid for by Intermountain Health Care, owner of the hospital. His visits brought remarkable relief to us and to those with whom he met on those too-brief visits. The problem was, once he left there was nobody to carry on the work with us. We had his book *Post-Traumatic Therapy* and the book *Victims of Violence*, but were still in need of someone to guide us.

As Susan tried to deal with her feelings in her own way, I wanted to help and became increasingly depressed at not being able to "fix things and make them all better." Unfortunately, I was experiencing my own problems with recurring nightmares that included watching the hospital blow up from the bomb carried by the killer. We were growing steadily apart and unable to communicate. Even though we loved one another, we were overwhelmed with trying to deal all at once with the stressful effects of

- the criminal justice system,
- opportunistic "helpers,"
- my not being able to concentrate when I returned to work immediately following the incident,
- sleep deprivation,
- "therapy" groups that were formed primarily to gratify the need of some individuals to become "insiders," and
- the never-ending attempts by the media to get a scoop.

The weeks turned into months, with Susan not able to return to nursing for fear of a panic attack that would jeopardize patients' lives. In my frustration at feeling I was no longer needed or important to her recovery, I made an appointment with an attorney to discuss a divorce. The day before that appointment was to be kept, I canceled it, realizing just how unhealthy the situation had become and that divorce would merely compound the difficulties.

Finally, nearly a year after the hostage crisis, we started seeing a psychologist who was a colleague. He was at first uncertain of the propriety of our working together and establishing a suitable patient-therapist relationship. After serious soul searching and his decision to consult with Dr. Frank Ochberg and others on how to deal with our PTSD-related problems, Susan and I started several months of rebuilding our relationship and dealing with the aftermath of the trauma that had affected us both deeply but differently. We will ever be grateful to Dr. Leonard Haas for his professional and personal support that made it possible for us to begin to heal and move on.

In 1994 we moved back to Hawaii where new jobs awaited us. Susan had not done any clinical nursing since the night of the hostage crisis. With the promise of help and support from old friends and colleagues in Hawaii she was able to return to the profession she so much loves, that of bringing new lives into the world. It took a while, but she was finally able to overcome her fears and she proved to herself that she could again function as a competent professional nurse.

What happened next is truly remarkable. One afternoon, while looking up a phone number in a Salt Lake City directory which we had taken with us to Hawaii, Susan saw a listing for the National Institute for the Prevention of Post-Traumatic Stress Disorder. Having experienced most of the negative effects that accompany PTSD, the inference that it could have been prevented was intriguing. On an impulse she called that number, and so began what has developed into a relationship that has impacted many lives. Barry Richards, the president of what has now been renamed the Wound and Injury Recovery Center of America, had in fact worked as a member of the initial trauma team at Intermountain Health Care's largest hospital. While there he and several of his colleagues, physicians, nurses, and administrators developed a traumatology program. Richards had left the hospital's employ, but continued to develop and refine the protocols that are today the IRO-STEPS© tutorial (educational) tools. (IRO stands for Injury Recovery Orientation.) Those tools are emphasized in this book and are the basis of Richards's current work with survivors of trauma.

After a number of telephone conversations and study of the literature Richards sent us about his work, Susan and I came to recognize that the information he provides up front to help people avert the disastrous consequences of PTSD are in large measure what we had to discover on our own through much trial and far too many errors. Our questions to him were, "Where was this information when we needed it? Why wasn't it made available to us? Why are so many trauma survivors suffering needlessly?"

Several months later a major crisis occurred in the hospital where Susan worked. She consulted with the management and human resources personnel and they agreed to have Barry come to Hawaii to work with those who were affected. In a word, we were impressed. Richards's grasp of the needs and feelings of those who had been traumatized, as well as the specific tools and information he provided to help them understand and deal with the issues they were facing, was radically different from the uncertainty and confusion we had experienced in our own situation. We were struck by the proactive nature and clarity of his approach. Since that time we have had the opportunity to work with Barry Richards and meet and speak with many of the clients he has helped. His track record is remarkable.

In this book you will find examples of different people who received help from Barry Richards, functioning in his role of clinical traumatologist. The term itself sets a professional traumatologist apart from the bulk of those who deal with trauma survivors. Typically, emotional wounds of survivors are ignored until the survivor develops serious problems that are either the symptoms that forewarn of the condition or are the actual manifestation of PTSD. The strategy of clinical traumatology is to resolve these potential problems early on before they fester into a psychological abscess that may never heal. The case accounts show that the IRO-STEPS intervention should ideally begin as soon as possible following the injury or traumatic event. However, we present striking evidence that the STEPS tutorials are valuable even when begun years later.

Because of our own experiences and the evidence we have gathered concerning the effectiveness of clinical traumatology, Susan and I have attempted to apply our professional expertise to the task of helping produce this book. Barry Richards has graciously cooperated, making available his material, refining the text, putting us in touch with his clients, etc. Darla Isackson is both a co-author and the editor, and comes to the project for similar reasons. In the aftermath of a serious accident, without the benefit of prompt, definitive help of the kind described in this book, persistent emotional wounds created havoc in her family, including a divorce four years later. Although now happily remarried, Darla understands too well the long-term destructive power of unresolved emotional trauma.

It is our sincere desire to help other survivors of trauma avoid the suffering and family disruption we have felt so strongly. These negative effects are largely preventable through the timely acquisition and application of the information available through clinical traumatology as presented in this book. Intense experiences can help us to put things into perspective, to organize our priorities and determine what really matters. Eventually that happened to us and we have healed. By following these same principles I believe others can, too.

I will end this preface with the letter Susan wrote to her family while being held hostage. It is intensely personal, and I share it with you in hopes you will recognize the grief and pain our family experienced—and the potential for healing from such pain through the sound principles in this book.

> *My Dearest Husband and Family,*
>
> *Many thoughts and feelings have been racing through my head all night. The overpowering emotion is that of love for all of you. I have made many mistakes in my life that I wish I hadn't, but they seem quite insignificant in light of what has been going on tonight.*
>
> *One right thing I did, which I have never regretted for even a moment is marrying Ross and together bringing five choice children into mortality. Each of them has enriched our union and brought many blessing into our lives.*
>
> *I certainly am not looking forward to dying at this time, but I really do not feel fear. I'm not really sure what exactly the emotion is I feel. I have prayed that the Lord would help us through this and all I can say at this time is that it is in the Hands of the Lord.*
>
> *One time while [Richard Worthington] was in the other room, four of us knelt in prayer. Although we have prayed for deliverance we will just have to be patient and accept what comes. We really don't have a lot of choice.*
>
> *I miss you and wish so much that this wasn't happening and we were together, safe, and at home. Tonight I witnessed death and then birth within about four hours and it reminded me again of the eternal nature of things... Life is eternal and I have no doubt about it.*

You know, it's strange to me that for so many years I've seen in movies, etc. that when you are faced with death you have a flashback or an instant replay of your life. I haven't experienced that at all. My only thoughts are of my family and the deep love and gratitude I feel for each of you. I'm usually anything but poetic but I've been thinking about two songs. One is "Love One Another" and the other is "You Are the Wind Beneath My Wings." And you have all been that for me.

Please never forget my love for you. It is eternal. Go on with your lives as you would, had I been with you. In fact, try to do even better.

Saying thank you doesn't sound like much but it's the best I can come up with at this moment, so it will have to do. Please be happy. Love always,

(Unsigned)

Susan's letter was left unsigned because she felt she would be surrendering her faith and acknowledging there was no hope left if she finalized the letter with a signature. Little did she know she would survive, yet because of the trauma—*life would never be the same again.*

———•———

Introduction

- A bomb explodes in Oklahoma City killing 168 men, women, and children.
- A shooting spree in Littleton, Colorado, leaves thirteen dead, a nation stunned.
- A multi-car accident wipes out a family of three and injures seven others.

Every two seconds in the United States an accident or trauma shatters lives, limbs, and dreams. Medical trauma teams using the latest technology are keeping many people alive in miraculous ways. However, mounting research indicates that *quality of life* for those saved is questionable unless health care providers give more attention to emotional wounds. Untreated *emotional* wounds are causing alarming delays in physical healing. More long-term disabilities and problems can be traced to emotional wounds than to physical injuries. *Sudden Trauma* will explain the latest developments in effective aftermath care that can prevent these current trends. **Trauma survivors could be receiving that care right now, but they are not.**

Few Will Escape

Catastrophic events and physical injuries are only two of many sources of emotional wounding. All those involved in a horrifying event are at high risk for emotional wounds, whether they are physically injured or not. Close family and friends of the survivors may suffer even greater emotional trauma than those directly involved in the incident. Parents and spouses of those who are killed or severely injured are especially vulnerable. When we consider the current rates of accident-related injury and death and the probability of exposure to violence and natural or manmade disaster, there is little chance any of us will escape unscathed from some form of significant emotional trauma.

Real People, Real Suffering, Real Triumphs

Sudden Trauma! When Life Will Never Be the Same Again tells the stories of real people. With one exception, their actual names are used. Whenever possible, their stories are in their own words. They have "been there, done that, and felt what it's like" to suffer and then to benefit from the tutorial guidelines of clinical traumatology. They willingly share their experiences with the hope of helping others triumph over the turmoil created by traumatic events.

For example, at age eleven Gene Hockenbury lost his parents and sister in a car accident. Gene suffered for forty years until he found long-needed knowledge by engaging in the clinical traumatology tutorial process. Gene's experience is contrasted with the rapid recoveries of Larry Rowley and Art Van Tielen who received immediate attention. Rowley suffered an industrial accident that left him a paraplegic, but received effective emotional care tutorials in the emergency room and during his hospital stay. Van Tielen, a bus driver who was involved in a fatal accident, benefitted from **Specific Early Educational Directions** (SEEDs) initiated at the accident scene and was back to work in days. Phil Webber, a police officer shot in the line of duty, returned to work against all odds because of timely response to his nonphysical wounds. All received the STEPS tutorials.

What Are the Tutorials?

Tutorials are key educational procedures that teach people how to more effectively manage the emotional aftermath of trauma. The instructions are empowering and are based on the messages of the STEPS acronym (**S**timulate positive thinking, **T**ackle unrealistic fears, **E**ducate about options, **P**lan for the future, and **S**top unrealistic expectations).

The individual stories by trauma survivors presented in this book illustrate how several of the tutorials are employed and it will become clearer, as you continue to read, what principles underlie the tutorials. A more complete explanation of the basic six tutorials is contained in Appendix 1 pp. 147–69. Also, in Appendix 1 pp. 170–76 you will find a summary of the auxiliary tutorials. The Glossary contains explanations and definitions of terms used in clinical traumatology that are important in comprehending the tutorials more fully. The following concise descriptions of the six basic tutorials are presented to help the reader understand how the tutorials were used as the individual stories are recounted:

1. *Memory Bank* stimulates awareness of key thought processes that will promote the ability to bounce back emotionally.
2. *Psychic Energy Battery* provides the motivation to identify and engage the most effective sources of support during convalescence.
3. *Rule of Thumb* cautions against making major changes impulsively, i.e., changing residence, employment, marital status, etc., which often impede progress. The survivor is advised to seek professional guidance to assure that decisions in these areas protect their interests and give attention to long-term needs. (See Structured Settlements in Glossary.)
4. *Fear Wheel* identifies the five most common after-crisis fears and how their negative impact can be minimized.
5. *Basic Necessities and Human Stimulants* discusses the three basic human necessities: recognition, acknowledgment, and acceptance. It identifies the four critical stimulants: touch, talk, activity, and material possessions that are keys to thriving after surviving.
6. *Drivers, Fatal 5s and Injunctions* caution about unrealistic and problematic substitutes for learning and successfully using the IRO-STEPS to resolve the impact of life-changing events.

Bedrock Principles and Survival Realities
The people who share their experiences in this book, as well as all others who acquire the tutorials of clinical traumatology, are first introduced to the bedrock principles and survival realities. They are

Bedrock Principles
- Survival is only the beginning.
- Learning means less suffering.
- The sooner knowledge is acquired the more quickly complete recovery can be anticipated.

Survival Realities
- Life will never be the same.

- Complete recovery is both physical and emotional.
- Early response to emotional wounds is just as important as emergency care for physical injuries.
- Just because a person looks fine (or says they are fine) doesn't mean they *are* fine. No two people recover exactly the same and you cannot predict with any degree of certainty how long it will take for any survivor to recover.

Clear Directions

SUDDEN TRAUMA is not a conventional self-help book that relies on hyperbole and inflated promises for change that usually lead to disappointment. This book offers important information, simple assessment tools, and specific precautions and directions to minimize problems after trauma. It gives readers hope through information and direction for emotional wound healing. Clinical traumatology is not a panacea and is clearly not for those who want a "quick fix" or would prefer to shirk personal responsibility by expecting others to heal them. The information and the principles presented can be invaluable guides for those with the initiative and the presence of mind to apply them. This information is also of great benefit to loved ones of trauma sufferers and will help them to realize that psychological trauma is not the domain of the weak or ignorant.

This book does not diminish the importance of any service that promotes the healing of those injured or traumatized by a life-altering experience. It does, however, present a different focus and an approach to these problems that has been demonstrated to be effective. When the mind is fed with timely and appropriate information, there is no need for survivors to feel abandoned and helpless in overcoming trauma-related emotional problems. They *can* overcome the confusion, negativity, and frustration. Many previously without hope can now benefit from revolutionary strategies for emotional wound healing. These strategies employ the miracles of spirituality and promote the understanding of actions that must be taken to heal emotionally. Let the personal accounts and the strategies used in helping the survivors-turned-thrivers presented in this book be a beginning for change to an early intervention process. At last it is possible to be freed from the frightening uncertainties that come about after *sudden trauma . . . when life will never be the same again.*

1

Why Clinical Traumatology?

Chapter one may prove most interesting to professionals and caregivers. Trauma survivors may wish to skip this rather technical chapter and move on to chapter two where the real-life stories begin. Chapter one offers important background information—an overview of clinical traumatology strategies, scientific substantiation for them, reasons why preventive care for emotional wounds is essential, and why it has been abandoned by the current health care system. This chapter demystifies the resistance to the field of clinical traumatology and gives concrete reasons for making it available to all trauma survivors.

The Need Is Real

There are some who challenge the existence of emotional wounding and see themselves as virtually immune to the effects of trauma and horror. Even as survivors they feel emotionally fit and able to bounce back rapidly from traumatic experiences with great resilience. For example, a public transit supervisor stated: "I can't understand why all the difficulty. I personally witnessed the death of several teenagers in a fiery car crash without suffering any [disturbing aftermath] problems. People just need to be responsible and move on with their lives."

Perhaps his ability to witness and take in stride such an event was due to genetics combined with his environmental situation. He had a strong marriage and supportive family, reinforcing spiritual convictions, advanced education, secure employment and financial stability. Consequently, he had difficulty identifying with many of the obstacles that less fortunate survivors face. But we live in a less-than-ideal world where optimum circumstances are rare and where the chance of experiencing severe life-disrupting events seems to be escalating.

Yet, unless the present system is improved, few are likely to benefit from Specific Early Educational Directions (SEEDs), a strategy for the timely healing of emotional wounds that result from trauma. Failure to promptly deal with emotional trauma adds to the cumulative effect of the stressors that lead to physical and emotional disability—too often *total* disability. Although there are no hard and fast statistics, evidence from a number of studies of individuals exposed to horrific trauma, both civilian and military, indicates that approximately one-third can be expected to develop Post-Traumatic Stress Disorder (PTSD).[1] This percentage does not include those who have lesser, but still troubling, symptoms.

Cumulative Effects of Traumatic Events

Another concern is the potential for the cumulative effects of several smaller traumatic events to trigger PTSD or related problems. There is substantial evidence of an increased likelihood of post-traumatic stress problems when there is a history of previous stressful incidents that have not been adequately dealt with. Unfortunately, sexual abuse and/or rape is a common type of prior stressor. Obviously, rape by itself is capable of leading to PTSD. However, there are many individuals who suffer the horror of sexual assault and deal with it on their own. Whether or not they developed PTSD or any of the other trauma-induced emotional disturbances at the time is often a moot point since many were unable or unwilling to discuss the event and few received any sort of help. Consequently, having been previously wounded, they are especially vulnerable to developing PTSD from a subsequent traumatic event. The issue of previous emotional wounds that have not healed is discussed in the Memory Bank Tutorial (see Appendix 1, pp. 147–48).

---

[1] Trauma disorder high, new survey finds, *Science News.* 148, no. 26-27 (Dec. 1995): 422.

The Paradoxical Triad of PTSD

Although more will be said about the effects of PTSD and other trauma-related emotional wounds, there is a paradox (an illogical self-contradictory situation) that has been noted among PTSD victims. It has been described in various ways, but a useful concept is the "Paradoxical Triad of PTSD."

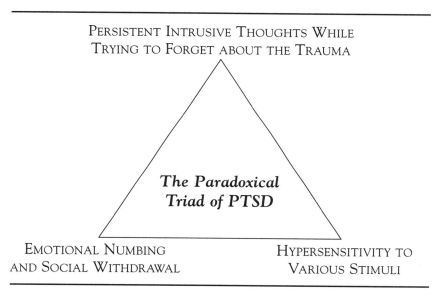

Figure 1
The Paradoxical Triad of Behaviors
in Post-Traumatic Stress Disorder

As you consider the diagram above, it is important to realize that all three of these effects are occurring simultaneously. It is easy to see why people who are developing the symptoms of PTSD believe they are going crazy. As the trauma survivor consciously tries to suppress their memory of the event, they continue to have intrusive thoughts about it. Sometimes these recollections, commonly referred to as flashbacks, are so vivid they feel as though they are actually reliving the event. At the same time they suffer dulled thinking, often reflected in a lack of expressiveness in writing, speaking, and personality, e.g., laughter, tenderness, appropriate anger. To complicate the emotional picture further, someone with PTSD will also overreact to various stimuli. One common example is a heightened startle reflex, where even relatively small noises or movements of objects may cause a panic reaction. These effects have a strong relation to chemical changes associated with emotional trauma.

Clinical Traumatology Can Prevent Disability through SEEDs

Most people who continue to suffer in the wake of horrifying events do so because they do not know how to change things for the better. No one has informed them that effective strategies exist to prevent most emotional wounds from progressing into psychological and physical impairment.

Clinical traumatology, a sound approach to help those with trauma-related emotional wounds, uses educational strategies to prevent the downward spiral toward disability. It arms trauma survivors with clear insights that increase the odds that they will thrive and not merely survive. The acronym SEEDs, which stands for Specific Early Educational Directions, is used instead of terms such as "therapy," "treatment," or regimen. This is done to highlight fundamental differences between clinical traumatology strategies and those employed by traditional psychotherapists, psychiatrists, and clinical social workers. Traditional methods are based on a "disease" model and often result in treatments that continue for years and tend to create dependencies and stigmatize the patient. The SEEDs approach of clinical traumatology is proactive. Rather than waiting for serious symptoms to develop, it is initiated as soon as feasible following the trauma (ideally within twenty-four to seventy-two hours). It encourages development of the skills necessary to continue the healing process after survivors have completed the structured education with the clinical traumatologist. Barring preexisting psychological disturbances, this educational process can be completed within thirty days.

Conventional Crisis Intervention Is Inadequate[2]

Current conventional crisis intervention, referred to as Critical Incident Stress Debriefing (CISD), is frequently inadequate because

---

[2] Beverley, R. and Meldrum, L., Does debriefing after psychological trauma work? *British Medical Journal*, Vol. 310: No. 6993, pp. 1479–81, June 1995.

1. It provides little in the way of continuous support. By definition, these interventions are brief and do not equip the survivor with the necessary tools to successfully deal with the array of problems that emerge after the intervention.
2. Crisis intervention fails to respond to the specific needs of the individual survivor: traditional group counseling and/or psychotherapy may not stop problems from progressing toward disability because they

- foster dependency,
- lack precision in delineating problems,
- are not uniform in the application of appropriate interventions for specific problems, and
- often stigmatize the survivor.

Tana Dineen's book *Manufacturing Victims: What the Psychology Industry Is Doing to People* clearly identifies the need for a change of direction in dealing with emotional wounds.[3] Endorsed by the popular radio talk show host Dr. Laura Schlessinger, Dineen's book points out failures that have occurred from traditional methods. She documents the common promotion of dependency on psychotherapy and the overuse of psychotropic medications (drugs that alter mental activity). Unfortunately, she recommends no effective alternatives.

What Is the Answer?
Clinical traumatology is an effective alternative for treating the survivors of traumatic events, providing the right care at the right time. Its primary tool is education as opposed to mental illness-oriented psychological interventions.

The discovery in the middle of the nineteenth century that simple hand washing could prevent the spread of infection heralded a great breakthrough in the medical field. However, the process was not without controversy. Between 1847–1849, Ignaz Phillipp Semmelweis, an Austrian physician, made a startling discovery in regard to the fever that killed thousands of women after childbirth. He proved that the doctors who went from one patient to another

---

3 *Manufacturing Victims: What the Psychology Industry is Doing to People*, 2nd Edition, by Tana Dineen, Robert Davies Publishing, Montreal, 1998.

performing their examinations without cleaning their hands were spreading the fever. Semmelweis's discovery was not popular among his colleagues and he was ridiculed for the rest of his life. He died a broken and despondent man in an insane asylum in 1865.

In the 1980s, hospital trauma teams pioneered clinical traumatology as early definitive intervention. It has been refined over the last two decades into the structured, uniform, precise response of the SEEDs strategy. Some health care professionals have greeted this new approach with the same skepticism and ridicule that beset Semmelweis's discovery. However, just as the act of hand washing stops the spread of infectious disease, the educational directives of clinical traumatology, expediently and appropriately delivered, prevent psychological crippling. Clinical traumatology represents a true breakthrough in the response to emotional wounds.

Clinical Traumatology—a Powerful Healer

Clinical traumatology's educational tutorials stretch the mind, instead of shrinking it. They encourage individual initiative, correct thinking, progressive self-reliance, and supportive attention from those who care the most, i.e., family and friends. The process of learning and applying these tutorials is incorporated into a structured format known by the acronym IRO-STEPS©. **IRO** stands for: **I**njury **R**ecovery **O**rientation. **STEPS** stands for **S**timulate positive thinking, **T**ackle unrealistic fears, **E**ducate about options, **P**lan for the future, and **S**top unrealistic expectations.

The concept behind preventing deaths from cancer through early intervention is identical to preventing PTSD though clinical traumatology. There is no known method of immunizing against either cancer or emotional trauma, but waiting to take action until the symptoms are pronounced, greatly diminishes the likelihood of a successful outcome. Informing people about the benefit of the SEEDs approach in clinical traumatology can be compared to informing women of the benefits of regular Pap smears. Women adopted this practice on a wide scale largely because of educational messages recommending it. Such education promotes detection of cancer in its earliest stages when treatment will be the most effective. Pap smears show evidence of cellular changes indicative of cancer long before there are symptoms of which a woman is aware. If surgery is performed at this point, the chances are high that the woman will have the same life expectancy as she would if the cancer had never occurred. As a direct result of these efforts, this testing procedure has become common and the number of deaths due to cancer of the uterus and cervix have dropped remarkably.

The same principles apply to emotional wounding. Immediately following the traumatic event a person usually doesn't recognize or doesn't understand the indicators of serious problems that lie ahead. However, if an appropriate assessment can be made and definitive intervention (SEEDs) started as soon as possible (ideally within twenty-four to seventy-two hours), there is a high probability of averting PTSD and/or other post-trauma emotional problems. In medical terms this type of prevention is referred to as secondary prevention. This means that the disease (or trauma) may not be preventable, but by early intervention its destructive processes can be arrested and its debilitating effects eliminated or greatly reduced.

Survival Training

The SEEDs process of attending to emotional wounds before they have grown to the point of causing irreparable damage might also be likened to the addition of survival education to the regular flight training given to military pilots. If forced to bail out over some unknown, hostile territory, flying skills alone wouldn't enable a pilot to stay alive on the ground. It is ridiculous to suggest that pilots take along a survival expert as a passenger on every flight or carry an extensive reference library to read when they are in serious trouble. Time has proven the value of thoroughly training military pilots in survival skills early on. They know their survival may depend on their ability to anticipate and deal with events as they arise. The ability to thrive after serious emotional trauma depends just as surely on being trained in what to expect and receiving the right information and the right tools as soon after the event as possible.

Self-Reliance Is the Foundation Principle

Clinical traumatology is the antithesis of those therapeutic approaches that tend to leave the therapist in a dominant role and promote dependent relationships. Clinical traumatology assesses the needs of survivors and presents them with carefully developed educational packages (tutorials). The tutorials consist of timely and precise directions tailored to meet the needs of each individual. These educational road maps give survivors the power to understand what is happening, or might happen to them. They forewarn survivors and empower them to make needed adjustments and changes that will let them maintain or reclaim their sense of control. The aphorism "an ounce of prevention is worth a pound of cure" applies to all preventive health care including clinical traumatology.

Following the SEEDs approach, clinicians introduce specific tutorials chosen from the forty-five available, according to survivors' individual needs. The basic six should ideally be completed within thirty days after onset of the trauma. Unfortunately most traditional therapies often do not even *begin* within thirty days. Delays are predicated on the current philosophy of "wait until it breaks and then try to fix it." These tutorials (described briefly in the introduction) form the basis of clinical traumatology's educational strategy. The basic six present those principles essential to thriving rather than merely surviving.

Family First

Another striking difference between the focus of clinical traumatology and conventional psychotherapy (in addition to timely emphasis on education and self-reliance) is the clear direction to strengthen family bonds, especially primary relationships. Husbands, wives, and/or other key individuals in the recovering survivor's life are invited to participate in appropriate parts of the tutorial process from the beginning. Couples learn and grow together; consequently, the whole process draws them closer. They are encouraged to support each other at every step and to devote significant amounts of time and energy to the process of nurturing each other. Among the many benefits to having such supportive relationships is that it reduces the chances that the loved one will suffer unnecessarily through secondary wounding and their own subsequent debilitation. Another is the sense of mutual growth that offsets the losses that inevitably accompany traumatic events. (If there were no perceived losses, events would not be traumatic.) Both survivors and their caregivers are taught to harness the positive potential of the mind to their mutual benefit. Without these mutual discoveries, the traumatic event often creates a chasm between survivors and their caregivers.[4]

The Mind-Body Connection

Clinical traumatology finds its primary power in the actuality of the mind-body connection. Biological researchers have largely ignored James Allen's significant work in the area of mind-body connection because he was a philosopher and not a clinician. However, scientists are providing increasing evidence that supports much of Allen's work. His discourse entitled *Effect of Thought on Health and the Body* effectively states in lay terms what has recently been recognized through physiological research. Health care practitioners should recognize his work as a truly pioneering contribution to understanding the effects of trauma—psychological as well as physical—on human functioning. Some call his work the all-time most significant contribution to modern-day disaster recovery efforts. Allen's classic works (which are available in two volumes: *As a Man Thinketh* and James Fedor's collection of Allen's sayings, *As a Man Thinketh, Volume Two*) expand on the same thesis, that of the incredible power of the mind. Both books continue to inspire millions.[5, 6]

Problems Faced by Survivors Are Not "All in Their Heads"

As a result of the mind-body interactions there are fundamental differences between the help needed by those emotionally wounded by sudden traumatic events and those who seek psychological help for other reasons. Prior to the horrifying experience that turned their very existence into chaos, the majority of trauma survivors had been reasonably content and functioned normally. Events over which they had no control suddenly changed their lives forever. The resulting sense of powerlessness caused measurable biochemical and

---

[4] Leske, J. S. and Jiricka M. K., Impact of family demands and family strengths and capabilities on family well-being and adaptation after critical injury, *American Journal of Critical Care*, Vol. 7: No. 5, pp. 383–92, 1998.

[5] *As a Man Thinketh*, by James Allen, DeVorss & Company, Marina Del Rey, California, 1983.

[6] *As a Man Thinketh, Volume 2*, by James Allen, compiled by James H. Fedor, Mind Art Publishing, Bountiful, Utah, 1988.

physiological changes in the brain and other organs of the body. Some of these changes are instantaneous—including the familiar "fight or flight" response associated with psychoactive substances such as adrenaline (epinephrine). Other changes are progressive, taking days, weeks, or even years to develop. The longer people go without obtaining definitive help, the greater the chance they will experience long-term disability.

The complications that emerge are not confined to *observable* behavioral abnormalities and psychological problems such as eating disorders, chronic fatigue, or heightened startle reflex. Complications often include what appear as purely physical ailments. For example, medical researchers have long recognized the relationship between certain types of stress and problems such as colitis and acute gastric ulcers.

Extensive Data Support Training the Mind to Take Control

Recently there has been a growing interest in the obvious interaction between the brain and the body's immune system. A scientific discipline called psychoneuroimmunology (PNI) now documents the process by which the central nervous system affects (mediates) the interrelationships between stress, the endocrine system (the glands that secrete hormones), and the peripheral immune system.[7]

There is mounting evidence that stress does alter the body's ability to fight off infectious agents. For example, caretakers of loved ones who have Alzheimer's disease have been shown to suffer disruptions of the immune system. These people have impaired responses to influenza vaccines and show delays in the healing of wounds, most noticeably following surgery.

Studies show that individuals who develop PTSD have altered levels of many neurochemicals such as dopamine, serotonin, and norepinephrine.[8, 9] Extensive data document the interrelationship between traumatic stress and a host of effects on the body as a

---

[7] Altman, F., Where is the "Neuro" in psychoneuroimmunology? A commentary on increasing research on the "neuro" component of psychoneuroimmunology. *Brain, Behavior and Immunity,* Vol. 11 pp. 1–8, 1997.

[8] Yehuda, R., Resnick, H., Kahana, B., et al., Long-lasting hormonal alterations to extreme stress in humans: normative or maladaptive? *Psychosomatic Medicine,* Vol. 55, No. 3, pp. 287–97, 1993.

[9] Charney, D. S., Deutch, A. Y., Krystal, J. H., et al., Psychobiologic mechanisms of posttraumatic stress disorder. *Archives of General Psychiatry,* Vol. 50, No. 4, pp. 294–305, 1993.

whole. Such data cry out for an increased emphasis on effectively dealing with aftermath problems before they spiral out of control. Aftermath problems are synergistic in that they feed off one another in a cyclical fashion; early intervention can break the cycle. The best way to initiate change is to harness the power of the mind. Therefore, the key to clinical traumatology is training the mind to take control.

Research indicates that individuals who develop PTSD have altered levels of many neurohormones and changes in many of the nervous system's regulatory mechanisms. In addition, other organs of the body are affected in response to hormonal alterations that disrupt normal interactive balances. A brief explanation of some of the terms and concepts related to these changes is provided in Table 1. If this is an area of interest we encourage further study. The critical concept, which facilitates emotional healing, is that early intervention using the power of the educated mind can arrest or reverse the measurable physiological changes produced by emotional trauma. Extensive data from hundreds of research studies document the relationship between traumatic stress and a host of systemic effects (changes throughout the body). It is clear from the research that these effects are far more complex than was believed just a decade ago.

Hormones (chemicals produced by specialized tissues throughout the body) have the unique characteristic of affecting organs other than the one which produces them. For example, most people are familiar with the hormone insulin that regulates the amount of sugar in the blood. Diabetes mellitus is the disease that results when the pancreas is no longer able to produce insulin in sufficient quantities to control blood sugar levels.

Adrenaline (also called epinephrine), a hormone produced by the adrenal glands (which are located at the top of the kidneys), targets many organs in the body. The term "adrenaline rush" is very common, referring to the sensation of power and speed that occurs when one is startled or threatened. This hormone protects the body against threats by producing a burst of energy and a mental sensation of excitement and power. There are many documented cases of people performing superhuman feats when stimulated by a surge of adrenaline. Hormones are powerful substances. When emotional trauma goes unattended, the resulting hormonal imbalances can cause serious physical and emotional damage.

The brain and the body communicate with each other primarily through hormones called neurotransmitters. These chemicals act as runners that deliver their message by locking onto specialized sites on individual cell membranes called receptors. Many different systems in the body respond to specific neurotransmitters. Many receptor sites are in the brain, but many others are located throughout the body. Variations in mood associated with the brain are communicated to many other places in the body. Research has demonstrated that emotions are not isolated events that occur in just one place in the brain, but are truly systemic.

The actions of the neurohormones are closely regulated. This is accomplished by a series of feedback mechanisms that allow the body to respond to excesses or deficiencies. By producing blocking agents (certain hormones that counteract the effects of others) and controlling the absorption or utilization of these neurohormones, the body is able to regulate the effects of these chemicals. The body of an individual with an emotional wound is unable to do this because the feedback systems that ordinarily work well are trying to respond to signals that are extreme. Consequently, either too much or too little of a given chemical may be present with corresponding variations in the emotions that are tied to the particular messenger. In Table 1, six major neurohormones are described with their common nonemotional effects and those which impact the brain and cause emotional disturbances. It cannot be overemphasized that the physical effects of emotional trauma are powerful and, if left unresolved, can lead to serious illness or even to premature death.

As you look at Table 1, consider the paradoxical triad of PTSD shown in Figure 1, (page 3). You will note that abnormal levels of the six hormones shown in Table 1 can account for virtually all of the problems associated with the three points of the triangle. Decreased levels of serotonin and elevated levels of noradrenaline are associated with disturbances in thinking patterns. Endorphins can produce emotional numbing which can be coupled with the perception problems and chronic fatigue from serotonin. Panic attacks and hypersensitivity can be precipitated by cholecystikinin and adrenaline elevations. This listing is an oversimplification, because the interactive effects of these chemicals and thousands of others all come into play. Also, the effects of these hormones tend to vary from person to person. What should be clear is that the presence of abnormal levels of these hormones, which are associated with emotional trauma, can produce many frightening and bizarre symptoms.

Table 1

Stress-Related Neuro-Active Chemicals: Their Effects on Emotions and Other Non-emotional Effects

Chemical and Status	Non-emotional Effects	Brain/Emotional Effects
Dopamine (elevated)	Changes in blood pressure	Causes severe emotional disturbances resembling schizophrenia
Cholecystokinin (elevated)	Alters function of pancreas and gallbladder resulting in digestion and glucose level disturbances	Released to counter effects of endorphins produced during stress; overproduction associated with panic attacks
Noradrenaline (elevated) Also called norepinephrine	Vasoconstrictor (constricting of blood vessels) reduces blood flow to arms, legs, and G.I. system; causes cold, clammy hands and feet and nausea	Affects mood with wide swings between depression and excitement; affects information processing and produces hyperarousal
Endorphins (elevated)	Opium-like substances that increase threshold of pain, similar to other analgesics	Causes emotional blunting that is similar to tranquilizing/euphoric effects of codeine or morphine
Serotonin (decreased)	Powerful vasoconstrictor (see noradrenaline)	Affects sleep patterns and moods, and alters perception
Adrenaline (elevated) Also called epinephrine	Increases heart rate and respiration; vasoconstriction	Causes feelings of panic, energy, high state of arousal (fight or fight)

Millions of People and Billions of Dollars at Risk

The real-life accounts in this book provide convincing documentation of the effective healing methods used in clinical traumatology. These people all completed the Injury Recovery Orientation-STEPS at the Wound and Injury Recovery Center located in Salt Lake City, Utah.

Widespread use of the SEEDs approach can lighten the financial burden currently incurred in treating those diagnosed with PTSD. Even more importantly, unnecessary suffering can be minimized or eradicated for millions of people.

Key Points Covered in the Introduction and Chapter One

Trauma-related emotional wounds can occur among those who are close to an event but were not physically injured. Witnessing a horrifying incident may lead to serious emotional difficulties including Post-Traumatic Stress Disorder.

In our society, trauma is a frequent occurrence. It is so pervasive that there will be few people who do not experience it firsthand, or have family or friends who have been traumatized.

Exposure to trauma has a cumulative effect. People who are victims of repeated emotional trauma may suffer serious emotional difficulties following a relatively minor event.

People who develop Post-Traumatic Stress Disorder often exhibit symptoms that appear to be illogical. The paradoxical triad of PTSD is explained (at least in part) by the release of neurohormones that cause seemingly contradictory behaviors.

Conventional "Critical Incident Stress Debriefing" (CISD) techniques are of questionable value in meeting the needs of trauma survivors. These interventions are too brief to provide an understandable foundation upon which most individuals can build.

Debriefing counselors provide support for only a few days, and survivors must often wait until serious complications develop before obtaining additional help. This "wait until it breaks" attitude means that serious problems often emerge which, if dealt with sooner, might have been avoided.

Clinical traumatology is an approach to dealing with emotional wounds caused by traumatic events. It is based on the principle of SEEDs—which stands for Specific, Early, Educational Directions. It differs from the traditional illness model because it relies on self-directed educational principles rather than the illness-based interventions commonly used by mental health workers.

Clinical traumatology (CT) requires survivors to accept responsibility for their own healing process. It specifically avoids providing rationalizations for an individual's behavior. It also avoids the tendency for people to become dependent on medications and/or the individual providing help.

The educational approach of CT uses a series of educational tutorials designed to teach the survivor how to anticipate and overcome the common problems of emotional wounding. The tutorials follow an educational model called the IRO-STEPS strategy. This acronym stands for Injury Recovery Orientation, to Stimulate positive thinking, Tackle unrealistic fears, Educate about options, Plan for the future, and Stop unrealistic expectations.

In the majority of cases, by intervening early using the SEEDs approach it is possible to prevent the later onset of serious debilitating emotional problems such as PTSD.

The SEEDs strategy is based upon the application of six basic educational tutorials which provide trauma survivors the tools necessary for best possible recovery from emotional wounds. These six tutorials are supported by the bedrock principles and survival realities.

Above all, the IRO-STEPS tutorials recognize the family or personal caregiver as key to success in the healing process.

The mind-body connection is presented to show that a high percentage of what we feel and the way we think can be altered by biochemical changes that are the result of trauma. However, these alterations can be arrested—and to a large degree reversed—by the application of appropriate mental and physical exercises taught through the IRO-STEPS tutorials.

Because of CT's revolutionary approach, there are some who challenge the value of the IRO-STEPS strategy. However, the principles upon which CT is based are time honored, with a substantial amount of current scientific research demonstrating their efficacy.

2

Collision!

Ideally, a clinical traumatologist will assess a survivor's specific concerns and needs and offer the tutorials within seventy-two hours of a traumatic event. In Gene Hockenbury's story, however, the principles of clinical traumatology open the way to healing forty years after his trauma.

That fateful Sunday, May 5, 1957, the Hockenburys—all eight of them—packed into a white 1957 Ford and started the drive home from Grandpa's place. Eleven-year-old Gene felt uneasy as his father picked up speed on the narrow road. His father's next decision changed all their lives forever. He swerved into the oncoming traffic lane at the base of a bridge, intending to pass a slower vehicle.

Collision

Out of nowhere came a black hammer of hell that produced a sound as deafening as the roar of a thousand trains and reduced their car to half its size. Darkness, thick and impenetrable, engulfed the horrified boy.

When Gene regained consciousness after the head-on collision, he was choking, coughing, and gasping for air. Twisted metal trapped his legs and terror gripped his whole body. Moments of absolute chaos felt like an eternity to Gene before someone grabbed his outstretched arms, freed his legs, and pulled him out of the wreckage.

Lying on the bridge, he could hear his oldest brother, Bill screaming out his name, "Help me, Gene! Help me." But Gene couldn't even help himself. He heard a man say, "Two of them are dead." Gene cringed, paled, and bargained with God. He would do *anything* to straighten out his life—even quit cussing like a sailor—if God would make it *not* be his mom and dad that were dead.

Emergency Room Terror

When multiple trauma cases arrive simultaneously, the hospital emergency room is pandemonium to the untrained eye, and it was terrifying to eleven-year-old Gene. The seemingly random movements of the staff as they attend to their duties and the clutter of waste materials gathering on the floor gave the impression of utter confusion. In reality, there was remarkable order to the shared responsibilities of patient assessment, wound cleansing, applying pressure dressings to stop external bleeding, starting IVs, stitching minor wounds, obtaining X-rays, and checking vital signs.

The doctors issued orders, directions, and questions that none of the children understood and the parents never gained consciousness to hear. Bright lights, sterile instruments, white coats, stethoscopes, and needles swirled together in Gene's mind. The patients' physical injuries were the focus of all this activity. The children were hurting, blood-smeared, dirty, cold, and covered with glass fragments. Some were thirsty, blurry-eyed and agitated, confused and cold with fear. They were experiencing their worst nightmare—a nightmare that seemed endless.

Left Alone

Gene, whose injuries were not life threatening, soon felt set aside, abandoned. The five surviving children were moved to separate rooms and now all Gene felt was loneliness. No one in his family could offer comfort or assistance. They were all hurt more seriously than he was.

When he learned that his six-year-old sister died at the scene and his mother died two hours afterwards, Gene wished he could have died too. Even before his father died two weeks later, he felt betrayed. He doubted that God had listened to his prayers on the bridge and he felt more alone than ever.

The Aftermath

The story of Gene's life after the accident reveals the most important reasons for this book. It graphically illustrates the necessity of providing more adequate interventions for those who suffer the ravages of injury, trauma, and other horrifying events. Here are his words:

The day after my mother and sister died was the worst of my life. There was no one to hug me, hold me, or comfort me. I felt totally abandoned and incredibly small. It was like standing on a mountaintop hollering and crying for help, but never receiving any reply, hearing nothing but the echo of my own voice. I felt I was in a time warp ... a vacuum.

Released from the Hospital

Three of my siblings were in the hospital for months, but my brother and I were treated, released, and sent to stay with my alcoholic aunt and uncle. That summer hangs in my mind like a hodgepodge from hell ... my aunt pushing me up to my father's casket and saying, "Take a good look—this is the last time you will ever see your dad!" ... my uncle in a drunken rage wringing cats' necks and throwing them against the barn ... my brother and me desperately searching through the pelting rain and terrifying lightning of a dark, stormy night for my aunt and uncle who had left us alone and gone to a bar ... awakening with nightmares of grinding metal, blood, screaming voices—and no one to comfort me or explain what I was going through.

But the worst part was the guilt. In my childish mind I was sure that the accident was my fault. If I had refused Mom's request to ask Dad to take us to Grandpa's, or maybe if I had yelled at Dad to slow down, it wouldn't have happened. I thought that if I could only find a way to get back to that stinky old house in Illinois where my parents fought constantly, everything would be okay. I would have given anything in the world to have things back the rotten way they were before the accident.

A New Home, But Not a New Life

In the fall my aunt from California offered me a home. I guess I thought things couldn't get any worse, so I accepted and left the rest of my family and moved to California. But my aunt and uncle didn't get along any better than my parents had. If that wasn't bad enough, my teenage cousin had mental problems and was in and out of sanitariums. "You've driven her crazy!" my aunt would say to me. I was smart enough to know my cousin's problem couldn't be my fault, but my aunt's words still hurt me.

I didn't get along from day one with my other cousin. He was nine months younger than I, and my aunt and uncle's favoritism toward him made my life hard to bear.

Since my Mom had started me in school early, I graduated from high school at the age of sixteen. I felt that my aunt was glad to get me out of the house. I floundered for a few years, wasting my accident settlement money, drifting from one job to another. Memories of the accident still plagued my mind, haunting me day and night, but I wouldn't discuss it with anyone. Instead, I denied my feelings, numbed out, and hid from the pain.

Side Effects of Trauma Continue after Marriage

I finally met Emy. Always searching for a better life, I had joined a church and Emy showed up in a Sunday School class I was teaching. I was immediately taken with her smile. About a year later I married her and settled down. I was twenty-three. However, I took all my emotional baggage into the marriage, and our family life became a reflection of my problems.

It still took me hours to get to sleep at night. Intrusive thoughts, such as "What if we hadn't gone to Grandpa's?" "Why did this have to happen?" "Is there anything anybody could have done to prevent it?" "What is going to happen to me now?" pounded through my mind day and night. Once asleep I awakened frequently, screaming in the night, my mind still tortured with replays of the accident. Sleep deprivation led to a deep fatigue which made all my other problems worse. I functioned poorly at work, with my family, in everything I tried to do. Feelings of loneliness and worthlessness led to resentment and frustration; I was fearful and belligerent.

About ten years into the marriage, physical symptoms compounded my personal and family dilemmas. I had severe stomach problems, loss of equilibrium, and blurry vision. Neurologists found nothing wrong physically; I was told my problems were emotionally based.

I always felt that my symptoms had something to do with the accident. However, when they continued for years, I thought if I suggested that possibility, others would say, "That happened so long ago. Why aren't you over it yet?" Some employers did say, "If you can't concentrate and function well, you're out of here!" So I had current stress added to my unresolved past stress. I didn't realize it then, but I was on the road to disability in a system that perpetuates dependence.

The feelings of helplessness that began when I couldn't help my brother after the accident ballooned into hopelessness. I couldn't help my brother then and I couldn't help myself now. I thought perhaps divorce would ease my burdens. However, by then I had children and my concern for their well-being made me want me to work things out

Eventually I saw a social worker who tried to resolve my problems, but the experience was a disaster. He made no connection between my condition and the trauma I suffered so long ago and I felt no compassion from him. He told me not to come back if I couldn't talk about something besides my physical ailments, so I quit going. Although I could see no progress, I kept going from one therapist to another because I recognized I needed to come to terms with my traumatic life history. Still, flashbacks and intrusive thoughts along with bloody nightmares continued to shatter my dreams of a better life. The stigma and humiliation of repeated referrals for psychiatric treatment compounded my feelings of inadequacy. Furthermore, none of the medications or psychotherapy made any real improvement in my life.

Family life was miserable and I became reclusive. I was prone to anger, so all of my relationships suffered. At home I continued to isolate myself from Emy and the children. I couldn't handle rejection, so I insulated myself from it. Family members didn't have a chance to reject me because I rejected them first, especially around any kind of holiday. Previous attempts to improve relationships suffered each time I lost my temper—I would burn any bridges we had tried to build. For whatever reason, I thought I should have died in the accident; if my family wanted me out of the house now, I somehow felt it would be justice.

A Breakthrough

In the late 1980s I began counseling with a therapist whose sensitivity to my long-term suffering became more and more helpful. At the end of each session, she offered a therapeutic hug. It took more than a year before I could accept one. The warmth and kindness of those hugs—my first ever—started a small degree of healing and kept me going back for treatment. I began to accept myself as a whole person—including all I had done to mess up my life to that point and the actual good that was inside me. I quit running away from myself and my problems. I had believed that if I couldn't do something perfectly, there was no reason to do it at all. This false belief had robbed me of motivation. Finally, it gave way to understanding that **any** progress is worth the effort, and I found the motivation to work consistently to resolve my problems. However, in spite of my hard work, my painful issues continued to wreak havoc in my life. Eventually, this therapist moved, and I lost the only trusting relationship I had ever allowed.

The Saving Connection

A few years later I met Ricki Landers, an accident survivor who has multiple sclerosis and works for the rights of the disabled. The first time I met her she said, "I don't give handshakes, I give hugs." She was a very helpful, supportive person. Ricki attended a presentation by a clinical traumatologist and suggested I go to see him. Because of her concern for others, I trusted Ricki and felt compelled to follow her advice. The referral she gave me was to Barry Richards at the Wound and Injury Recovery Center. I set up an appointment.

Taking Responsibility

The whole approach of that first appointment was different than any I had experienced. I found I was going to learn how to help **myself.** In the past I had always looked for relief from pills and professionals. I wanted someone else to fix my problems, or God to personally come down and heal me. I had never before been taught that it was possible to take responsibility for myself.

The traumatologist told me up front that he would be "in my face and on my case" (a description of his strategy to hold me responsible for my own progress). And that was all right. My previous experiences had taught me that confrontation was a necessary component for success. I could handle it as long as I felt sincerely cared about and wasn't being patronized. I simply needed to feel that my life and my progress mattered more than the "bottom line."

Being Heard

I was asked to describe my background, and together we pinpointed my major concerns. They were:

- Will I ever be able to overcome the long-term chronic symptoms and impairment the trauma had caused?
- Will I ever be accepted the way I am by those I care about?
- Will I once again be able to perform sexually?
- Will I lose my home because of the financial burdens I have accumulated?
- When will unwanted thoughts, ideas, and fears leave my mind?
- How long will my worry, remorse, grief, and other negative feelings go on?

With this list completed, I felt listened to, heard, and understood. This approach made more sense to me than previous experiences of being diagnosed and labeled mentally ill.

Thriving or Surviving?

Next I was given a copy of Richards's book, Thriving after Surviving.[1] *The title of the book made me reflect on the turmoil of my entire life. I confessed to Richards, "The idea of thriving has never even occurred to me. At very best I have been merely surviving, and it has been a fight to survive. I have wished thousands of times that I had died in the accident, and I have cursed God for letting me survive."*

———•———

Gene had been tolerating and enduring incredible confusion and misunderstandings about the accident. The painful consequences he had been experiencing came from not being prepared to deal with normal aftermath side effects, not being educated about those side effects, and not being given the tools of understanding necessary to learn "how" to thrive. Of course, Gene had not been old enough at the time of the accident to fully benefit from the tutorials even if they had been available at the time. The principles of clinical traumatology must be transmitted to children by way of informed parents or other loving caregivers who receive the tutorials and then give the children the reassurance and information appropriate to their understanding and maturity level.

---

[1] *Thriving After Surviving: How to Overcome the Devastating Emotional Wounds Caused by Accidental Injuries,* by Barry M. Richards, Hartley Communications, Murray, Utah, 1990.

Tools of Recovery

In that first appointment Gene was introduced to the tools of recovery—simple directions which are summarized in the Injury Recovery Orientation-STEPS (IRO-STEPS) which are

Stimulate positive thinking (by reading and memorizing upbeat thoughts, quotations, and lyrics)

Tackle unrealistic fears (by kicking unwanted ideas from the mind)

Educate about recovery potential options (such as learning new techniques to deal with anger)

Plan for the future (Gene was advised to keep the job he had but look for a better job)

Stop impractical expectations (such as expecting to win the lottery to solve financial problems)

At that point Gene understood on a deeper level that this wasn't going to be a hand-holding, nose-wiping, or shoulder-to-cry-on experience such as he'd had before; nor would it concentrate on delving into his past. Instead, clinical traumatology would provide highly focused "laser" learning and specific directions. Ideally, it is the right care given at the right time to prevent the festering of emotional wounds. It would have been best if Gene could have received clinical traumatology information and directions right after the accident. However, even forty years later he could still make use of them and start to take charge of his life. This approach made sense to him.

Normal Aftermath Feelings

Gene was given a list of the normal side effects and reactions that recovering survivors from trauma often experience, especially when their emotional wounds go unattended. They are

- Despondency, depression, or ambivalence about life
- Loneliness
- Sense of worthlessness
- Guilt about surviving when others died or experienced more serious injury

- Anger toward spouse, family, employers, and others
- Resentment toward those who fared better
- Humiliation over disabilities or dependency on others
- Frustration and desperation that the recovery is not progressing fast enough
- Feeling that there is no possibility of relief from pain
- Abandonment by those who initially showed interest, love, or care
- Fright or fear about things that are not understood or over which there is little control
- Emotional numbness or insensitivity
- Self-destructive feelings
- Maliciousness
- Belligerence
- Self-deprecation (condemning self)
- Helplessness about the current situation
- Hopelessness about the future

Gene (like many other survivors) readily identified with the above side effects of trauma. He said:

As I read that list I was stunned. It was a description of my whole life story! I was frustrated to learn that most of this could have been largely avoided had I received prompt and precise attention to my emotional wounds. Fortunately, it wasn't too late to overcome the pain of the past.

"The healing won't come from the outside," I was told, "but from within as you change your ways of thinking. And we're not just talking about positive mental attitude, either."

That was a relief! People had always told me that all I needed to do was think more positively, but that was bull. How could I? I had no understanding of what was going on or why I was controlled by such strong negative feelings.

Now I could see that most of my negative feelings and behaviors had come from my distorted thinking in regard to the aftermath side effects. What a revelation to learn that my problems were normal for the kind of trauma I had experienced! I learned that people who are educated about the normal and predictable side effects of a horrifying event don't withdraw or condemn themselves for having them. They don't interpret the symptoms and feelings they are having to mean they are weak or stupid or crazy as I had. Correct information stops the downward spiral. Consequently, the side effects experienced by informed people are usually short-lived—unlike mine, which had snowballed into unmanageable long-term problems.

Guilt Swept Away

We talked right away about the worst of my guilt issues—feeling that the accident was my fault, so I really didn't deserve to live. I finally understood that it was a distortion of reality to think there was a connection between carrying out Mom's request to ask Dad to take us to Grandpa's and the accident, or between me not yelling at Dad and the accident. I felt a thousand pounds of weight drop off my shoulders. I could finally see logically that I was not the driver, I was only a child. Consequently, I had absolutely no control over what happened. That knowledge was like pure oxygen that allowed me to breathe deeply, finally free of the guilt and confusion.

Psychological "Pus Pockets"

I learned that my thinking and judgment in all areas of my life had been contaminated by my intense unresolved feelings. A good example was my uncontrollable fear whenever one of my family was late. I would begin sweating and my heart would start racing because I felt certain they had been in an accident and been injured or killed. The later they were, the more upset and angry I would become.

Gene was informed that his untreated emotional wounds had abscessed into "pus pockets" that disrupted his psyche whenever something happened that remotely reminded him of his trauma (consciously or subconsciously). When told he would learn how to clean out the pus pockets so he could let go of the false judgments he had been making against himself and others, he felt reassured.

Mind Is the Master

James Allen's writings describe how to make this healing process work. Allen says,

"Mind is the Master-power that molds and makes,
And man is mind, and evermore he takes
The tools of thought and shaping what he will,
Brings forth a thousand joys, a thousand ills—
He thinks in secret and brings to pass:
Environment is but his looking-glass."

As a Man Thinketh, Volume 2, James Fedor's compilation of James Allen quotes, was given to Gene during his assessment. He claims it became a key resource in helping him overcome the consequences of the distorted thinking that had plagued him for so long.

What We Know Determines How We Feel

A tape-recorded talk by Stephen R. Covey (author of *The 7 Habits of Highly Effective People*) was another key.[2] Covey explains that we define each new experience by referring to all previous experiences stored up inside our minds. Consequently, an event never affects any two people the same way. For example, because of the differences in past experiences, the death of a pet may seem to be an insurmountable loss to one family member and only a minor inconvenience to another. Gene describes in his own words how Stephen R. Covey's message affected him:

I learned that I couldn't expect to make major changes in my response to outward events unless I stored new data in my mind. It would take new information to change the meaning I had assigned to things. Covey referred to this change as a paradigm shift. To illustrate such a shift he told of being annoyed by several unruly children during a subway ride in New York. When he appealed to the father, who was making no effort to control them, he learned that the man's wife had just died and he and the children were on their way home from the hospital. Overwhelmed with grief, the father was unable to cope with the disruptive behavior of his distressed children. In an instant this new information changed Covey's paradigm, which in turn dramatically changed his feelings and actions.

Covey's illustration provided the data I needed to make my own paradigm shift. I could see that each truth I learned could change my

---

2 *The 7 Habits of Highly Effective People: Powerful Lessons in Personal Change*, by Stephen R. Covey, Fireside, 1990

perspective, and consequently change the way I felt and the way I responded to things.

I sat quietly after the tape was turned off. I was overcome with emotion as I realized I had been given an idea that could make all the difference in the world. It was a sacred experience, a turning point. Now I could hope, for the first time in years, for a better future, for a better me. It struck me like a bolt of lightning that what Richards had explained to me was true: **I had within myself the power to change my life**. Teary-eyed, I sat there for about five minutes before I could compose myself. For the first time I made the clear connection between my thoughts and beliefs and the quality of my life. The idea struck me forcibly that I was really in control. This concept was like a door opening—freeing me at last from the false belief that I, by myself, could never change anything. So simple, yet so profound. Just what I had been searching for.

I finally said, "Do you mean to tell me that **I can change my circumstances simply by getting more information and changing the way I think?** Do you mean to tell me that all the while I've been relying on pills and doctors, and thinking that divorce might be my only avenue of escape, that **I have the power to change the situation and the way I feel about myself just by getting new facts and by taking control of my own mind?**"

This knowledge gave me an acute awareness. If I was ever going to get beyond the garbage I'd been struggling with for forty years, if I was ever going to get well, I had to implement what I had just learned. I needed to carry through with these ideas and learn to apply these principles. I walked out of the office with hope, committed and ready to work.

Sources of Support—the Three-legged Stool

When Gene came back for his first tutorial after the assessment process, he was introduced to the three most vital sources of support. Like a three-legged stool, all three sources of support are necessary. They are

> **Emotional support**—from those nearest and dearest to us, i.e., our caregivers (family, friends, and other loved ones), usually living within the walls of our own homes

Educational support—specific and precise directions and information from knowledgeable medical and health care providers

Encouragement—support from other survivors who have experienced and successfully recovered from a similar traumatic or horrifying event

Gene's reaction illustrates the importance of a spouse's support and understanding:

Early in the assessment process it was recommended that my wife Emy be involved and receive the same information I was receiving. I was told that her emotional support would be vital to my full recovery. I had never had close emotional involvement with Emy. Because of my background I didn't dare trust her, didn't dare trust anybody. I didn't want to weigh her down with my problems, and sometimes when I did try to reach out to her she would resist. But Emy came with me to the series of tutorials that continued to change my perspective. Feeling her willingness to be involved, that she really cared, gave our marriage new life and promoted my healing.

Several weeks later we had a particularly hard situation to deal with. For the first time in the many years we had been together, Emy nurtured me through it. I really felt her love instead of feeling like I was in trouble with her. I felt her concern, her caring. It made a strong impression on me and I felt very supported. In turn I was able to transmit that loving feeling to my daughter, an ability I had been lacking in previous years.

Accepting Emy into my life, finally realizing I could trust her, was a real breakthrough. She had always said she loved me, but now I was beginning to feel her love. She confirmed for me that I was important to her, that I really mattered.

Painting Life Pictures with M&Ms
*I began to feel kind of like an artist. I had had this tragedy and I survived. Now I could paint my own picture from here and finish my own ending. Now I was in control, especially after learning the "M&M" exercises for unwanted thoughts. The M&Ms stand for **M**emorize to **M**inimize intrusive thoughts and **M**aximize progress. Right away I began memorizing good thoughts and found I **could** control my mind and choose to "change*

the channel" from intrusive negative thoughts to something good I had memorized. Since I can't think about two things at once, "changing the channel" overrides the circuit and gets me out of fixating on the accident or other traumas in my life. All the good thoughts I memorized also contributed to a new mind set. As I was told so often, "The mind once stretched with a new idea never returns to its original dimensions" [Oliver Wendell Holmes]. My mind was expanding.

Two Memorials

Vietnam veterans have a memorial that symbolizes their commitment to help others avoid the hell they went through. Toward the end of the tutorials I was given the assignment to follow that pattern to memorialize my progress from survivor-to-thriver. The memorial I created was twofold. First, I decided to use my mind as a memorial, changing bad thought patterns that had nearly destroyed me to good ones that could create a better life for me and my family. I would also write my experience in hopes of benefitting others. The second memorial is in Butterfield Canyon where I frequently ride my bike. There, in a special place, I can pray, sing songs, meditate, and envision the best way of righting the situation I had been living with for so long.

Visiting Butterfield Canyon helps me in my ongoing quest to develop an enduring faith—even through trials and tribulations. I'm learning that God respects His own natural laws and He respects people's choices and doesn't often interfere with consequences. I'm now a hospice volunteer and am trying to strengthen my belief that God is there even when everything goes wrong and life seems hard to bear.

Within ninety days following the involvement of Gene and his wife with clinical traumatology tutorials, Gene's entire demeanor and outlook on life began changing dramatically. Gene has made continual progress: from sullen feelings of hopelessness and helplessness to enthusiastic interest in getting on with his life; from job dissatisfaction to more satisfying employment; and from dejected husband and father to committed family man. His wife Emy observed:

In past years, no matter how positive I tried to be, Gene was negative and would get mad and stay mad much of the time. The children would say, "What's Dad mad about this time?" I think that Gene was even mad at me for marrying him because he felt he wasn't good enough to be married to anybody.

But there has been a major change. One huge difference I've seen is that Gene comes out of the negative sooner, apologizes much sooner, things like this. We still get into the negative parts of life; everything isn't rosy yet. But now he can identify the negative and recognize that it's bad, and not get stuck in the feeling that everyone is against him as he used to do.

In that process of changing what had been a whole life pattern, Gene's visits to the Wound and Recovery Center steadily decreased. The more satisfying his marriage and family life activities became, the less he needed help. Within six months his Christmas celebrations were the most meaningful of his life. In his own words:

Five days after Christmas I went up Big Cottonwood Canyon, just below the Spruces campground, to go sleigh riding with my family. The brilliant blue sky was offset by an occasional fluffy cloud drifting aimlessly across the top of the mountains. The sun painted diamonds on patches of snow. But the best part of the scene was that my wife and I, my son, my grandchild, and my daughter were enjoying each other without bickering, without chaos.

It had been forty-one years since the accident, and suddenly the contrast of that engulfing black hammer of hell with the peace of the present seemed almost surreal. I drew my wife close to me. As we embraced I said, "this has been a great Christmas, and we can make next year even better."

The Best Gifts

This true spirit of Christmas peace, happiness, togetherness, and doing for others was finally there for us because of gifts I'd been giving myself for the past few months—the gift of self-control, the gift of peace without the pain of the past, the gift of health and happiness, the gift of progress in changing my thoughts and improving my life. These gifts hadn't been under the Christmas tree, but I knew they were real. I wrapped them myself, around every thought and feeling of my heart.

31

Key Points in Chapter Two

Emotional wounds that are not dealt with promptly and effectively can lead to a lifetime of serious problems. These unattended wounds are like infections; they fester and will poison the body. It is rare for a person who develops such wounds to be able to overcome them without help. Traumatized children need the guidance and reassurance of informed, supportive parents or other loving caregivers.

The list of negative behaviors and emotions common among trauma survivors who do not receive appropriate help are presented. Many people will experience some of these from time to time, but the emotionally wounded trauma survivor lives with many of them continually or intermittently. (For complete list, see Appendix 1, pp. 143–46.)

Feelings of guilt are typical in the aftermath even though trauma survivors realize intellectually that there was little or nothing they could have done to alter the events that led to the incident.

The power of the mind to heal itself when supplied with appropriate information and new behaviors is remarkable. This principle of the healing power of the mind is critical to the healing process.

Healing is achieved through education, emotional support from family and friends, and the knowledgeable encouragement of others who have also been victims of trauma but found ways to heal their wounds.

A key activity is memorization of uplifting and inspiring material. These memorized messages help to minimize intrusive thoughts and maximize progress. Consequently they have been referred to as "M&Ms."

Even though the ideal time to initiate the SEEDs strategy is within twenty-four to seventy-two hours following a traumatic event, or as soon as it is medically feasible, it is still possible to benefit from it years later. In Gene's case, over forty years had passed, yet he and his wife were able to change their lives dramatically by implementing the principles from IRO-STEPS tutorials.

3

Trapped!

Larry Rowley's story illustrates the benefits of early intervention beginning in the emergency room. As Larry learned firsthand, clinical traumatology, when appropriately employed, can minimize most serious aftermath problems and PTSD symptoms.

On a cold November Saturday afternoon in 1980, Larry Rowley sat on the front of a Bobcat mini-backhoe. He watched with fascination as the "arm" he controlled demolished a wall of a well-insulated cooler room at the site of his father's produce business. His father, Bill, was driving the Bobcat from his seat inside a protective cage.

An Inspired Rescue

Larry's fascination turned to terror when part of the heavy ceiling came crashing down on him. As a twelve-inch beam hit him across the shoulders, searing, blinding pain enveloped him. He screamed, "My back! My back!" Bill, who had been protected by the operator's cage, bolted over to Larry. He ducked under the beam, lifted the debris off Larry with his own back, then suddenly realized they were both trapped. If he moved an inch, the debris would crash back down on his son. But, if he did not move, how would they ever get help? No one else was in the building.

Out in the parking lot near the building, a friend who had delivered lunch to Larry and Bill was just leaving. As he turned the key to start his car, in his mind a quiet voice whispered, "You need to go back into the building." He argued with the voice, but finally listened and burst through the door just as the dust was settling. With Larry's screams ringing in his ears, he raced to the nearest phone and called 911, then ran back to help Bill and Larry.

Paralyzed

The arrival of the paramedics blurred in Larry's pain-filled mind, but the deep concern on their faces was clear. Within minutes Larry was strapped to a gurney and carefully positioned in an ambulance. Even today, Larry vividly recalls the ride from the accident site to the hospital. Although it was only a few blocks, the journey seemed to last forever. Each small bump in the road brought new waves of pain accompanied by a dreadful realization: there was *no* pain in his lower body. From the waist down he was completely numb. "What will Janet do?" twenty-two-year-old Larry agonized. He and Janet had been married only a year and a half. They were just getting used to each other and to their three-month-old baby. Life was getting better and better; would all that change?

At the hospital, the bright lights of the emergency room hurt Larry's eyes. As the medical personnel probed and prodded, Larry alternately screamed with pain or felt cold fear. Confused, panic-stricken, and filled with dread, Larry watched as they cut off his clothes. Multiple questions were hurled at him: "Where does it hurt? How much can you feel? How far does the numbness go?" His anxiety mounted.

Trauma Team at Work

Barry Richards had been on duty when the ambulance crew brought Larry in to the emergency room. After the initial barrage of questions was completed, Richards talked to him.

"Hi, Larry. My name is Barry Richards. I'm a member of the hospital's Trauma Team. Right now there are a lot of people here doing things to help you. Some of them you may never see again, but I am going to be with you a good percentage of the time from now until you leave the hospital. Remember my name: it's Barry, like strawberry, raspberry, and boysenberry—anything but dingleberry!"

Although unsophisticated, the comment had a precise purpose—to dilute the fear and insecurity Larry was feeling. He hung onto the name and the promise that Richards would stay beside him.

Focusing all his attention directly on Larry, looking him in the eye and anchoring his shoulder with his hand, Richards continued, "Everyone in here has a specific job to do and you are receiving the finest, top-priority attention. Together, with your help, we can get you through this ordeal with the best possible outcome."

When Richards used the phrase "best possible outcome" he was not promising that everything would be "okay." He didn't know for sure. No one knows how things will turn out for someone else. Instinctively, most people sense whether or not they are being told the truth, especially in uncertain circumstances. Trust engendered by forthright honesty can be a wonderful lifeline to sustain us in perilous times.

Selective Hearing

Richards continued, "I am going to be right here helping to explain who these people are and what they are doing." He then asked a question often forgotten in crisis situations: "How well are you understanding me?"

Trying to assess Larry's level of comprehension was crucial. With the body and the mind stressed to capacity by both internal and external stimuli, trauma patients typically become confused and distressed. Such situations sharply reduce normal comprehension and retention, increasing the probability of selective hearing. Patients more often than not let in only what they want to hear. The fact that Larry would remember little of what went on those first few hours was taken into consideration.

Reducing Anxiety

Continuing, Richards said, "Amazing things happen in here when we work together, Larry. Right now it's hard for you to think straight and believe what I am saying. But trust me; this will not last forever. Everything you learn from this point on can be of definite benefit to you."

Directing Larry's attention to a white marker board on the wall just beyond his feet, Richards observed: "Those are your vital signs—information that keeps everyone up to date on physical indicators of your condition. The nurse is charting them very carefully so that we can see how well you are responding to what is being done for you. Everything that happens here becomes a part of your record and will help us make your condition more stable."

This information, plain and simple, was immediately beneficial to Larry. It helped reduce his anxiety, change his thoughts, and diminish feelings of helplessness.

"Do you think you could help us?" Richards asked Larry. This question invited his participation and decreased his frustration and fear.

"Yes," Larry replied.

Very few patients say "No."

Family Support

In response to Larry's willingness to help, Richards said, "Right now you are hooked up to a lot of equipment that is really important: but I'm confident that there is something else that could be even more helpful. I'd like to bring your father in to see you right now, and then your wife as soon as she arrives. Is that all right?"

"Yes, I'd like that very much," Larry replied.

Although Larry may not have comprehended how this response was helping, he was doing himself a great service by moving his thoughts from fear of the unknown to positive interaction with those who cared about him. Larry's father, Bill, had arrived at the hospital with him in the ambulance. Shuttling between the waiting area and the emergency room, Richards had continually kept Bill informed of Larry's condition during those first tense minutes. Richards explained the technical procedures that were being carried out and why they were necessary. He provided the names of the doctors involved and told Bill where Larry would be taken following the first evaluation of his injuries. He explained his role as a hospital traumatologist and the specific role of each of the other trauma team members.

Orientation

Following these early reassurances, Richards explained the admission process, the layout of the hospital, and other important details. He informed Bill of the likely sequence of events for the first few hours and of the unfamiliar and intense feelings the family and loved ones could expect. Finally, he introduced Bill to the attending trauma physician who took him to see Larry.

When Larry's wife, Janet, arrived, Richards gave her much of the same information he had given Bill, letting her know she would likely experience an "emotional roller coaster" for the next couple of days. Knowing what to expect helped Janet and the other family members support each other as they combined their efforts for Larry's benefit. Consequently, in their first contacts with Larry they were able to be realistically reassuring and comforting—a far different scene than it could have been.

Mini-Miracles from Voice Contact

Typically, the connection between a trauma patient and family members is *first* made over the phone. At least seventy-five percent of the patients treated by Richards have quickly agreed with the suggestion that initial contact with family members be arranged using a speaker-phone. This facilitates conversation for those who might have difficulty holding the phone and permits the clinical traumatologist to hear and answer questions beyond the scope of the patient's knowledge or that the patient may not be thinking clearly enough to answer.

Those who opted not to have their family or close friends contacted in this way were worried about the reaction of these loved ones to the bad news or, sadly, were not able to name someone they felt close enough to call. But early connections made with a wife, husband, child, or parent provide the opportunity for encouraging words such as, "Honey, it's me and I've just had things explained. Hang in there. I'll be with you as soon as possible. Remember, I love you."

The loved one's voice most often steers the patient's preoccupation from uncertainty and pain toward something familiar and reassuring when it is most needed. Richards has noted that comforting words from a familiar voice almost always produce observable and measurable positive changes in the status of the trauma patient (such as the lowering of elevated blood pressure). Medical and technical procedures seem less threatening once contact with loved ones is established.

Reassuring Words and Directions

After Larry's brief visit with his father, Richards reinforced his previous statement of continued support. "Larry, there are several procedures the medical people need to conduct before you can be transferred to intensive care where you will be carefully monitored and stabilized. But I am going to be with you most of the time. I will let you know beforehand what to expect, what is next, and what you can do to help most with your recovery."

Immediate access to this information helped Larry understand the new realities he was facing so he could make smoother adjustments. These details helped stabilize the turbulent emotions that could slow or impede physical recovery. Such knowledge and direction can also inspire a determination and provide a way for survivors to gradually overcome even the most difficult obstacles they encounter in the recovery process.

Throughout his hospitalization, Larry and his family responded well to all of the specific directions and health care orientations that were provided. To help them avoid negative consequences common to the uninformed, they were given the "Dos and Don'ts" that apply to the aftermath of injury and trauma. (See lists of Dos and Don'ts in Appendix 1 pp. 179–84.) The sophisticated medical treatments and equipment used during Larry's hospital stay were explained. Other discussions encouraged a positive and mutually supportive attitude. They learned that a *realistic* positive attitude and family support during the healing process produce the best outcomes, that inappropriate or overly optimistic reassurances can be as damaging as pessimism. In Larry's words, here is what happened:

Before they took me into surgery, things had quieted down, the lights were dim, and all my family were gathered around me. We were better prepared and more peaceful as a result of the information we had received, beginning in the emergency room. That earliest information really helped us to help each other and, in my opinion, allowed me to feel more coherent, be able to talk openly, and be in a better frame of mind. I think it made a noticeable difference just before surgery, afterwards, and right up until the time I was transferred to the rehabilitation hospital.

No Sugar-coated Information

I have to admit that my rather unique circumstances worked to my greatest advantage. My spiritual convictions and close family relationships were invaluable from the very beginning. But even with all of that going for me, my life circumstances changed dramatically from the moment of my injury. At that point my family and I had to learn some very basic things. The educational process was especially beneficial to me and my wife as it related to what we could expect for the rest of our lives together. And the information wasn't sugar-coated, either.

―――――

The Link Between the Physical and the Emotional

Larry's entire family was taught about the impact emotional wounds can have on physical injuries—how emotions and stress are linked. Following injury and trauma certain physical symptoms are telltale evidence that nonphysical wounds need rapid attention—that the patient needs empowering information and direction. If emotional wounds are not attended to efficiently, complications and delays in ongoing physical recovery will likely result.

Probable Side Effects

The family was told of the probability that they would experience physical and emotional side effects of the trauma. The list of possibilities included headaches, dizziness, nausea, stomach and chest pain, loss of energy, restlessness, being easily annoyed, sleep disturbances, loss of appetite, and depression. (See Appendix 1, pp. 143–45 for complete list.) They were also told that the majority of these side effects usually go away within three weeks. They found it extremely valuable to know what was *normal* or typical so they knew what to expect. Braced with this information, Larry and his family were better prepared for the normal physical side effects and symptoms they experienced and didn't become unduly frightened by them. Still, they were oriented to the most common fears and their remedies. Unchecked fear is one of the most certain precursors of PTSD.

Fear and Homeostasis

Fear, including fear of the unknown, causes the release of numerous chemicals (such as the hormone adrenaline) into the bloodstream.

Because the chemicals are in the blood they are transported to all parts of the body, especially the brain. If they continue to be released for too long or in too large a quantity these hormones can overload the mechanisms that maintain a correct balance of psychoactive chemicals. For example, there are certain chemicals that promote actions such as excitability and others that help to calm us down. The key to normal functioning is for the psychoactive chemicals called "agonists" to act only as long as necessary to meet a specific need. When that need has been met, counteracting mechanisms—including the release of chemicals called "antagonists"—return the body to normal. This ability of the body to regulate itself and compensate for variations brought about by conditions that change from minute to minute is called "homeostasis." If fears persist, these chemicals (that are intended to allow the body to operate at a heightened level of awareness and escape threat) overwhelm the counteracting antagonist mechanisms, which become incapable of returning the body to normal. When that occurs, the body is no longer able to control pathways in the brain that are supposed to filter out unwanted (intrusive) thoughts and the impulses that cause impulsive behaviors.

Three Stages of Emotional Recovery

In a later tutorial Larry and his family learned about the three stages of emotional recovery that most survivors and their loved ones experience. This information helped them plan more effectively for the future. These stages are

Stage One: Survival Honeymoon—lasting from four to twelve weeks.

During this period, most trauma survivors have a great sense of indebtedness toward doctors and paramedics for their lifesaving expertise as well as to friends and relatives who offer help and support. Their sense of well-being is heightened by well-wishers and aided by medications that reduce pain and anxiety. Through this period of inordinate attention, survivors are generally protected from immediate stresses and demands and have not yet looked to the future. During this phase, survivors rarely grasp the full impact of possible physical limitations, changes in relationships, and lifestyle adjustments.

Stage Two: Adjustment Shock—lasting from a few weeks to years.

Recovering survivors experience diminishing attention from family, friends, and others and often feel isolated and abandoned. They become keenly, even obsessively, aware of physical changes, disfigurements, or limitations resulting from their trauma. Spiritual beliefs may change significantly during Stage Two. For example, survivors who expressed gratitude to God for sparing their lives or limiting their injuries during Stage One may become bitter and angry, even denying a belief in God, because they begin feeling punished and forsaken. It is important to recognize four reactions that are common during Stage Two.

1. Grieving. This is a normal response to injury-imposed limitations and losses, similar to the grief felt at the death of a loved one.

2. Selective Hearing. This is a common subconscious defense mechanism that "protects" the mind by blocking painful information. Selective hearing means letting in only those things that bring comfort and reassurance while filtering out negative information. Survivors of trauma are especially susceptible, which can be a serious problem. To assist in the healing process they may need to understand and respond appropriately to certain negative facts concerning their condition.

3. Disequilibrium. This reaction is characterized by disruptions in the normal feedback-control mechanisms that maintain homeostasis (physiological stability) in the body. As discussed above, stability is maintained through a series of coordinated mental and physical feedback mechanisms that react to conditions. When left unchecked, disruptions to these mechanisms can be harmful or even fatal. For example, when we exercise strenuously our hearts beat faster and we breathe more rapidly. The faster heartbeat transports more blood to the lungs where the faster respiration allows excess carbon dioxide to be exchanged for the oxygen needed to sustain activity. Without these homeostatic mechanisms we would pass out and possibly die from even moderate exertion. Thousands of such mechanisms in the body control processes vital to both physical and emotional well-being. When the mind and body are out of sync, life becomes a roller coaster of mental and physical highs and lows.

4. Anniversary Reactions. These are reactions that typically happen during a period of sustained, successful recovery. Around the anniversary date of their trauma or some closely associated event, recovering survivors may lapse into painful recollections of their traumatic experiences and subsequent losses. They may become nervous and hypersensitive about accident-related topics, brood over their recovery progress, and/or develop unreasonable fears about the event recurring.

Stage Three: Recovery—length of time varies.
Recovery is defined differently according to the unique situation of each survivor. It may be when a person regains his or her original state of health or well-being. However, in the case of disabling or disfiguring injury, the best possible outcome may be when the survivor has established a new, but different, meaningful and rewarding lifestyle. For all those who thrive after surviving, recovery is the point when physical and emotional healing are maximized, and the determination to move ahead with life has replaced the shackles of trauma.

There was no doubt that Larry's life would never be the same. He and his family were taught that the most important factor in the transition would be nourishing relationships. They learned how to best handle potentially threatening issues such as insurance, loss of income, and future employment. They were told what to expect when Larry was transferred to the rehabilitation hospital. Because they could see some resolution to their situation, the outlook seemed less bleak.

Larry continues his story:

Losses and Limitations vs. Future Success
It was during my rehabilitation procedures that the information given to me previously really began to make sense. One day, when I wasn't progressing as quickly as I felt I should and was feeling sorry for myself, I met a sixteen-year-old boy who could only move his head and right arm as a result of injuries received in a joy riding accident. Suddenly things clicked for me about the importance of focusing less on losses and limitations and more on future success. I had full use of my upper body, so there were

countless things I could still do! No matter how bad things seemed to be for me, the preparation I had received earlier on being as optimistic as possible during times of frustration was invaluable. I had learned how to make the best of a bad situation. With the ongoing information and reassurances I received I came to believe what James Allen said in As a Man Thinketh, Volume 2:

> The cause of all power, as of all [limitations] is within; the secret of all happiness as of all misery is likewise within. There is no progress apart from unfoldment within and no sure foothold of prosperity or peace *except by orderly advancement of knowledge.* (Italics added.)

Anniversary Reaction

I can't say that I haven't felt sorry for myself since seeing that young man, but being prepared for the normal ups and downs minimized my depression and helped me tremendously. Every year since, I have experienced a bit of a depression around the time the accident happened. However, we had been warned about "anniversary reaction." It has been particularly helpful to have Janet there to help pull me out of my doldrums very quickly.

Life Is What You Make It

Since that fateful day of my accident, I've had my share of trials and frustrations. My paralysis was irreversible, and I have lived my life in a wheelchair; but even if I had not been hurt, many trials and frustrations simply go along with living. What I have learned and how I used that knowledge has allowed me to go on with life in a positive manner. I have become the proud father of four beautiful children, and I have an active role in each of their lives. I have served as a soccer coach, boat driver, horse wrangler, scoutmaster, camping partner, and lay leader in our church. All this has been possible by learning, gaining new perspective, and planning realistic goals and objectives. Today I am privileged to serve as a 4-H council president over some three hundred youth.

I've learned that my life is what I make of it. I have been strongly directed by the knowledge I was given of how to control the way I feel about setbacks, difficulties, and frustrations. My spiritual convictions sustained me at that time and continue to give me the faith to keep trying. I know I'm not always going to be in a wheelchair. Having a strong belief *that there is something better after this life helps me and my whole family to cope. My youngest daughter often tells me she is happy her daddy will be able to walk again someday.*

Sometimes I reflect back on what happened to me. I know that my strong beliefs and the concern, comfort, and help from family and friends made the most difference, coupled with the invaluable information and guidance we received. Because all these things were there when I needed them most, I am who I am today with a family and life that I enjoy and love. I have succeeded in ways I never anticipated or expected.

Noted author and International Rotarian Marion D. Hanks has said, "Every human being is trying to say something to others, trying to cry out, 'I am alive; notice me, speak to me, listen to me, confirm for me that I am important, that I matter.'" In emergency rooms or other urgent care settings there are many factors that interfere with that message being sent, received, or understood. Obvious life-threatening injuries and the detection of unseen physiological damage must be top priority. However, with focused effort, a trained and discerning person can hear a patient's verbal or nonverbal cries for attention. Patients need to be heard at a time critical to their overall recovery. Their emotional wounds need early attention too—preferably using the SEEDs approach. As noted in the introduction, emotional disabilities can have a profoundly harmful effect on physical healing. Here is a recipe for continuing tragedy: rescue trauma victims from death, then do nothing to help them avoid the conclusion that their future holds no promise and life is not worth living. Such neglect of emotional needs demonstrates callous indifference.

"You Matter Most"

When people perceive that their thoughts, feelings, and anxieties are being taken seriously, they feel valued and are sustained by a sense of self-worth. The dehumanizing effects that are a part of many traumatic events are arrested. This principle was eloquently described by Viktor Frankl, author of *Man's Search for Meaning*, as "the consciousness of one's inner value being anchored."[1]

---

[1] *Man's Search for Meaning*, by Victor E. Frankl, with Gordon Allport, Washington Square Press, New York, 1998.

The Right Information at the Right Time Promotes Thriving

Fortunately, most accident survivors do not suffer losses as catastrophic as Larry's. This gives rise to the question: "How much information is essential for the average injury or trauma survivor?" There is no pat answer since the needs of individuals vary according to religious beliefs and/or level of spirituality, previous experiences, severity of the trauma, elapsed time before intervention, degree of support from family and friends, and whether or not the event involved criminal actions. This high degree of variability underscores the need for early and accurate assessment. Trauma Severity SPEED scores (see Appendix 1 pp. 134–42) and the IRO/STEPS Assessment Process (see Appendix 1 pp. 143–46) are key methods of determining the need for professional help as well as the type and amount of information that needs to be provided. As Gene Hockenbury came to realize, "The mind once stretched with a new idea never returns to its original dimensions." Without vital recovery information, prolonged impoverished thinking has painful and unnecessary consequences.

Fortunately, almost anyone who survives a traumatic event through the intervention of modern medicine and technology can now learn to thrive and to shorten the process of emotional wound healing. No one should suffer for decades as Gene Hockenbury did. Timing is the key and even in the most severe circumstances, almost anyone can be empowered and enabled to overcome emotional roadblocks and change their lives for the better. It is a matter of having emotional wounds attended to and having the right information provided at the right time. The Rowleys exemplify this process and the words of James Allen:

> *You may bring about that improved condition in your outward life which you desire, if you will unswervingly resolve to improve your inner life.*

Key Points in Chapter Three

Ideally, the specific, early, educational directions (SEEDs) strategy is initiated within twenty-four to seventy-two hours. It is possible for it to begin even sooner as pointed out in this chapter. Messages of positive thinking and support provided in the emergency room often have a beneficial effect on the management of physical injuries as well as on the healing of the survivor's emotional wounds.

A key to healing is accurate information. The mind is better able to deal with facts—even though the facts may not be positive—than it is with the questions and fears of the unknown.

Involvement of family in the healing process is a principal factor in the success of the IRO-STEPS tutorials and the entire SEEDs strategy. Family members, especially primary care-givers, should be involved as much as possible to ensure that they are providing positive support as well as having their own emotional wounds attended to. Family members are at risk for developing serious problems as a result of their identification with the traumatic event. It is not uncommon for the spouse or parent(s) of a trauma victim (either a survivor or deceased) to develop PTSD as a result of the incident and the aftermath events that often follow.

The lists of specific "Dos and Don'ts" mentioned in this chapter provide loved ones with helpful guidelines for offering the most effective support. (These are found in Appendix 1, pp. 183–84)

There are three stages to the recovery process. Understanding these stages and the events that typically accompany them is important to the healing process. They are the "Survival Honeymoon," the period of "Adjustment Shock," and finally the time of "Recovery." It is important to realize that recovery doesn't mean returning to exactly the same state that existed before the trauma. This is often impossible, as it was in Larry's case. Recovery is characterized by adjusting to current realities and maximizing the abilities the survivor has to resume a productive and positive life.

4

Rescue from the Rapids!

The urgency of obtaining structured, educational directions in response to emotional wounds can scarcely be overstated. George Miller's story illustrates the serious consequences of even a few weeks without informed direction. His experience also highlights the value of two of the six basic clinical traumatology tutorials: Psychic Energy Battery and the Fear Wheel.

The high-spirited launch of five rubber rafts onto the Salmon River began like George's hundred other river running trips. George loved the breathtaking scenery of the Salmon River as it snaked its way from central Idaho northward, then turned west into the River of No Return Wilderness Area. The river ran high, the water splashed cold and clear, and the first day's travel exhilarated all twenty rafters.

Adventure of a Lifetime

George had handpicked experienced oarsmen for the five boats and organized every detail of this expedition. The six leaders and four-teen Boy Scouts had been anticipating this adventure of a lifetime for eighteen months. George felt that without his leadership and logistical planning, the trip could not have happened.

Recently weakened by the effects of medications he had taken to treat a hepatitis C liver infection, George had been running a low-grade fever for days before departure and knew his stamina was poor. His wife LaRee had pleaded with him to cancel the trip. But after all those months of preparation, how could he say, "I don't feel so good. Can't we just stay home?"

Down the River

The second morning, the scent of pine trees, campfires, and rain-washed air heralded a magnificent new day. By 10 A.M. the five rubber rafts floated peacefully down the river; however, George realized he was tiring much too quickly. Midafternoon they stopped at a natural hot spring. The 105-degree water felt so good to aching muscles that no one wanted to leave.

Dark rain clouds filled the sky when they finally pushed off. The wind had started to blow and George was beyond tired. His back hurt and his arm muscles were strained from so much rowing. With boys whooping and cold water splashing, George led the group successfully through Big Mallard, one of the trickiest rapids. He felt relieved, but twenty minutes later, one of their smaller rafts overturned. During the frantic rescue efforts, George cut the palm of his hand and scratched and bruised his ankle. The natural protection his skin would have provided against invading microorganisms was compromised—a fact that would later prove significant.

Soon they continued down the river, caravaning closer together this time. The tone of the group was subdued. Some were shivering and wet, and the wind was becoming more brisk by the moment. Those who had been in the water were dangerously chilled and hunger gnawed at them all. To top it off, George was bone-weary and his head felt foggy; they *had* to find a place to stop and get warm.

Elkhorn Rapids

Frantically searching both shorelines for a suitable campsite, not one of the leaders noticed the silence that always precedes the most dangerous white water. Too late, George's mind snapped to attention. He only had time to think, *Oh, no! How could I let this happen?* before his boat capsized. As they hit the rapids sideways, all four occupants fell into the icy water. Screaming, gasping, they catapulted head over heels through the rapids. The force of the water shoved George headfirst toward the river bottom. He struggled furiously against the wild currents, his lungs screaming for oxygen. He finally broke the surface, pulled in great gasps of air, then glimpsed the black bottom of another rubber raft. Two rafts were capsized! Would there be anyone left to save them?

"Help!" he yelled as he went down again in the swirling white water. George was numb with cold and frantic for air. When would this nightmare end? *I can't breathe! God, help us!* he prayed.

Rescue

The raft carrying Tyler, George's son, had reached the bank safely. Tyler was able to throw George a rope and pull him to shore. George collapsed onto the muddy bank, chest heaving, blood flowing from the back of his right leg—the third place his skin had been broken. George sprawled face down, exhausted on the wet rocks on the edge of the Salmon River. "I can't believe I'm really alive," he said.

George sighed with relief when all were accounted for. The boys were crying, shivering, and shaken. Mike, the other adult thrown from George's raft, was glassy-eyed. George knew that the wind and the misty rain increased the possibility of hypothermia. The teary-eyed, ashen-faced crew drew close to regroup. Several had been miraculously snatched from the very clutches of death—and they knew it!

They decided to set up camp for the night, then try to find an immediate way out of the canyon. Most of their food and supplies had been lost. The two days of river travel it would take to float out of the canyon would be too great a risk considering their condition. Prayers for rescue soon rose above the smoke of the campfires they had built to help them endure the cold night.

The next morning a large jet boat rounded the bend. When George and the others yelled and waved frantically, the boat slowed to a stop. A large sum of money and a promise to load quickly convinced the owner to rescue them. They all fit into the large boat— barely!

Heading Home

Thirty-six hours after the accident, the bedraggled group loaded into cars, trucks, and trailers and started the ten-hour drive home. At their first rest stop, George gingerly put weight on his injured leg. A rush of searing pain let him know his troubles were not over.

Finally, about 11 P.M., George made his way wearily into his house. LaRee gasped when George showed her his leg. Flaming fingers of red, black, and blue traveled from ankle to knee. The whole area was hot to the touch and George's temperature had spiked to 104 degrees.

Emergency!

LaRee called 911, and minutes later an ambulance rushed George to a nearby emergency facility. His leg had swollen to almost twice its normal size. The doctor told him that his immune system, compromised by the medications he was taking for his liver problems, could not fight off the serious infection that had invaded his body through his wounds. The infection could be strains of staph, strep, or both. George's condition was critical. He needed immediate hospitalization for treatment with powerful intravenous antibiotics and plenty of rest.

An aide pushing George's gurney from the emergency room to a hospital room asked him what had happened. He listened with interest to George's summary. "Well, it's like falling off a horse," the aide immediately countered. "You fall off, get back on, try again. I suppose you'll be wanting to go river running as soon as you get better."

George surprised himself with the intensity of the feelings that colored his reply. "No! I will never set foot on another river trip again and I am going to sell all my stuff. That's it!" As much as he loved the river, George could not bear the thought of ever again feeling that much responsibility for so many people. Besides, George wanted to grow old with his family, not die at the bottom of some cold, dark river.

The Aftermath

After the hospital released him, George expected to feel relief and closure to the whole incident. No one had died. His leg had healed. It should be over. But constant flashbacks compounded the difficulty of George's recovery. Whenever he shut his eyes or let his mind wander, the churning white water of Elkhorn Rapids sucked him under again. He repeatedly relived the terror of the experience. The trauma of "what could have happened" seemed to distress him almost as deeply as if it *had* happened. George suffered from sleep deprivation and became irritable and difficult to live with.

Partly to prove to himself that he was "okay," he went back to work earlier than advised. He felt annoyance with his work assignments, but tried to put up a good front. He exemplified the "fake it" temperament, acting fully in charge and repelling any offers of TLC.

Relationships, especially with his wife, deteriorated rapidly. LaRee had no way to understand George's descent into sullen darkness. However, George dutifully reported his sleep problems, headaches, and depression to his doctor, who prescribed four additional medications. George sensed that some of his problems stemmed from the strong medications he had been taking long term and he didn't want to take any more. Consequently, he did not fill the prescriptions.

Relapse

On a trip to southern Utah, George had a relapse and landed in the hospital again. The doctors gave him an additional ten-day course of intravenous antibiotics.

Home from the hospital, George's anger and explosive behavior mystified LaRee and the children. She had no answers when they asked, "What has happened to Dad? Why is he acting that way?"

George's symptoms became more pronounced each day as he sank further into despair. He said,

I found life terribly dull or full of fear. I had no interest in anything and I could not sleep. I suffered recurring nightmares of suffocation, and several times each day I would see myself on the river approaching the rapids. I would shake myself or get up and walk around trying to "snap out of it." I felt I was sliding down a slippery hill of depression and anger. Since I didn't know what was causing the problem, I could not help myself. The realization hit me that if something didn't change, I was going to lose my family, my job, or even my life! I was to that point after only two and a half months. I felt I was living in a never-ending nightmare.

Reaching Out

George remembered the help his son had received from visits to the Wound and Injury Recovery Center (WIRC/America) several years earlier. However, he repeatedly convinced himself that he could slay this dragon single-handedly. Finally, seventy-six days after the accident, the situation had become intolerable; he picked up the phone and made an appointment at the Center.

"I can't believe I did that!" George berated himself. He could not bring himself to tell LaRee that he was falling apart and needed help for *himself*. So he made up a story about going to the Center to get some information for their son, Tyler, who had recently had a motorcycle accident.

Here, in George's words, is what happened when he went "to get information" a couple of days later:

My first experience with clinical traumatology was not what I expected. I began by describing what I had been doing . . . about the hepatitis C and about my recent injury in a rafting accident. I recounted the planning and the first two days of the trip. When I came to the accident, I knew I couldn't just say, "I fell overboard and hurt my leg." It was much more significant than that. I explained what it was like to row a raft down the river and the skills, strength, and stamina needed to successfully negotiate the rapids.

I described the river the day of the accident—the dark clouds, wind, and rain. I explained my terrible fatigue from illness and from rowing and enduring the river for twenty-four miles already that day. My eyes closed as I started to explain what it was like when we had suddenly come upon Elkhorn Rapids. I described how I felt when the raft flipped over, throwing us into the icy water.

Flashback

What happened next was simply out of my control. A terrible lump filled my throat and my stomach knotted up. Tears filled my eyes, and in my mind I was back in the river. I pulled my legs up close to my chest and it was as though I were under water again, unable to breathe. I repeatedly called out for help and sobbed uncontrollably until I felt Barry's hand on my shoulder. Then I slowly pulled myself upright and started to breathe normally again.

I felt embarrassed at first and apologized, but learned immediately that I had just experienced a normal (although extreme) example of a flashback episode. Most of my sensory systems had been triggered regarding my near-drowning.

Lightening the Load

During the next half hour or so I didn't say much, just listened and learned about normal aftermath reactions. I was told they can be so intense that it is not uncommon to feel that the impact of the accident is never going to end. Flashbacks are a common experience for trauma survivors. Wow! If only I'd known that, I could have prevented weeks of suffering. It felt so good to unload my burden on someone who understood.

I guess I was typical of most men; when we are sick or hurt in an accident, we usually respond by acting big and tough. I wanted to believe I did not need help, that I could get better all by myself.

With just that little bit of information about flashbacks, clearly and simply explained, the terrible weight I had been carrying began to lighten. I had not felt this good for almost three months.

Why Early Intervention Is So Important

Barry said to me, "Your experience shows the importance of routine early intervention. Most people have no idea what the experience has done to their emotional shock absorber. Nor do they anticipate what lies ahead. Feelings of resentment, hostility, fear—even terrifying nightmares—can magnify past problems beyond reason. If someone does not tell survivors that such reactions are normal, then depression, anxiety, and withdrawal—such as you have been experiencing—are likely to follow."

Side Effects and Mind-Stretching

I was asked to review a list of side effects and symptoms (see **Normal Aftermath Feelings,** *chapter two, pg. 24) and circle the ones that had been causing me the most problems. I was surprised at how many of them I checked. Everything I described was taken very seriously.*

I learned that many of the things we might discuss after completing the assessment procedures would go much deeper than the events on the river. Why? Because the ways I had learned to deal with problems in the past were absolutely relevant to how I was dealing with them now— unsuccessfully! I felt better knowing I would learn more effective ways to resolve the problems that had mushroomed ever since the accident.

I was given a profound Oliver Wendell Holmes quote I will never forget, "The mind once stretched with a new idea never returns to its original dimensions." *That phrase was referred to every time I visited the Center.*

In that first appointment and in all those that followed, I received clear and simple directions that were invaluable to me, food and exercises for my **mind***. I was given a copy of James Allen's* As a Man Thinketh, *Volume 2, along with a written "prescription" to begin reading it. I was told to memorize quotes that made the most sense to me. Two of the ones I chose from Allen's book to memorize were*

> You may bring about that improved condition in your outward life which you desire, if you will unswervingly resolve to improve your inner life.

> If circumstances had the power to bless or harm, they would bless and harm all men alike. But the fact that the same circumstances will be alike good and bad to different souls proves that the good or bad is not in the circumstance, but only in the mind of him that encounters it.

A Joint Pursuit

I had not shared any of my fears, uncertainties, or feelings of inadequacy with LaRee, but now I learned how important it was that she be involved in everything I was learning. I was to share my written assessment with her and bring her with me to the rest of the tutorials so we could work together. It was really hard at first, but proved to be a prime factor in my recovery.

IRO-STEPS

Before I left, I was introduced to the Injury Recovery Orientation-STEPS (IRO-STEPS):

> **S***timulate positive thinking*
> **T***ackle unrealistic fears*
> **E***ducate myself*
> **P***lan for the future*
> **S***top impractical expectations and distorted thoughts*

I realized that these steps of active recovery were going to give me the ability to help myself rather than make me dependent on something or someone else. It all made absolute sense. The key to success was right in

54

my hands (the book *As a Man Thinketh, Vol 2*) and all I had to do was understand, and then apply the principles to my own personal circumstances.

Getting the Facts

Within an hour of my initial assessment procedure I was back at my office, my appetite whetted for more information. Ten minutes of simple research on the Internet revealed the expected side effects of the massive doses of the medications I had been taking (mostly treatment for hepatitis C). I had experienced all of them: significant depression, fatigue, sleeplessness, headaches, and lethargy. I had not once been warned of any of them, so had not made the connection. Knowing my symptoms were normal—and realizing that those symptoms had increased the side effects of the trauma—reduced my anxiety enormously. I started to realize that many of my fears could be dissipated by stretching my mind with the facts rather than saturating it with more of the medications that had been dulling my senses and decreasing my ability to thrive.

Learning this principle of "getting the facts" as quickly as possible saved me a lot of trouble a short time later. I visited a clinic for a routine blood analysis to monitor my hepatitis C. The lab technician remarked that my blood sugar level was so low that he wondered how I was walking around. "By all rights, Mr. Miller, you should be dead right now," he said. Someone from the clinic called me at home that evening and said, "Mr. Miller, are you okay? The doctor analyzing the lab report wants to send an ambulance to your home." Well, those comments set off a terrible amount of anxiety. However, having just learned how important it was to gather accurate information, I tracked down my own physician who checked with the laboratory technician and let me know it was "all a mistake" and that my blood sugar level was fine. Talk about a paradigm shift! My anxiety left immediately.

I know now that I need to make it a daily practice to focus my energy on getting the facts rather than dissipate my energy on worry, fear, and anxiety. Helpful information is usually available if we just put forth the effort to obtain it.

Psychic Energy Battery

A later tutorial (educational session) called "Psychic Energy Battery" gave George the motivation to make needed changes in his lifestyle (see Psychic Energy Battery Tutorial, Appendix 1, pp. 149–50). He quickly related to the following metaphor: a car battery can be recharged easily, and when it is fully charged the battery makes it possible to start the engine or to play the radio, turn on the lights, open electric windows, etc. before the engine is started. We each have a *psychic* energy battery that needs constant recharging through proper diet, rest, and physical and emotional nurturing. A charged psychic battery gives us the resiliency and bounce-back energy we need to function well.

If the psychic energy battery is not recharged, if we have not done what we need to do to recharge it, then a major troubling emotional incident or traumatic event can

1. Drain the "charge" of available psychic energy (essential to effective thinking, reasoning, and problem-solving)

2. Limit the ability to recharge the battery

3. Result in insufficient power to handle other stresses that come along

Even before the accident, George's lifetime accumulation of unresolved events had put a major drain on his psychic energy battery. Then, his near-drowning experience (which would severely drain even a fully charged battery) reduced what little energy he had left. Just as appliances and other electrical devices do not function optimally and may be damaged when they receive a voltage that is too low, so too can the intricate homeostatic mechanisms that keep our bodily functions regulated be damaged when there is insufficient energy. George's regulatory system was becoming seriously unstable. Anything that isn't maintained properly will eventually break down; like most of us, George hadn't maintained his psychic energy battery to keep it well charged. Consequently, when his situation deteriorated, he didn't have the emotional energy to handle it.

Our psychic energy batteries can occasionally be jump-started—by exhilarating experiences or a "quick fix" from chemicals. However, jump-starting does not fix the problem long-range. Our psychic energy batteries need slow and regular charging through proper self-care and ongoing nurturing from family, friends, and other loved ones.

Bed rest and medical procedures may assist in the recharging, but alone they are not sufficient. In times of greatest need, the most valid and long lasting recharging comes from the nurturing of our closest loved ones. It comes from mutually expressing our feelings and concerns and then working together for positive outcomes. Honestly sharing our responses to events, relationships, or tragedies with those we love—giving and receiving emotional support—charges psychic batteries and changes many negatives to positives.

In times of emergency, if we don't share our feelings with close family members, how can we expect them to give us the help and support we need? LaRee didn't know of George's emotional struggles after his accident because he did not tell her. Since she didn't understand what was happening, her own fears escalated and she could not respond well to George. When two mutual caregivers, husband and wife, don't understand each other and are not nurturing one another, they create a vicious cycle of ineffective communication. They routinely deplete each other's energy level as they hide behind self-made walls of frustration and isolation.

After the accident, George was starting each day with a low level of psychic energy. Then difficulties throughout the day took him even lower. At home each night, he and LaRee were inadvertently draining each other's energy. Combine that cycle with the effect of the drugs, and it is easy to see why George was soon unable to cope with the demands of work, marriage, and family.

As the level of his psychic energy battery kept spiraling downward, he eventually reached the point that he had to do something about it. Some people at that point turn to illicit drugs, alcohol, or obsession with recreational activities—all attempts to artificially recharge. George simply withdrew, but after a few weeks was wise enough to reach out for help.

By the time George began acquiring the health care tutorials, extreme fear was already taking its toll. It was essential for him to learn about the "Wheel of Fear" (see Fear Wheel Tutorial, Appendix 1, p. 166–69) that explains the most common indicators of protracted fear. They are

1. Prolonged medical problem(s)
2. Accident-proneness
3. Neurotic tendencies
4. Excessive work-focus
5. Chemical dependency, etc.

The most effective remedy—often overlooked or neglected because of fear—is attention from the most caring "significant other," most often a spouse. Positive attention charges the psychic energy battery. The common tendency to push away or keep that caring person at arm's length physically and emotionally was robbing George of his most ready source of strength—his wife.

The Fear Wheel

The Fear Wheel illumination helped George change his perspective in much the same way that Gene Hockenbury changed his by listening to the Stephen R. Covey tape. George said:

It was a great relief to learn that unrealistic fears are a normal part of recovery from a traumatic experience. If I started to feel threatened, I would say to myself, "Oh well, these fears are normal and to be expected." Now, whenever I start to feel anxiety, confusion, or frustration, I am able to put things in proper perspective. I review in my mind the facts I learned and say to myself, "this is all part of the recovery process." Previously, my negative thoughts would turn on my adrenaline. [Adrenaline triggers the "fight or flight" reaction, which can cause negative side effects such as those listed on the Fear Wheel Diagram. These side effects can have a damaging effect on the brain if allowed to continue without disruption.] *I would start to think I was losing it because my whole body would react to that overload of adrenaline. It was a great relief to learn how to avoid that downward spiral.*

Ambitious
- Driven
- Win at all costs
- Inadequate
- Inferior
- Ruthless
- Manipulative
- Lonely
- Shallow

Chemical and Other Dependence
- Alcohol
- Prescribed drugs
- Illicit drugs
- Deep emotional pain

Suicidal
- Ideation
- Distortion
- Threats
- Gestures
- Attempts

Psychotic
- Paranoia
- Delusions
- Hallucinations

Deviancies
- Pedophilia (child molesting)
- Rape
- Exhibitionism
- Prostitution
- Pornography
- Voyeurism
- Promiscuity

Medical Problems
- Dizziness
- Headaches
- Stomach disorders
- Heart disease
- Cancer
- Kidney disease

Non-conformist
- Antisocial
- Withdrawn
- Loner
- Aberrant
- Eccentric
- Kinky

Accident Prone
- Preoccupied and distracted
- Transfer of psychological problems to physical incidents

Neurotic
- Phobias
- Eating disorders
- Fanaticism
- Obsessions
- High anxiety
- Sleep disturbances
- Hyperactivity

Criminal Tendencies
- Hostility
- Passivity
- Compulsive
- Ritualism
- Obsessive
- Manipulative
- Controlling

Recognition

Acknowledgement

Acceptance

Accessibilitiy =

Self-worth
Self-esteem
Self-confidence
Self-respect
Security

Making Progress

I now realize there are no magic pills for recovery. However, simply "getting the facts" through these health care tutorials has made a big difference. Receiving this pertinent information in a more timely fashion would have decreased my crippling anxieties and fears. Because of the educational processes I've gone through, I have gradually become more confident and realistic in my expectations and not as prone to wild fluctuations of emotion.

A few tutorials into the recovery process, I could see real improvement. As I continued to surround myself with good thoughts, ideas, pictures, music, reading, and poetry, I moved from being lethargic to being energized. LaRee and I are doing more things together, and I often spend time in the evenings helping her with computer work.

As a Man Thinketh, Volume 2, has inspired me with good insights. I have always believed that we shape ourselves and our environment, that we follow a path of our own choosing and design, and become what we think. But now I am really implementing these ideas instead of just believing them.

Reflections and Renewal

The other day I reflected on the river accident and the events before, during, and after. Previously, such reflection would have brought considerable anxiety. Now it is no big deal. In fact, now I would even like to run the river again—and that's major progress! I am at a point of renewal, and the change is exciting. I can once again look forward to and really enjoy each new day with my wife, family, and work.

Key Points in Chapter Four

Flashbacks are a relatively common occurrence among victims of emotional trauma. They are a significant indication that emotional wounds are not being resolved and should prompt the survivor to seek help. Unfortunately, many people feel that admitting the existence of flashbacks will label them as being weak or mentally unstable, or both. Without intervention, flashbacks may persist for years and lead to further problems.

When people are in good mental and physical health, they have a great deal of resilience to external insults such as injury. After an illness, however, the ability to bounce back from additional injuries or diseases is compromised. If we rode in a car with worn out shock absorbers, we would feel every bump. When emotional wounds have weakened our emotional shock absorbers, ordinary life events tend to create great distress.

Active involvement is a critical component in the successful process for healing emotional wounds. One cannot be "treated" in a passive way; healing requires active participation and involvement in the process. A paradigm shift is required, so that instead of waiting to be told what to do, one seeks answers and learns the power of applying what is learned.

Just as resistance to disease and emotional disruption are affected by poor health, long-standing unresolved problems leave the mind seriously weakened. The principle of the psychic energy battery helps demonstrate the effects of unresolved problems which place a constant drain on the system. If not reversed, they can deplete the energy to a point where normal functioning begins to fail. Practicing the principles taught in the tutorials will provide a steady charge of the psychic battery. There is no long-term benefit to trying to speed up the charging process with drugs, alcohol, and other chemicals—only further damage.

One of the most common effects of unattended emotional wounds is fear. The fear wheel tutorial describes the many forms that fear can take and the variety of damaging behaviors it causes. People will do almost anything to make the pain of fear go away. In many instances, however, the methods they use lead to added pain and more intense fear.

5

Fatality!

Art Van Tielen's story highlights the effectiveness of the SPEED scoring scale and the importance of early reconciliation. Author E. H. Chapin stated: "Never does the human soul appear so strong and noble as when it forgoes revenge and dares to forgive an injury." Over 2,500 survivors have received STEPS tutorials. Those who have healed most rapidly and with the least problems have reconciled quickly with the other parties involved. Delay is disastrous. Enmity, avoidance, or resistance to peaceful reconciliation impedes recovery. In contrast, willing efforts to confront, forgive, and be forgiven facilitates rapid recovery in a manner that nothing else can.

Rabbi Harold Kuchner, author of *When Bad Things Happen to Good People,* said, "God inspires people to help other people who have been hurt by life."[1] Rapidly applying this principle is one of the best responses to emotional wounds. Failure to reconcile is poison, and when you seek an antidote for poison, timing is everything. The following experience epitomizes the outcome of early reconciliation.

On January 24, 1998, Art Van Tielen was driving a public transit bus southbound on a narrow street in Salt Lake City. Just as he went through an intersection, Art caught a glimpse of a young woman on a bicycle approaching from the west. She had a stop sign, so he wasn't alarmed. However, this twenty-year-old college student did not stop, but crashed into the side of the bus. Instantly Art applied the brakes. Before the bus stopped, he had the sickening, horrible realization that the wheels of the bus had just run over the young woman.

---

[1] *When Bad Things Happen to Good People,* by Harold S. Kushner, Avon Books, New York, 1981.

Reporting the Accident

Art flung open the bus door and leaped out. He took one look at the woman lying on the road, then ducked back into the bus. Art had been sent to the scene of numerous tragedies in his previous job as an accident investigator for the Salt Lake City Police Department. He didn't need a closer view; he knew she had been crushed to death.

He notified his dispatcher on the radio phone and within minutes police and paramedics were on the scene. Even though Art had investigated many accidents with fatalities, this was the first that had any personal connection to him. Art describes his response with the following words:

After making all the necessary calls, I slumped in my seat. One fear after another raced through my mind: Would I lose my job and be unable to support my two sons? [One was doing missionary work in a foreign country and the other was a college student.] *Would I ever drive again? How would the parents of the young woman react and would they sue? I had seen years of drawn-out litigation in similar cases. Would I be dropped into the pit of a court battle? How much responsibility did I have for the accident? Could I have done anything to prevent it?*

Plagued with Questions

With my investigative sense, the biggest question plaguing my mind was "What had caused the accident?" The investigating highway patrol officer could offer no explanations. The only witness, one of my passengers who saw the young woman hit the side of the bus, could add no additional insight.

In the hours that followed, I went over the scenario in my mind a thousand times. Each time I asked myself the same question: "Is there anything I could have done differently?"

Support at the Scene

Something happened, however (and happened quickly), that helped me get the whole experience into perspective and led me to a rapid recovery. Two years earlier my employer, the Utah Transit Authority (UTA), had initiated a new policy. Every employee involved in an accident or traumatic event received an immediate professional response to the emotional upheaval, whether they were injured or not. Usually within an hour following initial investigative procedures, Barry Richards, from the Wound and Injury Recovery Center, met with the person at the emergency room, at his Center, or at the UTA offices. I was fortunate enough to have him come to the scene of my accident within minutes.

Richards clearly stated that he was **not** offering psychological treatment. Instead he wanted to inform me what to expect in the next seventy-two hours and give recommendations for dealing with the questions and concerns flooding my mind. I knew that many of my bus driver colleagues had benefitted from the health care directions he had provided and that I had the option of accepting or declining. I immediately accepted his help.

I was living my worst nightmare and was in a state of numbed-out shock, but was fortunate that the police officers who responded to my call were supportive; I had known them in my earlier career as a policeman. I immediately related to Richards when I learned of our shared history in law enforcement. The brotherhood and the BDF-factor of "been there, done that, and felt what it's like" are immediately acknowledged among police officers, and this bond comforted me (see "BDF Factor" in Glossary).

I was informed that my wife, already awaiting my arrival at the bus station, could be with me in future tutorials. Richards would meet with us at the UTA offices right away and help us get through the next seventy-two hours in the best possible way.

Immediate Response

When I was taken back to the UTA offices, I was apprehensive and nervous. After talking with the workers' compensation officer and security officer, however, I calmed down a lot. They were supportive and understanding.

Our first clinical traumatology tutorial, within an hour following the at-scene investigation, introduced us to a growth process and relieved our apprehensions.

———•———

No one survives trauma turmoil in a vacuum. Those who love the survivors are always affected. In Art's case his wife, Charlotte, would be a secondary victim. Art and Charlotte were informed of the most typical side effects and symptoms common to trauma survivors so they would know what to expect. The basic guidelines for dealing with these side effects are the **IRO (Injury Recovery Orientation)-STEPS:** (**S**timulate positive thinking, **T**ackle unrealistic fears, **E**ducate about options, **P**lan for the future, and **S**top impractical expectations).

They were warned that people often make comments that could be painful, known as "secondary wounding," and taught the "Rule of Thumb" that survivors should not change job, residence, or marital status, or make major financial decisions within one year following the trauma without wise objective counsel.[2]

They were given a brief explanation of future tutorials such as "*in vivo* desensitization" and a copy of the book *Thriving after Surviving* (see "*In Vivo* Desensitization" in Glossary). The "Dos and Don'ts" guidelines from the book and listed in *SUDDEN TRAUMA's* Appendix 1, pp. 179–84, can also help people avoid setbacks and recover more quickly.

After Trauma Assessment

The following day during the "After Trauma Assessment Procedure," Art and his wife spent about two hours explaining their personal circumstances and receiving additional directions (see After Trauma Assessment Procedure in Glossary and Assessment in Appendix 1, pp. 143–46). Like most survivors, they were at a crossroads and wanted immediate information relevant to the decisions they had to make.

SPEED Scoring Scale

Then Art and Charlotte were introduced to the Trauma Severity SPEED Scoring Scale—the simple device that can determine the urgency of additional health care directions relevant to individual trauma recovery situations (see Appendix 1, pp. 134–42). It helped them understand the basis of clinical traumatology and the purpose of the health care tutorials.

---

[2] Note: "Secondary Victim" and "Secondary Wounding" are not the same thing. A secondary victim is someone who suffers emotional injury because of their close association with the primary victim, such as in this case. Secondary wounding refers to the re-wounding of survivors during the recovery process. The re-wounding is usually unintentionally caused by someone asking insensitive questions or making an offensive remark such as telling the survivor they are fine and nothing is wrong with them, inferring that they are malingering.

The concept is simple and straightforward. Harvard scientists pinpointed the things most people need to succeed and feel good about life.[3] Specifically, they are security, economic well-being, a sense of belonging, recognition, and control over personal circumstances. Major problems in any one of these areas magnifies the current trauma and indicate a threat to future functioning and a need for additional help. SPEED stands for

Severity of trauma

Perceived loss of income from trauma

Estrangement from family and loved ones

Environmental skepticism—Demonstrated by people who downplay the possible impact of the trauma (especially where there is little apparent injury)

Damaged sense of control over a person's future life circumstances

Emergency room scoring devices determine how serious and life-threatening a person's physical injuries are. The SPEED Scoring Scale accomplishes the same thing in regard to emotional wounds.

SPEED scoring considers a person's total circumstances immediately before the trauma and their likely impact on both physical and emotional healing. With the SPEED Scoring Scale, Art and Charlotte were able to pinpoint the tutorials and clinical procedures that would be most beneficial for Art personally, such as *"in vivo* desensitization," and also those procedures that would aid Art and his wife together.

Survival Realities and Stages of Recovery

Art summarizes: *Within that all-important two-hour appointment, all our major anxieties and concerns were specifically addressed—such as the possibility I would lose my job, and how I would continue to support my family. We learned the Survival Realities, the Stages of Recovery, and what to* expect at each stage. [See Introduction and Glossary for Survival Realities and Appendix 1, pp. 144–46 for Stages of Recovery.] *Even*

---

[3] Getting to Yes: Negotiating Agreement Without Giving In, 2nd ed., by R. Fisher and W. Ury, New York, Penguin Books, 1991, 49–50.

with all the uncertainties that we faced, our most urgent questions and concerns were answered and resolved quickly with specific directions.

In Vivo Desensitization

Two days after the accident I felt ready and willing to get back on a bus and participate in the recommended "in vivo desensitization." ["In vivo" is a Latin term meaning "in the natural setting."] I knew that the longer I delayed, the stronger my fears would become about driving again. With UTA permission, Richards and I boarded an empty bus identical to the one I had driven the day of the accident. I sat in the driver's seat and Richards sat in the passenger seat directly behind me. He explained the procedure clearly and told me I could stop any time I chose. I felt uneasy, but trusted that the procedure would be beneficial.

I drove the route I followed the day of the accident and was encouraged to freely discuss whatever came to mind. As we neared the scene, I was directed to recall exactly what had been going on just prior to the accident. I was to stop the bus if I became too upset.

I drove directly to the area and parked the bus on an adjacent street. We got off the bus and walked over to the scene of the accident. I was asked to describe in detail what happened that day, how I had felt, and what I was feeling right then.

As I relived the accident, I had a big emotional outpouring that was very helpful. For a half hour we went through what Richards called a "resolution procedure." I don't know why it helped so much to be supported through the expression of my feelings about that traumatic incident, but I felt intense emotional relief. Immediately afterward I felt I could continue my job as a bus driver!

Unfinished Business

One area of "unfinished business" still troubled me, however. Ever since the day of the accident I had clearly stated my desire to express my feelings of deep sorrow and regret to the family of the deceased. I wanted to tell them how sorry I was that the incident had occurred. The people at UTA were quite reluctant at first because of liability concerns, particularly about statements I might make that could be construed as an admission of personal responsibility for the accident. But I did not give up on the idea, especially when it was being encouraged throughout the IRO-STEPS procedures. Clearly, I learned that my desire to give and receive comforting reassurances was normal, healthy, and important. A reconciliation would help me heal sooner and put the whole matter into a healthier perspective.

As much as I wanted the meeting to happen, my anxiety grew like a monster weed, gradually taking over my mind. Every time I thought of the family of the deceased, I couldn't help feeling afraid that they would be too upset at me or too angry to even consent to a meeting. Also, my police experiences kept the real potential of lengthy litigation lurking in the back of my mind. For three days I felt exhausted and my stomach was often upset.

A Meeting Is Arranged

Then, by an amazing grace, arrangements were made for me to meet with the family. Though somewhat relieved, I was still anxious. How would they react? Would I say the right thing? Would this visit make things better or worse for all concerned?

As we drove to their home, I learned astonishing things about the family. I was told of their sincere desire to visit with me—that they had expressed their concern for me to the police officers who had delivered the terrible news. Even in their great loss, their heartfelt desire was to comfort me! They had not known what to do or how to arrange a meeting, but were very relieved when they were contacted.

Reconciliation and Relief

As Richards and I walked up to their front door I could hardly control my emotions. I met the father first and we embraced. I cried a lot and expressed my sorrow, then did the same with the mother, who reassured me that this meeting was not about blame. I was struck with their sincere concern for me.

I was welcomed so warmly into their home, and the parents shared with me some very personal experiences and details of their daughter's life. She had lived exuberantly, even recklessly, and her father had a premonition for years that a policeman would someday come to their door to announce a tragedy. The father ended by reading from his daughter's last diary entry where she recorded that she had finally found peace in her life. The experience was touching and emotions flowed.

I was invited to kneel down and pray with the family. Just after we finished, a scripture came into my mind as clearly as can be: "Come unto *me, all ye that labor and are heavy laden, and I will give you rest." A feeling of calm came over me, a feeling that only comes through spiritual intervention from God. My subsequent feelings of anxiety and fear that I could be blamed for the accident left me entirely. It was a marvelous experience in which grief and compassion were freely expressed for the suffering we were all experiencing.*

As I was about to leave, the father mentioned he would have nothing to do with any attorney who might call wanting to represent the family. So even my fears of a lawsuit were put to rest. I walked away feeling deeply relieved, having peace of mind, knowing I could go on and that everything would work out.

The Funeral

I felt good about attending the funeral, where special seats were reserved for me and my wife. I was elated and grateful that my employer acknowledged the good that had come from my meeting with the family and had approved my attendance at the funeral, even in the face of legal concerns and possible liability factors.

Life Is Not Ideal

Admittedly, not all bereft families or other affected parties in a tragedy are as kind and forgiving as the one in this story. Consequently, not all survivors will experience such a positive reconciliation. But whenever possible, the opportunity should be given. Rapid reconciliation is clearly beneficial.

Back to Work in Record Time

Resuming work just four days after the funeral, I felt some physical signs of stress and exhaustion. Still I felt good about returning and felt a new appreciation of my value to my employer, evidenced by their understanding support and the timely help they provided. I realized I had been spared most of the intense side effects and symptoms that could have plagued me. Clearly, ongoing guidance from a clinical traumatologist made an incredible difference, not only by stimulating my mind with positive information, but also in arranging my visit with the family.

Silver Linings

My rather miraculous, rapid recovery and return to work involved a lot of people. Thanks to them and to receiving early intervention where the facts were provided, I didn't suffer in ignorance. I had a learning and growing experience all along the way.

I cannot emphasize enough the importance of the spiritual aspect of my healing process, combined with the opportunity to reconcile with the woman's parents quickly. The two books I read (Thriving after Surviving, and As a Man Thinketh, Volume 2) *and the tutorial instructions I received helped me put things into proper perspective. This combination helped me deal with my fears and helped me plan realistically for the future. The tutorials, along with support from family members, former and current work colleagues, and the family of the deceased, turned the whole experience from something that could have seriously affected our lives adversely into something uplifting and good.*

All trauma survivors deserve to have prompt information and crucial directions. They need to be empowered by patterns of right-thinking; they need to avoid prolonged dependency upon others, and they need realistic incentives to thrive versus merely survive. Experiencing "*in vivo* desensitization" within seventy-two hours, and reconciliation as soon as possible, cleanses emotional wounds and prevents them from festering into psychological abscesses.

Lifting and Reassurance

Response to real needs is the basic concern of clinical traumatology. Confusion, uncertainty, and anxiety can best be handled with immediate and simple directions. During survival aftermath, realistic assurances are critical. People need to express their feelings and have them responded to, the sooner, the better. Rapid reconciliation (perfectly illustrated in Art's story) is a vitally important part of this process. By calling on and sharing available spiritual and emotional strength, survivors and those who care the most about them can effectively lift each other out of their agony and into a better future.

Key Points in Chapter Five

One of three essential support systems is encouragement from other survivors. It is important to have people with credibility who can identify with the survivor and encourage them in the steps that need to be taken to avoid long-term effects of emotional wounding. This is referred to as the "Been there, Done that, Factor" (BDF).

Failure to recognize secondary trauma, such as occurred with Art's wife, will create a situation where each person is dealing with their own problems in ways that are not mutually supporting. Nurturing between family and loved ones can occur even if both are suffering, if each one learns and applies the principles of recovery.

In vivo desensitization is the process of going back to the scene of the trauma with survivors and helping them gradually overcome intense fears and flashback symptoms often associated with the location of a traumatic experience. This process is commonly used in the SEEDs strategy. The procedure takes preparation (such as arranging for vehicles, obtaining permissions, time off work, etc.) and may require multiple visits to the accident site before the survivor resolves the phobic-anxiety associated with the scene or circumstance.

All people are not at the same risk for experiencing disabling psychological consequences from trauma-caused emotional wounds. An assessment is vitally important to identify those at greatest risk for prolonged symptoms that could lead to life-disruptive consequences if not attended to adequately.The SPEED scoring system is a simple and accurate method of determining the likelihood of serious side effects from emotional trauma. Although training on the use of the system is desirable, if the guidelines are followed almost anyone can perform the assessment. However, it should be performed by someone who is not experiencing post-trauma effects themselves.

Reconciliation is a critical activity in the healing process. In many cases trauma survivors hold others responsible for their injury. Even if others are responsible, holding onto animosity and grudges can destroy other efforts to overcome emotional wounding. The peace and resolution that come through reconciliation can significantly aid the recovery process.

Although no one wants to experience the pain of injuries, the process of healing and the insight one gains about interacting with others and about life's priorities can be a positive. Until one has experienced the pain of trauma and learned to overcome the challenges that come with the healing process, it is difficult to fully appreciate the blessings of life. This understanding characterizes those who thrive as opposed to merely survive following a traumatic event.

The process of recovery is often a spiritual experience. Whether or not we are affiliated with an organized religion, we may find strength through prayer and spiritual meditation. The key is acknowledging a higher power in our lives that guides and directs us when our own resources are inadequate.

6

Plane Crash!

Scott Paterson's story highlights the consequences of delayed reconciliation, a vivid contrast to Art Van Tielen's experience. It also illustrates common phobias that interfere with recovery, the essential need for *"in vivo* desensitization," and how the IRO-STEPS tutorials can solve emotional problems more effectively than conventional psychotherapy.

January 15, 1990, Scott Paterson was a passenger aboard a SkyWest commuter plane flying from Salt Lake City to Reno. A blinding snowstorm decreased visibility to zero as the pilot began his descent on approach to the Elko airport, the last stop before Reno. Suddenly a ridge appeared through the haze—directly in the plane's path.

Passengers screamed in terror as the plane nosed sharply upwards. The belly of the aircraft struck the mountain about four feet below the crest. Because of the upward angle of the plane, it skipped like a rock and bounced over the top of the ridge. Then the plane slid down the other side, carving a groove in the snow and in the dirt beneath. Airborne briefcases, purses, and glasses sailed over Scott's head and pummeled the forward compartment. Bouncing and skipping again, the plane turned in midair, barely avoided plummeting over a ledge, and miraculously came to a stop about two-thirds of the way down the mountain.

Stranded on a Mountain

At first Scott thought they had crashed on Elko's runway. Since he was sitting next to the exit, he opened the door and jumped out. Stunned, he saw they were stranded on a snowy mountain. The smell of fuel was heavy in the air and Scott heard a drip ... drip ... sizzle ... from the engine. Realizing the plane could explode and burn, he dashed back into the plane, and began to shout, "Get out of the plane! Quick!" Stunned people looked at him blankly but did not move until he addressed them in more colorful language. Then one after another of the fourteen passengers began stumbling toward the exit.

Scott went back in to make certain everyone was out and found that the pilot could not move. Scott went to get help and noticed red liquid dripping outside the plane directly beneath the pilot's seat. Was it blood? Was the pilot bleeding to death? He could not leave him to die! He ducked back into the plane and talked calmly to the pilot, trying to see where the blood might be coming from.

Suddenly feeling confined and panicky, Scott thought, "Oh no, I'm back in this plane and it's going to blow up and I'm going to burn and die." Fear immobilized him until the copilot appeared and said, "Everything's okay outside. We're not going to burn. We don't have to move him." The pilot had multiple leg fractures, but was not losing much blood. The red liquid dripping from the plane turned out to be hydraulic fluid.

Rescue

Helicopter rescue teams soon landed on the snowy mountain. In good time all survivors were evacuated. Scott rode in the helicopter with the copilot, who was feeling the weight of some responsibility for the tragedy. He repeatedly said, "I'm sorry. I'm so sorry."

Miraculously, only four of the sixteen people on board had serious injuries, and no one was killed. Twelve passengers, including Scott, were quickly treated and sent home. The medical personnel released him, but his tormenting memories did not. Scott had previously piloted small aircraft for recreation and had been a frequent passenger on commercial flights for his sales rep job. However, for the next three years, he developed an escalating phobia of flying. Here, in his own words, is what happened:

I thought I would slowly get over my fear of flying. But instead, a daily obsession with the crash plagued me. Tapes of it played over and over in my mind and spawned fears of injury or death befalling my family, especially my daughter, Sarah. My fears, strongest while we were on our frequent boating trips, motivated me to see a psychiatrist. However, my problems only mushroomed.

I became obsessed with watching the weather forecast and planned all of my travel to avoid storms. Whenever I arrived at an airport, I increasingly found myself thinking of fires and death. As I entered a plane, I began to visualize the passengers up and down the aisle as skeletons or the grim reaper.

Panic Attacks

In January of 1992, almost two years to the date after the accident, I boarded another flight to Reno. Snow flurries and poor visibility reminded me of the weather the day of the crash. I was assigned a window seat by an exit. Feeling nervous, I asked to trade seats, but no one was willing to move. I became more and more fearful as I watched the snow swirling outside the window of the plane. I tried to calm myself by reading a Psalm in the Bible while waiting for takeoff, but soon bounded out of my seat and ran toward the door.

"What's wrong?" asked the surprised flight attendant.

*"This is **not** a good day for me to fly. I need to get off this plane **now**," I stated emphatically. I all but ran over her in my urgent need to escape the situation.*

My heart pounded as I retraced my steps out of the plane and back into the terminal. I sat down in tears, wondering what was happening to me. How could I be this upset? I just wanted to call my wife or my mom.

I attempted a trip the next day, but rushed off the plane again, overcome by anxiety. During the following spring and summer I determinedly kept trying, but continued this pattern. One day I tried three times. I ran off two flights, left the airport, turned around and went back to try again. But after my speedy exit from the third plane, I gave up and drove to my destination.

*I can still hear people saying, "Scott, don't you understand the odds against you crashing and surviving and having this happen again? It is just **not** going to happen." My countering thought was, "Baloney! My odds are that it **did** happen and it **could** happen again."*

Full-Blown Phobia

Later that summer I had to go to Joplin, Missouri, my company's corporate headquarters. The first date I scheduled to fly I exited the plane in a complete panic. I rescheduled, and with the help of anti-anxiety drugs I boarded a flight. This time, in spite of two near-panic attacks, I stayed on the plane. However, once there I realized I was in Missouri without a car and did not feel I could possibly fly home!

I spent the next three days going in and out of fear, anxiety, and panic. What was I going to do? What if I got on a plane and it crashed and burned? What if something happened to my family and I was stranded and not able to get home to help? I could not eat or sleep. I had nightmares of flying and crashing.

The only way I could feel moderately comfortable was to take the Xanax™ [a brand of anti-anxiety medication] *my doctor had prescribed for me to use during flights. I repeatedly called my wife, Peggy, to get comfort and to ask her what I should do. I finally rented a car and drove home, defeated. This problem* **was not** *going away.*

The Anger Trap

As time went on, my anger and resentment toward the pilot and toward SkyWest grew. On a trip to Lake Tahoe my wife and I decided to go look at some glider sailplanes, one of the small aircraft I used to love to pilot. The realization hit me: because of my terrible fears, there was absolutely no way I could go up that day as a passenger, much less be the pilot. I broke into tears, looked at my wife, and said, "I'm so damned mad because SkyWest took away what I loved so much. I can't fly anymore, and it wasn't my choice not to be able to fly."

The worse my phobia became, the more angry I got and the more I wanted to sue SkyWest. I decided to meet with a lawyer who was representing four other passengers who were suing them. My lawyer sent a letter to SkyWest explaining what I was going through.

A representative from their insurance company called and offered me a settlement, which I accepted. However, the settlement did not decrease my anger. I would have given the money back in a heartbeat to be able to erase the whole experience and its terrible effects on me.

Increasing Anxieties and Allergies

The following January my wife Peg tracked me down at my friend's business to tell me my dad had died. I had fond memories of flying in small aircraft with my father and somehow his death made an irrational connection in my brain: plane crash = death of father. My anxieties increased, attacking me with tremendous strength. I began having panic attacks even

76

when I was on road trips and my throat began to swell, adding to my other phobias. I began to focus on my throat and it seemed that when I was out of town it was always swollen and I often choked when I ate. I worried that my throat would totally close up and I would choke to death.

My doctor saw nothing wrong and referred me to a specialist who said I had become allergic to pollens, molds, and dust. My job required me to travel, yet travel pushed me into so much anxiety I couldn't stand it. Every doctor I visited found a new problem that I believed in. I had a whole shoe box full of pills that were supposed to "take care" of my problems, but all of those pills only seemed to make matters worse.

Downward Spiral

When I drove out of town I took two Xanax™ every four hours, two Valium™ every three hours, and drank Scotch at night. Being dependent on drugs was very demeaning. I also lost more confidence each time I drove halfway to Reno, panicked, and turned around and went home.

I remember saying to my wife, "Peggy, I don't understand anything anymore; what am I going to do? What is wrong with me? Am I going insane?" She did her best to comfort me, and it was only her love and support that made my life bearable.

I finally went to my priest and told him I wasn't sure whether I was crazy and needed to be committed to a hospital for treatment or was just going through a weird stage. He referred me to another psychiatrist, who prescribed more medication to help stop my anxiety and fear. It did not fix the problem, but may have kept me from going all the way over the edge.

By this time I didn't even like to go out of my house. I was obsessed with the fear that my allergies were going to put me into anaphylactic shock [a serious, often life-threatening allergic reaction, characterized by low blood pressure and difficulty breathing]. I never left the house without the supplies I needed to give myself a shot just in case. My self-worth had vanished.

The only positives were unfailing family support and great peers at work. My boss said, "Scott, don't worry; you stay home and get your problems taken care of. I'll cover for you." With the fear of losing my job taken off my shoulders, I was more free to deal with myself. But that "self" was a walking basket case full of anger toward the people I felt were responsible for all my misery. I felt I had not come through for my family and had let my company down.

Referral

Finally an uncle who had survived a head-on collision (fatal to the other driver) referred me to the Wound and Injury Recovery Center where I got the help I so desperately needed. From the very beginning I learned things I wish I had known right after the plane crash, things that made sense and immediately gave me hope that there was a cure for my symptoms.

I learned about specific health care directions that survivors need as soon as they are medically stable. My father was a physician, but that hadn't helped me get the treatment I needed for my emotional wounds. If I had received specific guidelines for dealing with my side effects and symptoms early on, they would have diminished instead of becoming progressively worse. Although a traumatic event may not even cause a scratch physically, the intensity of the experience may result in severe psychological crippling unless immediate attention is given to the emotional wounds that are inevitable. I was a case in point!

Mind-Body Connection

Without any beating around the bush, I was told that I was in control of the only remedy for my symptoms, which was learning to use my mind productively instead of painfully obsessing about what had happened to me. The key idea is in a James Allen quote:

The body is the servant of the mind. It obeys the operations of the mind, whether they be deliberately chosen or automatically expressed. There is no physician like cheerful thought for dissipating the ills of the body; there is no comforter to compare with good will for dispersing the shadows of grief and sorrow.

The IRO-STEPS tutorials focused my energy in a positive direction. I began to experience a welcome relief from my dependence upon pills and the endless need for professional treatment. I was excited about my rapid progress.

Memory Bank

In the Memory Bank Tutorial, Scott learned that painful life experiences often cause reactive behaviors later on. The five most common categories of disruptive reactions in the face of fear are fight, flight, fake, fold, and freeze (see Memory Bank Tutorial, Appendix 1, p. 147).

Negative habits of thought and behavior from the past had seriously crippled Scott in his recovery. He could see how they connected to his current personality and victimization. He was taught to identify and understand the mental stumbling blocks that were not letting him thrive after his survival. Experiences he did not even remember were affecting his current thinking, actions, and personality. Gaining an understanding of why he thought the way he did and learning that he could choose a better way to think made all the difference. By taking correct steps and keeping focused on the goal of recovery instead of on losses and limitations (living in today and tomorrow, not yesterday), he was assured he could overcome his problems and pain.

Psychic Energy Battery

The Psychic Energy Battery Tutorial was given to Scott immediately after his assessment. (This tutorial is explained in George Miller's experience, pp. 56–57, and summarized in Appendix 1, pp. 149–50.) Negative programming and outdated ideas from Scott's early life were stored in his memory bank. They had drained his psychic energy battery and left him susceptible to psychological problems. This tutorial was a key to new successes because it helped Scott make the necessary changes to begin recharging his psychic energy battery.

Hour of Power

One of the important changes Scott made that is still important in his life was to implement the Hour of Power. To this day he usually gets up, reads for twenty minutes, exercises for twenty minutes, and meditates for twenty minutes. This practice became a critical means of stretching his mind, learning to think in positive ways, learning why he felt certain ways and why certain things happened to him. Faithfully practicing the Hour of Power was a big part of learning to thrive rather than just going through life as he had before (see Appendix, p. 176).

The Importance of Other Tutorials

The Basic Necessities and Human Stimulants Tutorial informed Scott and his wife of the seven basic elements for effectively nurturing their relationship (see Appendix 1, pp. 152–58). They were also taught that the most important factor in healing emotional wounds is having primary nurturing relationships, and Scott recognized that it was only Peggy's sensitive support that had kept him going to this point. Together, Peggy and Scott learned that if they kept their priorities straight and spent prime time nurturing each other first, they would experience the enhancement of self-worth necessary to thrive versus merely survive.

Tutorials number 4, 5, and 6 (Human Intimacy, the Drivers, and the Fatal Five Compensations) cautioned them about "be busy" activities and false successes that could build walls rather than encourage positive family interactions (see Appendix 1, pp. 159–66.). Scott and Peggy learned to decipher thoughts and ideas they had stored in their minds that were now outdated and interfering with current relationships. Scott was then able to identify the fear that was undermining his frantic efforts to overcome the trauma of his plane crash. He continues his story:

Reconciliation with SkyWest

Surprisingly, an essential part of my recovery was made possible by the concern and compassion of SkyWest. Their willingness to help with this process was even more amazing because of my threatened lawsuit and the settlement they had already made the year before. Barry and I wrote them a letter explaining my situation, what we needed for the "in vivo desensitization" process and why. They graciously offered to help in any way they could.

When we met with them I could see their sincere concern for my emotional well-being and how much they wanted to help. The corporate face really was human! After interacting with these officials, much of my anger dissipated, and I actually felt I owed them an apology for threatening to sue. They went out of their way to help me, and their attitude and actions renewed my faith in people.

Because of this reconciliation, late as it was, I moved from terrible anger to writing a "Letter to the Editor" of our local newspaper, singing SkyWest's praises and thanking them publicly. I know that everyone makes mistakes—the SkyWest pilots made some big ones that hurt a lot of people. I made the mistake of harboring anger toward the pilots and the company. But it is what you do to rectify the mistake that counts. SkyWest did their best to rectify the mistake, and if I had made reconciliation earlier, I could have saved myself all that counterproductive anger.

To this day I still think about the pilot and copilot and wish I could have had some closure by meeting with them. I heard that the pilot quit flying because of the accident and was running a bar in Montana. I also learned that the copilot had never gone back to work and was on psychological disability. It is too bad they did not receive the tutorials and an opportunity to reconcile with the passengers.

In Vivo Desensitization

Each tutorial I received was invaluable to help prepare me for the "in vivo" desensitization [discussed in Art Van Tielen's story, p. 68 and in Appendix 1, p. 171]. I feel that this process finally freed me from the phobias and aversions that had held me hostage for such a long, painful time. Here is the process I went through, one step at a time, to become desensitized from my exaggerated fears:

1. SkyWest Airlines arranged for me to spend time in a small aircraft similar to the one I was on that crashed. I went into the maintenance hangar at the airport and boarded the plane, but broke into tears and ran out of the aircraft.

   We went back the next day and this time I successfully completed the preliminary clinical procedures. Sitting in the aircraft for several hours, I gradually adjusted to being on a plane again and felt comfortable there.

2. On a later visit, we boarded and the pilot taxied all around the airport tarmac.

3. Next, SkyWest's Senior Vice President, John Ligtermoet, and pilots Jim Christopherson and Kyle Smith took Richards and me on a flight around the Salt Lake Valley for approximately an hour. During the flight I was applying everything I had previously learned—especially the "M&Ms" (Memorize to Minimize intrusive thoughts and Maximize progress). That

81

process kept my thoughts more positive and finally gave me some control over the panic and aversions that had built up over the years.

As I exited the plane I realized that it was God's spirit that had given me the peace of mind I needed to enjoy the flight. I hadn't thought about dying; instead, I had remembered pleasant times spent flying with my dad. I got off the plane a proud person.

4. *The next clinical procedure was to fly to the crash scene. As I looked down at the mountain where we had crashed, I felt excited that I was putting that experience in the past. I was actually flying again without anxiety or panic!*

    Over the years since the crash, I had visited the executive air terminal about six times, but couldn't consider going on a flight because of my fears. But the day after my excursion to the crash site, I made an appointment with an instructor to pilot a small aircraft—another clinical procedure I had requested.

5. *That day I felt more excitement than fear as Richards and I walked toward the plane and boarded. I got into the pilot's seat, taxied, and took off with no problem. I was actually flying again! What I had missed most was finally back in my life. Excitedly I gave a "high five" sign. The flight went fine and I loved it. I finally had some confidence again.*

6. *The next step was to fly on a jet to Reno, but the day I scheduled the flight a severe snowstorm blew in. The airport closed so I did not have to fly that day, but I was beating myself up because of my anxiety. "**Nobody** would want to fly on a day like this," people said repeatedly. However, I was still not feeling good about myself because of my fears.*

    The following day we set off on our second attempt to complete the final clinical procedure for aircraft phobia. I didn't know whether I was ready or not. It had become so much easier for me to run out of the plane rather than stay on a flight, but I realized that what mattered most was my happiness and my family's happiness. I had to do this for all of us.

My mind was racing in circles as I boarded the jet aircraft. Three times I won the battle with my familiar desire to run out of the plane by repeating to myself quotes I had memorized, such as

- Whatever the mind can conceive and believe it can achieve.

- That which I persist in doing becomes easier, not that the nature of the thing has changed but that my ability to do has increased.

- If it is to be, it is up to me.

At takeoff I was finally calm. I talked peacefully with others throughout the entire flight and actually enjoyed the flight. On the return trip I boarded the plane without a problem and felt amazingly relaxed on the flight home.

Dragons Slain and Dreams Come True

Two days later my daughter and I realized a dream we had shared for seven years. I took her flying in a small plane—with an instructor, of course. I took off, flew, and landed without any fear or anxiety. That was four years ago.

After the trauma of being in a plane crash, a serious phobia became my enemy, my dragon. I thank God for leading me to the help I needed to slay that dragon and realize my dreams. I am a living example that seeking, learning, and loving can make the difference.

Key Points in Chapter Six

Too often people who survive traumatic experiences believe their symptoms are merely a passing phase and will go away on their own. As a result, help is delayed until the problems have grown to the point that they begin to interfere with daily living. A key principle is: don't wait! Apply the principles taught in this book, seek help, and take positive control of your life.

Trauma survivors who have emotional wounds frequently become caught up in the maze of the medical care system. Because there are both physical and mental components to emotional wounds, patients are often seen by physicians and other health care providers in a variety of specialties. Often each individual provider will add to or modify the treatment regimen with different drugs. The result can be disastrous because of the numerous interactions between medications, including nonprescription drugs. It is critical to let each physician know exactly what medications you are taking, including the nonprescription items, before more medications are added. As noted earlier, emotional trauma results in a general depletion of the body's energy; thus, medications can affect the body differently than they normally would—and often these effects are unwanted.

Fear is an almost universal emotion among trauma survivors. In the presence of fear there are several different behaviors that can emerge. An easy way to remember the most common reactions to fear are the "Five Fs": fight, flight, fake, fold, or freeze. Fight is often demonstrated as blind anger and fighting against everything in sight. Flight manifests itself in the many forms of escapism, some physical and some emotional; too often the escape is into a bottle of alcohol or drugs. Fake is typified by the facade that "I'm doing just fine." To fold is literally giving up and letting every imaginable physical or emotional problem render the person incapable of even minimal productive activity. Freeze is the sheer panic that is felt in ever-increasing episodes by survivors with unresolved emotional wounds.

The Hour of Power is a tool used successfully by many people to prepare for the day. It consists of three, twenty-minute blocks of time for physical exercise, learning (generally reading uplifting books), and meditation or prayer. This hour often proves to be critical in changing the negative patterns of trauma survivors.

As a part of the Basic Necessities and Human Stimulants Tutorial, the importance of a nurturing relationship is emphasized. Generally this relationship is with a spouse or parent; whoever it is, the person is integrally involved in the healing process. Without such nurturing it is extremely difficult for anyone to heal on their own. This is not a relationship that can be established with a therapist or other "outsider" whose interests in the survivor are not extremely personal.

When fears have reached the point of becoming phobias, the process of *in vivo* desensitization has proven to be an effective technique in overcoming them. This is the step-by-step process of conquering extreme fear by a series of successive activities that involve live encounters with the object of fear. Each activity brings the person into greater contact with the object of their fear in an environment that is safe and supportive until they are able to deal with it on their own.

7

Rape!

Marianne Carson's story highlights the effectiveness of clinical traumatology in conquering trauma-related depression, even when the memory of the trauma has been repressed. Currently, the basic principles of clinical traumatology are effective life-management tools widely taught piecemeal. When implemented as a whole package, the concepts in this book have the power to benefit any person regardless of circumstances. For more than forty years, Marianne could not remember the trauma that had so negatively affected her life. The symptoms and re-traumatization were evident, but the original event continued to elude her. Its life-damaging effects were frustrating beyond measure until she engaged in the IRO-STEPS tutorials that gave her the skills (enabling her to stop recycling her terrible trauma-related depressions) and the motivation to embark on a healing journey.

In this chapter we will use the term "pus pockets" to describe the festering emotional wounds that continued to plague Marianne. "Pus pockets" is a metaphoric clinical traumatology concept used to describe the consequences of emotional wounds left unresolved which consequently lead to thought contamination, dysfunctional behavior, and disturbed relationships. "Brain boils" is another term sometimes used for this condition. The process of working through Marianne's trauma was more lengthy than most others we have described. Like Gene Hockenbury, her initial trauma happened long ago and she received no help at the time. The longer the time that elapses from trauma to treatment, the longer it may take to heal. The process that finally freed Marianne, although it took over three years, was a healing journey. At a cost of these years of hard work she bought back a productive and happy life. Because of the sensitive nature of her material, Marianne has used a pseudonym and has changed the names of those involved. **But her experience is painfully real. She shares it in her own words.**

My oppressive, chronic depression was beginning to take on a fatal feeling. I had always loathed this cycle, but this time I was beginning to hate being alive to experience it again. All I wanted to do was curl up on my bed in my dark room with the door closed. Yet with four teenagers and a demanding husband, my hollow hibernation was frequently, startlingly interrupted.

One Sunday morning when I would not, could not move off the couch to leave for church, Stuart asked in desperation, "What do you want me to do, Marianne?"

My response to him was, "I don't know and I don't care."

Looking for a Lifeline

Frightened and frustrated, Stuart went to our minister for advice. He referred us to a clinician he knew and regarded highly. When Stuart told me about the Wound and Injury Recovery Center and asked me to make an appointment, I said, "Whatever." It didn't really matter to me. Nothing mattered anymore.

I was worn down, burned out by twelve years of sporadic failed therapeutics, and had no will to go on. Our two oldest children had recently been hospitalized because of their own destructive acting out. The new concepts we learned in family therapy during their recovery held out tiny moments of hope—short-lived because of my inability to change old thought patterns and behaviors. The profound emptiness remained; the aftermath was bitterness.

Still, to get my husband off my back, I called the number he gave me. Quite frankly, Barry Richards's enthusiasm and optimism over the phone irritated the hell out of me. Who was this "happiness pusher," I thought? I didn't have the energy to deal with him. If he was this way on the phone, I could skip the "sunshine" of an office visit. Even if I cared, I didn't have the strength. This guy made me tired.

I'm not sure why, but I kept the appointment. The deep, dull ache in my soul made my legs feel leaden. My movements were lethargic as I located the elevator and pushed the button for the fifth floor. "Why, why am I trying again?" I wondered.

First Tutorial—Memory Bank

My memories of that first meeting are a blur... Evaluation... Introspection... Have your husband come with you next time. Would your children come in for a family session?... Read in The Road Less Traveled*... Memory Bank Tutorial. To top it all off, as I left the first educational tutorial with my head spinning, Richards added another ton to my misery by interjecting, "I think it is significant that you have decided to come to a male clinician. The cross-gender work is very powerful in healing"* (see Cross-Gender Work in the Glossary).

Right, I thought to myself in sarcastic inner monologue, Whatever you say. I don't expect this to last long anyway, so whatever.

*He **was** different, I had to give him that. And the Memory Bank Tutorial explaining "pus pockets" from unhealed past experiences did spark my curiosity. But that drivel about my ability to become a "creative achiever" versus staying a "victim creature"—I could not fathom that possibility for my life. It's too late for me, I thought. Ninety-nine percent too late.*

Soul Surgery for Survival

I had to maintain my sarcasm, my fatalism, my hopelessness. Risking the one percent held fear on both sides. It was my last shot and if it didn't succeed, I felt I'd surely die. If it did succeed, I had a terrible fear of the unknown—where would that success lead me?

I sensed I was being offered more than bandages, more than behavior modification, more than hand-holding sympathy. I had always hoped to find a clinician who could teach me how to nurture and be nurtured in return. But I could not trust what clinical traumatology offered me—not yet.

I was worn out and my temporary infusion of spunk soon ran out. I had not come to this new experience as an identified "trauma" victim. I had no visible current fractures or open wounds. Yet my empty, broken spirit said to me, "This is about surviving." Both "surviving" and "thriving" were frequently said in the same phrase, same breath, but I was not ready for "thriving." Still, no matter how much I recoiled at the idea of discovering my hidden wounds and fractures, I somehow knew I had finally found a path that would lead to healing from them.

I began to sit in the humble student's seat and through the density of my depression began to absorb small infusions of hope from the tutorials.

What I would soon realize, however, was that this process was going to be soul surgery, minus dependency or numbing anesthesia. These early therapeutics would be called "ICU (intensive care unit) days" and that meant I could be in contact with the Center as often as necessary, but not just for comfort. I would have to be learning and applying the correct principles that were being taught in the tutorials. Somehow, I believed the IRO-STEPS principles enough to act on them.

The Gauntlet

Thus began a difficult, and sometimes discouraging journey. I knew it was THE journey for my life. In the directed reading I came upon this quotation from Scott Peck's The Road Less Traveled:

> These possessions [delayed gratification, a sense of worth, and trust in the safety of existence] are ideally acquired through the self-discipline and consistent and genuine caring of [one's] parents; they are the most precious gifts of themselves that mothers and fathers can bequeath. When these gifts have not been proffered by one's parents, it is possible to acquire them from other sources, but in that case the process of their acquisition is invariably an uphill struggle, often of lifelong duration and often unsuccessful.[1]

Now that I understood what clinical traumatology had to offer me I could not, would not accept the edict of "often unsuccessful." Now I had hope; now I knew that I could recover from the deep losses of my childhood. I had the trust in Barry that I had never had in a therapist before. Now that I knew recovery and growth were possible I couldn't accept any less. Peck's quote was a literal gauntlet thrown at my feet. I felt the deep meaning of his words, and I knew this was the journey of my soul's survival. So I bent and reached for that gauntlet and picked it up. I felt both excited and terrified.

This process of clinical traumatology was so blatantly different from the conventional psychotherapy I had been involved in. It wasn't about depending on someone to hold my hand while I talked. It was about pro-active involvement in my own growth and encouraging my own independence.

---

[1] *The Road Less Traveled*, by M. Scott Peck, MD, Simon and Schuster; Touchstone Books, 1983

The tutorials gave me specific steps, specific assignments, specific focus. I was required to make efforts on my own behalf, to learn better ways of thinking and doing. Reciprocal work was expected. The outlined tutorials were the source of inspiration and new direction for my life, and I was determined to succeed.

The Only Way Out Is Through

The long journey back to an unknown destination was excruciatingly painful. But one truth I've come to know soul-deep is that "The only way out is through." I have often wanted to transform that saying into a concrete object and throw it over a cliff. I have hated its truth, yet no matter how I raged against it, I have known how deeply true that saying is.

So I took the maps of the tutorials and lessons learned from clinical traumatology as my guide on the journey to find the source of the monsters, the reeking "pus pockets," of my life. Much of the time my husband, Stuart, was with me. The Principle of Equivalency taught us that we were drawn to each other because of the similarity of our painful past experiences (see Principle of Equivalency in the Glossary). *It felt familiar to be together.*

A Difficult Decision

When I began to thaw from the deep freeze of my depression, I began to realize another truth. I wanted out of my painful marriage and I wanted to be justified in that decision. Stuart and I had a turbulent and empty relationship. It began when we married on the rebound and I was pregnant. Somehow I had thought that the security he represented would be enough. I even thought that I could learn to love him and that we could grow together.

*I had become convinced that I could heal personally, but too much pain in our lives together, too much negative history, barred my belief that we could heal the marriage. I could not imagine that **any** number of tutorials or changes of paradigm or restructuring could make enough difference.*

To my dismay I became convinced that we needed to give our marriage one more shot before we could think of declaring "no hope." The description of what we would have to do was summarized in Peck's book: we were now embarking upon "an enormously difficult process of completely restructuring a marriage." We had invested over twenty years of our lives into this family. We had had six children together; two of them we had buried as newborns. We had a home and had built a life in our community and church. Most definitely, we were encouraged that our marriage was worth a very great effort to rescue, restructure, and try to breathe life into. Stuart agreed wholeheartedly.

With patience and encouragement I was finally persuaded to try. Soul weary, I reached inside to search for any fragment of strength or energy I had left. I found a few grains of strength in my fear of going it alone if we divorced.

Basic Necessities and Human Stimulants

Very slowly, hope and sporadic growth became realities for Marianne. Gradually Stuart and Marianne learned to recognize what was so painful and missing in their marriage and that they could choose to make necessary changes. They were taught about the Basic Necessities of relationships—Recognition, Acknowledgment, and Acceptance. They also learned about the Human Stimulants—Touch, Talk, Activities, and Material Things (see Basic Necessities and Human Stimulants Tutorial in Appendix 1, pp. 152–58). They tried, struggled, and committed themselves to do "Preventive Maintenance"—defined as providing the Basic Necessities and Human Stimulants in the relationship at regular, frequent, and predictable intervals. They were encouraged to acknowledge the progress and efforts both were making and to clarify each other's needs and expectations in the relationship. Their communications had previously been so sparse that they felt they were starting at ground zero. Marianne continues:

Small Miracles and Low Places

The Principle of Equivalency helped me recognize that I was bringing shortcomings to our marriage from my damaged life every bit as much as Stuart was bringing shortcomings from his. I became more humble, more willing to accept my part of the responsibility and do my share of the work before us. There were times of small victories that seemed gigantic to us and then there were times of discouraging relapses that felt almost insurmountable. Many times I felt like packing it in and saying, "That's all, folks." But each time, a small miracle would bring me back to the healing journey and the gauntlet that I had picked up for myself.

The Human Intimacy Tutorial was especially painful for me. I realized how deprived of necessary nurturing both Stuart and I had been in our families of origin (see Human Intimacy Tutorial, Appendix 1, p. 151). This had negatively impacted our marriage and our parenting abilities. A deep chasm seemed to open before us to keep us from the effective implementation of the principle of nurturing in our lives. It marked a real low point in our work.

Boomerang

After struggling through this discouraging phase, progress began again. I experienced months of positive and negative events, to be sure, yet I seemed able to handle them all. It was one of my strongest times since beginning the tutorials, but lasted only until our daughter's first child (our first grandchild) was born in late summer. Instantly, a mental and emotional boomerang took me back to the traumatic circumstances of my pregnancy twelve years before.

Soon after being confined to bed for complications of my pregnancy, tests revealed that one of our twins was deceased in the uterus. By the time labor was induced and births accomplished, both baby girls were stillborn. I felt that my world and life had ended. For medical reasons this had to be my last pregnancy. I'd always wanted twins—such a perfect way to finish our family. But suddenly the unthinkable had happened and I did not believe I could live through it, nor did I want to. I thank God for our young children who were still in need of their mother's care. If it had not been for them, I would have given up.

Triggered by our granddaughter's cesarean birth, all my traumatization from twelve years earlier resurfaced. From my viewpoint, the death of my babies had been the single most traumatic event of my life. With the help of clinical traumatology, I began processing the unresolved trauma I had suffered after that loss. To the clinical eye, my response to this trauma signaled the probability of other unresolved traumas in my past. So we began mining my life story for clues to repressed traumas.

Detective Work

I turned back to tread old territory I'd covered earlier with the Memory Bank, Psychic Energy Battery, and Fear Wheel tutorials (see Appendix 1, pp. 147–50, 166–69). I wondered how this backward journey into the "pus pockets" left by betrayal, abandonment, and tragedy could bring about anything positive. I did, however, recognize one major positive— how deeply I had come to trust the healing work of clinical traumatology.

Yet by spring I felt that much of the progress we had previously woven was unraveling before my eyes. I was depressed again and felt I was limping or crawling from one crisis to another. I didn't realize that a deeply hidden past trauma might be keeping me in the camp of the "walking wounded." I was in such pain that I inadvertently created daily problems for myself.

With Stuart's input added to my own, we began to form a composite list of my recurring symptoms. Mounting clinical evidence pointed to a significant sexual trauma of which I had no conscious memory.

Was It the End?

When it was hinted, even suggested to me by Stuart (during one of our couple tutorials) that I go hunting this monster, I emphatically refused. I would not go there and no one could make me. I could not go there. If I should find this monster, I thought it would surely kill me. I'd rather just move ahead and do the best I could. Look at what I'd accomplished, the distance I had covered. How could anyone ask me to go further, look deeper? No, I could not. This was the end of my quest.

It even appeared to be the end of the marriage. I needed to get away from Stuart, from it all. I moved in with my friend, Hannah, in a neighboring town and felt some temporary relief. But soon I felt as if all hell was erupting inside me. My pain became so intense, mentally and physically, that I almost began to believe again that "the only way out is through." That thought terrified me beyond any feeling I had ever felt. Only my weekly contact with Barry Richards gave me the courage to explore my past more deeply. What I already knew of my life and past traumas was bad enough. But if I had repressed all memory of something even worse, uncovering what had happened could be more hellish than the excruciating pain I was already living with.

The Search

I had no idea how to even begin a search for that which caused my amnesia of an elusive past trauma. Yet it seemed that even the thought of beginning brought people and books and events into my life that helped me start the journey. I met Kelly at my new job. She was currently working through her own traumatic childhood experiences. We connected instantly and I felt kinship with her on many levels. We shared many ideas and interests and she was very supportive of me in my new circumstances. Not by chance, I was given two books: As a Man Thinketh, *Volume 2 by James Allen, and* Family Secrets, *by John Bradshaw.[2] These books helped me to begin pulling at and loosening the edges of the scab covering the deepest pus pocket still trapped in the recesses of my memory. From the former book, one quote proved invaluable to me:*

> You may bring about that improved condition in your outward life which you desire, if you will unswervingly resolve to improve your inner life... As you proceed, golden opportunities will be strewn across your path, and the power and judgment to properly utilize them will spring up within you. Genial friends will come unbidden to you; sympathetic souls will be drawn to you as the needle is to the magnet; and books and all outward aids that you require will come to you unsought.

Pieces of the Puzzle

The day I took my photo album with me to my tutorial, I was introduced to the "in vivo desensitization" procedure of the Injury Recovery Orientation-STEPS (see Appendix 1, p. 171). Soon thereafter, Barry and I drove to the neighborhood of my early childhood. Walking around my old yard and neighborhood stirred mostly happy, fond memories. I talked about all the things I could remember from age three to eight. It was a pleasant excursion and I felt there was nothing to be discovered in that place.

The next day was a different story. By late morning I was developing the worst migraine headache of my entire life. The physical problems and nightmares I had experienced over much of my life immediately intensified. I was assured this meant progress. The trip to my old home, reading about lost memory, and my growing friendship with Kelly combined their strength to pull the scab off my deepest emotional wound.

Somehow during this time, Stuart and I were reconciled to the degree that I moved back home. Amidst the turmoil of my search, Stuart was supportive of me and hopeful about our future. As I drew closer to my

---

[2] Family Secrets, by John Bradshaw, Bantam Books, New York, 1995.

most horrific memory, I needed to be in the safety of my own home where I felt a measure of comfort with Stuart and my grown children.

I continued to meet with Barry Richards at intervals and he encouraged me to keep applying the principles I had learned in the tutorials. He also assured me I could find the courage inside myself to continue my search.

The work was slow and painful. Then, metaphorically, I came to the edge of a cliff. I could not look over it nor step off it into the dark unknown. There seemed nowhere else to go. How could I ever discover the incident which so eluded me?

Ironically, at this difficult time I found an unsought expert—my estranged sister. I soon discovered she had been traveling a similar path. It seemed such weird timing, so strange that she would be sharing anything with me. She told me that until she had been able to accept and embrace her "inner child self" that had been the victim, she could not progress in her healing. These shared concepts offered by my sister turned out to be a turning point for me, a breakthrough concept for my process of memory retrieval.

Slowly, over a period of several weeks, I had a framework and a few clues, yet the actual traumatic event still continued to be totally elusive. I realized I would have to mentally and emotionally reconnect with myself as a child in order to find the puzzle pieces that finished the "picture." I tried diligently to find them on my own, but could not. Finally, I phoned Dr. Cardwell, an expert in memory retrieval that I had been referred to and made an appointment. [Dr. Cardwell, another pseudonym, is a clinical psychologist who specializes in memory retrieval using hypnosis.] Thus began the final miles of this journey.

Over a period of five weeks, with Dr. Cardwell's help, I uncovered the pieces to the picture of my six-year-old self being raped. Betrayed by a teenage uncle whom I adored, I had been raped while he was in a rage, then threatened with horrific scenarios of death and dismemberment of my parents if I told anyone. He left me in a dark basement room where I lay curled and paralyzed, bleeding and broken in a rough, cold concrete corner. And he ran.

The Aftermath and Healing

This was the monstrous act at the bottom of my cliff. For days after the memory returned, I felt as though my forty-six-year old self had just been raped, fallen off the cliff, and I experienced all the aftermath of rape *trauma.* **Now** *there was a current trauma aftermath to treat with the IRO-STEPS.*

From that moment on, I went concurrently through all the stages of recovery work of a rape victim. But I did not go alone—Stuart and Barry Richards were my stability. I went through the "ICU" process once again and had times when I needed the intensive care of immediate support and validation. I felt so torn apart from normal. I had to be reassured that the symptoms I was experiencing, such as panic attacks, startle reflex, and anxiety attacks, **were** normal and to be expected in the aftermath of rape. Those contacts provided the acceptance, support, and reassurance I wasn't receiving anywhere else

Just knowing that my reactions were normal somehow helped me to cope. Sometimes I was reminded of portions of previously learned tutorials that helped connect my fragmented feelings. I felt dirty and damaged and not worthy of acceptance. Richards validated me as a person, and knowing that he was not repulsed by me was vital to my healing. Because I trusted him and the clinical traumatology process, I was able to tell him anything I was feeling, no matter how ridiculous it sounded. He would tell me I had every right to feel that way and that I was progressing, that I would get better and that I wouldn't always hurt this badly. I had to take it on faith, as I had in the beginning, because I didn't know if it was true. But little by little I started to believe it.

My friends, Kelly and Hannah, were most supportive; my children and some of my siblings were there for me too. In time, blessed time (a period of several months) and with my ever-growing spiritual convictions, I began to heal.

Years later, I am still amazed at the resiliency of that precious, tiny child within. I cannot in my adult mind imagine how that child survived that ordeal. I honor her as my hero and I know I can do anything difficult in this life because she is part of me. We have been to hell and survived. Together we would now be able to THRIVE with the perfect love of God. He loves all his children and will **always** provide a way for them to overcome the past.

The Rewards of Perseverance

The procedures and information of clinical traumatology work together best for those who are able to combine their own determination with support from those who care the most; family, friends and other loved ones. The outcome for those who persevere can be freedom from the past and ongoing personal fulfillment. No short-cuts exist. A price must be paid in time and energy as well as money. The time frame with the IRO-STEPS tutorials is usually weeks or months. With Marianne, it was longer, partly because of the initial hopelessness she felt after struggling through so many years of con-ventional psychotherapy to no avail. It was difficult for her to muster the strength to believe there was something different that could actually help her.

Today, Marianne is a role model to many. She is acquiring her advanced education and contributing to her community. She is a source of encouragement to those who learn of her triumph over early childhood abuse. Though her marriage eventually dissolved, Marianne's increasing inner strength has seen her through the tran-sition and she is doing incredibly well. Her life is evidence of the reality that "a mind once stretched with new information" can ulti-mately transcend the pain of the past.

Key Points in Chapter Seven

The mind's ability to repress horrifying events is truly remarkable. However, even though an event has been forgotten, the wounds that it caused are still present. They often continue to fester, leading to behaviors and feelings all the more frustrating and frightening because the event that precipitated them is not available to the conscious mind. Victims of repressed traumas which still produce negative and inappropriate emotions and behaviors will benefit from the "Specific, Early, Educational Directions" (SEEDs) strategy.

Repressed traumas will generally take longer to resolve than those which are recent and remembered. If the SEEDs interventions are implemented within twenty-four to seventy-two hours after a trauma, the process of going through the IRO-STEPS tutorials and the associated learning activities can be accomplished in four to six weeks. In the case of long-repressed trauma the process may take four to six months, or longer.

Although the details (or even the nature of the event) behind repressed traumas are not remembered, there is a conscious feeling that "something" happened in the past that causes great pain and confusion.

The SEEDs approach requires active participation on the part of the trauma survivor. Healing cannot be accomplished in a passive mode. This means that the person must commit to be an active part of the healing process because it cannot be done **to** them, it must be done **by** them.

The maxim "The only way out is through" is central to SEEDs. There are no shortcuts; there must be active learning and participation that takes the survivor through the process of transformation and healing. The way out of the pain and suffering is through the active learning process which enables the mind to heal.

Too often people who have unresolved trauma develop a self-image that pushes them toward relationships and activities that are unhealthy. Another reason that early intervention and help is so important is to prevent serious mistakes in choosing mates and associates that tend to reinforce illness rather than encourage healing. This is a part of The Principle of Equivalency.

Human intimacy is a vital part of healthy, productive living. Without such intimacy, nurturing is lost—along with the healing power that can come through it. From the time of birth the need for tender and nurturing contact is present. It is well known that infants in neonatal intensive care units (NICU) who do not get held and cuddled regularly are at a greater risk of dying than those who do. Consequently, volunteers or parents are brought into the NICU solely to hold and nurture these tiny babies. This need continues throughout life.

As noted previously, unresolved traumas compound the effects of additional traumatic incidents. The effects are additive—which means that events that would ordinarily be distressing (but could be dealt with adequately one by one), cumulatively produce symptoms that overwhelm the victim. Get help, regardless of what others may say. Following the suggestions outlined in this book is one effective way to begin that helping process.

8

Gunfight!

Phil Webber, a Provo City (Utah) police officer, shares an experience that emphasizes the necessity of health care tutorials for effectively minimizing the negative effects of difficult pre-trauma experiences on recovery.

Saturday, July 6, 1991, I was working a night shift on the west side of Provo, Utah. It was a warm summer evening, and Utah County Sheriff Deputy Mike Morgan and I had been conferring about a stolen car report. When we parted I headed west toward the boat harbor, and he drove east toward Provo.

Call for Aid

I'd traveled about a mile when my radio crackled to life. It was Mike.

"337, are you still in the area?"

"Yes, I am."

"Do you remember the dirt lane I was talking about? I have three men involved in a fight and I'm on that lane. I need a cover unit."

"I'll be right there."

I put my patrol car into gear and sped to Mike's aid. When I arrived and saw two obviously drunk men, I quickly labeled it a routine intoxication call—if any police call is routine. Mike and I got out of our cars and started toward the men. I instantly changed my assessment when the third man appeared from behind a small house about 125 yards away, menacingly pointed a rifle at us, and began shooting. We took cover behind Mike's car and returned fire.

Slow-Motion Tragedy

There was no time for emotion. Reflexes and training took over, my every movement calculated for survival. I had been thrown into the whirlwind of a life-and-death fight, but the whole scene seemed to be playing in slow motion. The man took hits from both Mike and me—twelve in all. We were not shooting to kill, and he was so drunk he barely seemed to notice he had been shot. I kept thinking, "This is not real; it is not happening." I'd never before had a drunk and disorderly call turn into a gunfight.

As the fourth round blasted from the man's rifle, the bullet tore through the trigger guard of my gun, nearly severing my right index finger. The bullet fragmented and ripped into my right shoulder. I dropped to the ground in stunned disbelief. My arm instantly went numb and at first I thought the blast had severed it from my body. I could see blood squirting out of my neck in an 18-inch stream each time my heart would beat. I was sure I'd be dead in two minutes. The way the blood was pumping, I knew the carotid artery was severed.

Who will help Mike? I wondered. There was a crazy gunman in front of him and two disorderly drunks behind him who might grab my loaded gun.

Who was going to tell my wife I had been shot and killed? was my next thought. I didn't want her notified by phone.

[For the reader's information, the shot that injured Phil was the gunman's last. He had been seriously injured and his weapon had been disabled by one of Mike's shots. One of the drunk men was stunned and submissive and helped care for Phil before the paramedics came. The other drunk man jumped Mike after Phil was shot; Mike had to threaten him with his life to get him to back off.]

Hanging On By a Thread

I faded in and out of consciousness and have only fragments of memory from then on... Mike holding a cloth to my neck trying to stem the bleeding... Paramedics working on me...

Somehow I hung on long enough to get to the emergency room. Nurses I had worked with for many years took care of me. I still believed I was dying: it was just taking longer than I first thought.

Then the doctor examined me and said there was no way the bullet could have hit the carotid artery. By this time I was not bleeding at all.

But four paramedics, two other officers, and the two drunks had seen the proof along with me, the blood pumping out like a geyser with each heartbeat.

*The X-ray vividly showed the bullet fragment. Before it had entered my shoulder, it had severed my trigger finger. However, it was now split like a three-pronged treble fishhook with the prongs wrapped **around** my carotid artery. My wife and I believe an angel saved my life. There seems to be no other explanation.*

With the comforting realization that I might not die after all, I lapsed into total unconsciousness for the next three days. I was so heavily sedated for the week following that I remember very little about what happened. I don't even remember when my wife was with me and when she wasn't.

Karen, Phil's wife, remembers clearly the day Phil was shot. Their fourth grandchild was born the night before and the day of the shooting was their first grandchild's birthday. Karen expected it to be a day of celebration. Instead, it was a day of near tragedy.

Phil Webber's circumstances could have played out like those of so many others in law enforcement who are involved in a shooting. Statistically, most never return to work. If they do, it is generally after a two-year break. But for him, it would be different.

Approximately six months earlier, Chris Glem, the worker's compensation insurance claims adjuster now assigned to Phil's case, had learned about the urgency of providing immediate attention to emotional wounds. Chris Glem knew exactly what Phil needed and made rapid arrangements. As a result, Phil would beat the statistics.

Phil Webber was an experienced police officer who had a reputation for being a "street cop" who had been involved in several high-risk incidents. Still he had never before been injured on the job. Phil knew his job and the level of performance expected. Consequently, dealing with physical recovery and the possibility of facing the future without a trigger finger presented some ominous challenges. He was aware of the politics of his profession and the impact they had on his whole life. What could he expect?

Personal Dilemma

Not unlike others in law enforcement, Phil's background provided ample experience and preparation for both personal success *or* failure. Phil was always ready to take decisive action and do the job "the right way." He seemed undaunted by any emergency. He prided himself on being precise, organized, and detailed.

However, Phil saw things as either black or white, with little tolerance for any gray middle ground. This had occasionally resulted in problems with administration. Phil was extremely concerned about what his superiors would think and do in regard to this incident.

Karen was the daughter of a Los Angeles deputy sheriff. The risks involved in Phil's career were "life as usual" for her. Still, Phil did not know how Karen would respond to this new challenge. Typical in the world of police work, Phil's tough-guy "cop mentality" had put a strain on their marriage, and he had expected more from his children than most fathers. Phil had always felt he could handle whatever happened—and he expected his children to do the same. His toughness had been hard on them, even when they became adults.

Resistance to Structured Early Educational Directions

Three days into Phil's recovery Barry Richards walked into Phil's hospital room. Phil was immediately on guard. His first response to Richards' explanation for his visit was a very perturbed, *"What?"* He assumed that Richards was a "shrink," and he had no intention of talking to one, not now, not ever! Here is Phil's description of how things developed:

The first time I was coherent, about three days after the shooting, this guy came into my room who said he was a former police officer. He brought me a newspaper article about another officer he'd worked with who had also been shot.

"I'm Barry Richards," he said. "The worker's compensation claims adjuster requested that I visit you. My job is to tell you what you can expect to happen—in the hospital, when you get out of the hospital, and in the next days and weeks."

I listened to him for a few minutes just to be polite. When he asked if he could visit with me another time, I said, "Sure, I'll talk to you, later."

But I had no intention of talking with him again. Police officers are a very independent breed.

Questions and Confusion

For the next few days I have to admit I worried constantly. What was going to happen to me? Was I going to keep my job? Could the doctor repair my severed trigger finger so I could still shoot? What had happened to the man with the gun? What had happened to Mike and the two drunks? Who was going to take care of my wife if I lost my job? People told me later that I often seemed alert those first few days. But in reality, I didn't remember most of what I was told. I was very confused for a long time because everyone assumed I knew what was going on—and I did not.

The twelfth day after the accident, I was discharged from the hospital knowing I would be in and out of doctors' offices for follow-up exams and physical therapy. I could not get straight answers from anyone—not from my doctors about my medical prognosis as it related to my future, not from the physical therapist about my treatments, nor from my boss about my job. They all told me "maybe this and maybe that." One thing was clear: The police chief said pointedly that I would have to pass demanding psychological and physical tests before I could return to work.

Generally, most trauma survivors involved with the health care tutorials of clinical traumatology are making steady progress by this time. Without them, Phil was going downhill, but was still very reluctant to admit that he needed directions or information. Several things pushed him to the realization of his need for clinical traumatology.

Over a period of time following the shooting Phil was subjected to a series of investigative interviews in which his judgment was questioned and negative inferences were made regarding the way he handled the incident.

He was incredulous when he learned of insinuations about his character and work performance. He also became aware of himself as the target of departmental political debates. Some favored recommending him for a medal while others wanted disciplinary action. No wonder he had strong doubts about his worth to the organization and was cynical when Richards talked with him about the issue of "morale building" and career advancement. Here is what Phil says about that period of time:

*The trauma specialist called me several times at my home, but I was not going to talk to him; I was a cop. I did not need help from a stranger. I could handle this like every other case I had handled. But this time I **was** the case. I just didn't know it.*

I was getting more frustrated with the department heads at work and the doctors who were treating me. I felt the Police Chief was being unfair. I became so angry that I decided to find another job. I was getting better physically, but mentally I was on a roller coaster. I wondered when I was going to get my life back together and if things would ever be the same.

Questions Answered, Trust Established

Finally, I agreed to see Richards in his office. By this time I knew I needed to get the direction I had been offered and had been turning down. But the policeman in me would not let just anyone access my thoughts and feelings. Before we could proceed, I needed to resolve many major concerns and serious questions in my mind. Such as: how could I make a clear distinction between "psycho babble" and clinical traumatology and accept the health care tutorials at face value? To get in better shape emotionally, did I really need to go through the processes I was being told about? Why did I need to deal with problems from my past to solve current ones? What could the IRO-STEPS do for me and how did the After Trauma Assessment differ from a psychological evaluation?

It took several visits before I would let down my guard, let go of the "cop" attitude and let myself trust the process. However, it was not too difficult for me to understand how clinical traumatology had evolved from emergency and trauma team services, much as physical therapy had evolved from nursing. But I needed more facts, and facts were exactly what I was given.

Within six weeks Phil was looking at options and alternatives for his future well-being. Like Gene, Scott, George, and Art, he became converted to the "If it is to be, it is up to me" prescription. He eventually invited his wife to participate in the tutorial procedures and accepted and carried out specific assignments to change his pessimism into optimism.

The Goal of Thriving

Rapidly, Phil came to realize that focusing on the goal of thriving was a major key to his success. This approach made more sense to him than choosing the predictable consequences of looking at all the obstacles and lamenting losses and limitations. Phil's story is a good example of how trauma experiences provide opportunities to make new decisions, move in new directions, and solve problems that otherwise might have been left unsolved. He grasped the reality that it *was possible* for him to turn his career-threatening experience into a positive outcome. He could make choices that would take him to an even better place in his life than before the shooting.

The Loss of a Trigger Finger

Six months into the process, the doctors said they could not save Phil's trigger finger. The bullet had destroyed too much of the bone.

However, by then Phil was a different Phil, and the complexion of his marriage relationship was different, too. Though Phil said that losing his finger was the hardest thing he had to deal with, he was prepared by what he had learned. Even more important was the reassuring comfort Phil felt from Karen. She, too, had benefitted from the tutorials—they had been a catalyst to greater closeness and understanding in their marriage and had improved her ability to give meaningful comfort and reassurance.

———

Karen remembers:

I initially told the doctor, "If Phil loses his trigger finger he loses his job." So the doctor had put it back on the very best he could that first night and Phil had physical therapy for several months. By December it was not improving. He couldn't bend it and it had never healed right. He went to see a specialist in Salt Lake City who said, "My best advice is to have it amputated right away." The news hit Phil hard. Instantly he was dizzy and sick as a dog and had to throw up. He was afraid he might pass out on the way home.

When Phil got this terrible news, I was at work about forty miles from the doctor's office. I had no way of knowing what the doctor had told him, but for some reason began to have flu-like symptoms and thought I was going to throw up. I went home early and found Phil there. We were so close by then that I had sensed the feelings he was experiencing miles away. I was able to comfort him and he handled the disappointment well and got over it very quickly.

Gratefully, Phil observed:

Through all the stress (brought on by the shooting), our marriage stayed together rather than pulling apart in a divorce. We spent a lot of time together during my recuperation, and once Karen began coming to the tutorials vital changes in perspective occurred as we resolved things from the past. Karen also came to realize that unresolved personal issues from her childhood had been hindering our marriage and had been magnified by the trauma of the shooting. We drove to California to talk to Karen's parents and they were very helpful. They explained that she was not the only child in the family who had the problem she was discussing. Karen experienced great relief from the pressure she'd felt from all the years of keeping her concerns inside. Her increased well-being somehow improved our relationship; and that is only one example of things we worked through that really enriched our marriage.

Again, in Karen's words,

Phil changed a lot after the shooting. Seeing things differently, he softened toward the children and toward me. Much of that was spiritual. We became more convinced over time that Phil's recovery was miraculous. Mike told me that he was certain Phil was dying at the scene and would never make it to the hospital. The X-rays are proof of our miracle. We believe in angels and believe that God saved Phil for a purpose. That perspective has given a new dimension to the time we spend together. We feel differently about life and blessed to be given more time to spend together. We want to make the most of it.

Phil concludes,

Statistically, officers involved in a shooting do not go back to work at all, or if they do go back to work, it is after a two-year break. However, because of the direction I had received, I passed all of the physical and psychological tests and went back to work in eight months. I passed the shooting test, shooting against the chief himself. I outshot him with my left hand and he never said another word about my lost trigger finger.

The first week I returned to work I drove to the scene where the shooting took place. I intended to get this flashback thing over with. It didn't happen, and never has.

Benefits of Responsible Application of Principles

I did the studying, I did the research, and everything I was asked to do in the IRO-STEPS tutorials. Consequently, even today, when challenges come up in regard to the shooting, I know they are normal and I know how to deal with them more positively.

Knowing what to expect and being prepared so that I understood what was going on made a huge difference. Everything I was told in the tutorials was right on. The information rescued me from the uncertainty and negativity that plagued me at first.

The shooting could have made me bitter toward life and toward the perpetrator—like other victims I have known. The man who shot me only got one to five years in prison. A gunman who committed a similar crime in Oklahoma got a life sentence with no possibility of parole. My wife Karen was amazed when the authorities asked me to testify at the parole hearing for the man that shot me. She could not believe I could put my bitterness aside and say, "If he can be a good citizen, I have no problem with him being out on the streets."

The IRO-STEPS tutorials put me back in touch with reality—what was going on, what my feelings were, why I was feeling what I was feeling. Because of my involvement with clinical traumatology, I went back to work early. And instead of being involved in a bitter struggle to survive, I have a positive attitude about myself and life.

The IRO-STEPS continually prove effective in resolving the problems resulting from unresolved trauma. Why do the tutorials work—whether with new or with years-old trauma? Because the process is the same whether the tutorials are begun the day of the event or forty years later. IRO-STEPS survivors such as Gene, Marianne, and Phil all learned the necessity of changing the way they think and look at life's challenges. They gathered more information, took charge of their thoughts, and focused them on uplifting and inspiring words and proven concepts for strengthening the mind. Consequently, they were able to effectively resolve both long- and short-term consequences of trauma aftermath.

It is a widely accepted fact that unresolved, inadequately addressed trauma leads to disabling psychological problems and prolonged physical disability. In his first book of the trilogy, *The Road Less Traveled*, M. Scott Peck points out how a trauma or series of traumas in one's early life often leads to serious problems in later life. He states that a psychiatrist can trace the origin of many physical problems and other dysfunctions back to an *unresolved* trauma, often with "an exactitude and precision that is seldom matched elsewhere in medicine."

In the final book of the trilogy, *The Road Less Traveled and Beyond*,[1] Dr. Peck convincingly addresses the issue of "failing to think well," a growing problem in today's society. He also describes the problems inherent in "thinking too little" (his description of illusions and neuroses) and the consequences of "not thinking for ourselves." In addition, he explains the ageless truth about our humanness—that we are the sum total of what we choose to think about (good or bad) and also *what we choose* **not** *to think about*.

Listening, Learning, and Thinking—All Crucial for Healing Physical and Emotional Pain

Dr. Peck indicates that it takes energy to listen, concentrate, and think well. He adds that people not only need to listen well, but they need to be *listened to* well, especially in the aftermath of trauma. When this actually occurs at a crossroads of life, amazing progress is made, as evidenced by Phil's experience and the other examples provided in this book.

Barry Richards states,

---

[1] *The Road Less Traveled and Beyond*, by M. Scott Peck, M.D., Simon and Schuster, 1998.

The process of rapidly learning about, understanding, and integrating the bedrock principles and survival realities into one's recovery experience enables trauma survivors to benefit the most from the IRO-STEPS tutorials. If they also receive the You Matter Most message, attentive emotional and educational support, and the right kind of encouragement from personal caregivers, survivors develop an unlimited potential for thriving after surviving.

Today's trauma survivors cannot be passive recipients. They need directions about what to expect and how to avoid escalating problems. Only if we acknowledge this need early on and respond appropriately with the right care at the right time are we honoring the Hippocratic Oath: "First do no harm." Our combined efforts to effectively and efficiently respond to the needs and expectations of survivors are vital if our ultimate goal is to promote the healthiest recovery possible.

Key Points in Chapter Eight

Previous experiences and beliefs will influence the way in which people deal with trauma. In some cases, prior experience in dealing with others' trauma, such as the experiences Phil had as a police officer, may create unrealistic expectations of how to deal with trauma of their own.

Sadly, the attitude of many employers and administrators toward trauma is: "if there is no physical injury or those physical injuries have healed, then there is no need to deal with the emotional issues." The practice of putting people back to work into the environment where they were traumatized, without recognizing the need to deal with inapparent but serious emotional wounds, is the cause of much needless suffering and disruption.

Previously formed attitudes about people with emotional problems and the professionals who deal with them can threaten trauma sufferers with an unnecessary stigma and is a principle reason many victims refuse to get help when they need it.

Simply being exposed to the IRO-STEPS tutorials or knowing some of the facts of emotional trauma does not lead to successful resolution of the problems. Learning in the SEEDs strategy is an active process, and unless the principles are actually practiced they are of relatively little value.

Sadly, in traumatic incidents where there is an issue of liability or criminal wrongdoing, there is a strong probability that the victim will be accused of causing their own injury either deliberately or through negligence. This practice of blaming the victim, either directly or by innuendo, leads to re-victimization or secondary wounding which prolongs the healing process and can exacerbate symptoms.

Not all health care providers appeal to every person who may seek their care. In some instances the patient is acutely uncomfortable. In such cases it is important to either resolve the issues or find another provider. Similar backgrounds and beliefs may make it easier for the patient and the provider to work together. Do not be afraid of offending a clinician by finding someone else if you are not satisfied that you will be able to work with him or her.

Do not be surprised to find that your primary caregiver (spouse, parent, etc.) is unusually perceptive about what is happening to you as you both proceed through the IRO-STEPS tutorials and activities. As in Phil's case, you may actually find that there is a level of communication that is inexplicable to others.

Forgiveness and resolution have a remarkable power to heal and let the mind move beyond the events of the trauma. If one harbors hatred and revenge for those who may have injured them, it is virtually impossible for healing to occur since there is too much energy devoted to negative and unproductive activities. This is one of the chief sources of psychic energy drain. Scott Peck described it as "failing to think well."

9

A Perspective on Healing

In the aftermath of horrifying experiences when the whole world seems filled with chaos and uncertainty, people often feel self-conscious, anxious, and insecure. The dominant emotion is that of having lost control of some of the most basic aspects of independent living. In the face of such overwhelming insecurity, the suggestion that they need a "shrink" is likely to be regarded as yet another assault. Seeking the help of a mental health professional is interpreted by many trauma survivors as a sign of weakness—a weakness that compounds feelings of loss and that challenges an already diminished sense of identity.

Education and Self-Reliance, Rather then Dependency

In general, traditional psychotherapeutic techniques are relatively effective in the treatment of mental conditions which have a fairly long developmental phase or are related to organic disease such as brain tumors or lesions. Such problems are complicated and frequently the sufferer has been labeled as mentally ill. However, trauma survivors generally have different needs—especially the majority who have no prior history of psychological illness. When applied in the immediate aftermath of trauma, traditional techniques may actually add to the problems of recovery for survivors rather than helping them regain normal function. For example, traditional psychotherapy often creates an increased sense of dependence, when the survivor most needs a restoration of self-confidence. The educational approach of clinical traumatology, as presented in this book, is primarily structured to help survivors regain their sense of security and independence. Clinical traumatology teaches survivors how to rely on their own inner strengths and spiritual resources, rather than the strengths of professionals.

Early Intervention

It has been emphasized that the IRO-STEPS assessment and the tutorials should be initiated as soon as possible following the traumatic event. The SEEDs strategy of early and specific educational directions has proven to be highly successful. This early intervention is significantly different from traditional approaches. Indeed it is a fundamental principle of this book—that unless definitive care of emotional wounds is undertaken as soon as physically possible, recovery will be unnecessarily delayed. Definitive care must begin by helping the survivor identify goals and strategies to achieve the best possible outcome.

Road Maps for the Journey of Recovery

Identifying the goals of the recovery process and learning how to achieve them is as important as having a good road map when traveling in a strange country. There are dangerous places that we should avoid, and without a clear map we may not safely navigate our course. If someone familiar with the rough terrain provides a map and points the way as the road becomes more hazardous, we'll have a safer journey. Following the map makes it possible to get to the destination sooner, without needless detours and costly breakdowns.

Physical pain and emotional turmoil are better tolerated with a point of relief in sight. But, when a survivor has no idea what to expect in the aftermath of trauma, and the side effects and symptoms just keep happening without warning, the pain (both physical and emotional) seems endless, and the suffering may seem unbearable.

Knowing what to anticipate does not eliminate all the serious and difficult issues inherent to the recovery process. Some injuries lead to physical disabilities that make once commonplace activities difficult or even impossible to perform. For example, a professional pianist or a surgeon who loses the use of a hand must make difficult decisions regarding the future. Such changes can spell major financial challenges—even economic ruin—if not handled with the kind of emotional resilience encouraged by clinical traumatology.

Trials, Determination, and Silver Linings

The story of Douglas Bader, a British pilot, is worthy of note. Prior to World War II, Bader had been an outstanding young aviator with an almost unlimited future. However, tragedy struck when he was involved in a flying accident that resulted in the amputation of both legs. He was nursed back to physical and emotional health through the caring of a young nurse who became his wife.

He faced a flyer's worst nightmare, especially since he had only one dream—to serve his country in the Royal Air Force. He could easily have given up hope of ever flying again; indeed, many encouraged him to do just that. However, through undaunted faith in God combined with his wife's belief in him, he qualified to fly again. He was initially restricted to relatively simple aircraft, but was not satisfied with the restricted flight certification. He had his sights set on something greater—to fly high-performance fighters. He knew what it took to fly the "new" Hurricane fighter, a complicated and demanding aircraft, and was certain he could master the controls, even with two artificial legs.

As World War II broke out and the skies above the British Isles were filled with enemy aircraft, he became even more determined to fly as a fighter pilot. After months of repeated rejections by the Air Ministry, he was given a chance to demonstrate his ability to fly the Hurricane. Reluctantly they returned him to operational flight status in time for him to participate in and become a hero of the Battle of Britain, the single most important aerial battle of the war. He was not just competent, but outstanding in his performance in spite of his "disability." He became a triple ace, and at one point, his artificial legs actually saved his life. When his plane was hit by enemy cannon fire, the badly damaged cockpit trapped his legs. Only Bader could have unstrapped his legs, left them behind, and bailed out to safety!

The analogy is clear: the very things we see as our greatest trials can, in reality, be our greatest gifts. Bader was knighted for his valor in battle. Sir Douglas lived a full life and died peacefully of old age. Rather than wither in obscurity in the aftermath of both physical and emotional trauma, he surmounted obstacles and made good decisions that enabled him to continually progress.

The Importance of Educated Choices

Anticipating the decisions that inevitably follow traumatic incidents and learning how to process them intelligently, greatly affects the outcome. Author Clyde Reid treated this subject with insight in his book *You Can Choose Christmas*. The following excerpt gives his view on how choices are made following physical or emotional injury:

> *You can choose for nothing to happen to you from now on . . . You can hold onto your pain and your anger and your sadness. And many people do. Their sadness and pain and buried resentment feel good. They're like old friends they don't want to give up. At least they hurt and that is a feeling. To have some feeling is better than no feeling, many people reason. I have known quite a few. And I've hung onto hurt myself too often. If our energy is too occupied holding onto old pain and old grievances, there can be no happiness for us. No birth of hope. No deep joy. But we choose. We make the choice to hold on or to let go. We choose our own happiness—or our own lack of happiness.*

We all make choices every day; some are trivial, others have a profound and lasting impact on our lives. Some choices are about simple things, yet consistently making the right choice about these simple things has lasting consequences. An example of a simple choice most people make every day is whether to wear a seatbelt. As seatbelt usage has climbed, the number of fatalities has decreased, yet it has taken years to convince people to protect themselves by consistently taking this simple action. This change in behavior—increased seatbelt usage—has been brought about primarily by education that includes compelling information designed to motivate compliance. Driver's education teachers cite statistics and show movies of actual crashes that graphically illustrate the increased likelihood of survival in a crash through the simple act of fastening a seatbelt. This information, more than the possibility of getting a ticket and being fined, led to the change. The point is, we make decisions based upon information that we have internalized through education that motivates us. The more personalized and specific the information is, the more likely we are to use it to make correct decisions.

Sequencing and Personalizing Information

Trauma survivors are hungry for information. However, the use made of information will be in direct proportion to the degree it is personalized and made meaningful. The stories in this book are examples of sequencing the flow of information so that, as new decision points were reached, the information needed to make correct choices had already been provided and internalized. Simply handing survivors a textbook crammed full of good advice and scientific information will not meet their needs. Although the necessary information may be there, it is not likely to be in the most helpful form or sequence. As healing takes place and situations change, relevant new information can be made available. If there are no clinical traumatology services available, by familiarizing themselves with the post-trauma topics discussed in this book, caregivers, family members, or friends can help to sequence the information the survivor needs. (A likely sequence is illustrated in the order of information given in Appendix 1. This order can easily be modified according to individual needs.)

Passive or Proactive at the Crossroads?

Each trauma survivor's perspectives and recovery experiences are uniquely personal. Differences in background and the nature of the trauma cause people to react differently even though situations may appear to be similar. One commonality is that major events such as injury or death of a loved one bring people to a crossroads. Events that irreversibly change life as usual lead to turning points that take people in dramatically different directions. A choice is demanded of survivors—what to do next, how to change perspectives and patterns of time use, and what outcomes they desire. Decisions will be made, either consciously or by default.

Barry Richards recalls his acquaintance with two wheelchair-bound fellow students when he was attending college. Both had been paralyzed by similar diving accidents. One was outgoing, helpful, active, married and joyful; the other cynical, demanding, pessimistic, and lonely. Life was meaningful to the one, and to the other a burden of endless suffering and misery, according to the choices each had made in thinking and reaction. Any survivor may either be passive—letting the effects of the trauma control the mind—or proactive—taking control of the mind and turning these events into useful learning experiences. Then the "law of the harvest" becomes evident.

Knowledge and the Control of Suffering

Benedict De Spinoza, the 17th-century Dutch philosopher and mathematician, eloquently described how a person may choose to end suffering. He understood the power of the mind and its relationship to physical disorders.[1] In his treatise entitled *Ethics*, he stated that *"An emotion, which is passion* [suffering], *ceases to be passion* [suffering] *as soon as we form a clear and distinct idea thereof."* In other words, passion, in this case suffering, is something we hold onto emotionally because it serves some purpose, even though the purpose may be both destructive and subconscious. He went on to say that *"An emotion therefore becomes more under our control, and the mind is less passive in respect to it, in proportion as it is more known to us."*

Thus, knowledge of mind-body relationships and consciously putting things in perspective allows us to control suffering. Being aware of this early in the recovery process and learning how to resolve the suffering requires the accessing of relevant information. This is the purpose of the IRO-STEPS strategy as well as other effective post-trauma interventions. Once the appropriate information is obtained, it is up to the individual survivor and their personal caregivers to use that information effectively.

"Wait Until It Breaks To Fix It" Is Not Acceptable

The focus of this book has been on rapid intervention for the purpose of acquiring specific knowledge about the effects of injury and trauma on the emotions. Ideally, every trauma survivor should have

---

[1] *Ethics: Demonstrated in Geometric Order*, by Benedict De Spinoza (Translated by W. Hale White), Kessinger Publishing, 1997.

access to a well-trained and highly experienced clinician who can effectively present the definitive information contained in the IRO-STEPS tutorials. Unfortunately that is not usually the case and many trauma survivors are left largely on their own to find the answers. What is most important is that the victim-survivors understand that waiting for weeks on end until debilitating symptoms have taken a heavy toll is not necessary. The "wait until it breaks" philosophy is not beneficial to any mechanism, living or otherwise. There is little point in worrying about things we can't control, but much of the long-term emotional wounding caused by traumatic events can be prevented.

Note to Survivors of Trauma

Take personal responsibility by implementing the following:

1. Get your primary caregiver/loved one involved in your recovery. As illustrated in the case histories as well as the story of Douglas Bader, the support of a caregiver/loved one is an important, if not *the major* factor in the recovery process. When a person is receiving the IRO-STEPS tutorials, their spouse, parent(s), or other loved one should always be involved unless there is a compelling reason for them not to be. Too often, the survivor assumes that they are alone in their distress, that others are relatively unaffected and can carry on as though nothing had happened. The impact of trauma on others is greatly underestimated. The caregiver should not only be *providing* support, but also be *receiving* support through the critical information that will help them chart their own course for recovery.

2. Acquire knowledge about every aspect of survival recovery from *every* credible source available. When faced with uncertainty, information that will aid in the healing process should be made available as soon as possible. Military strategists are always reconnoitering, which means exploring the horizon to determine strengths and weaknesses—theirs and the enemy's.

Physical wounds are statistically less likely to limit one's recovery potential than emotional wounds left untreated. Unresolved emotional injuries leave the survivor vulnerable to the destructive, but mostly unintentional, acts of onlookers who don't understand the nature of the problem. It is important to remember that all of the information cannot be digested at once. It must be organized and prioritized to be optimally useful.

After reading this book, whether you are the survivor or the caregiver, you should be able to get a reasonable sense of the problems that are most likely to impact you. You may use the tools provided, such as the SPEED Scoring Scale to assess the magnitude of the injury and set priorities, determining the most pressing problem to deal with first. Don't become overwhelmed with the sheer volume of information. Start with issues that you feel are most important and take it one step at a time. The order in which you tackle your challenges is not as important as sticking with it and making slow but steady progress toward recovery. The elephant *can* be eaten one bite at a time.

Make sure your sources of information are credible and are focused on the future more than the past. Nothing is as important in determining the validity of information as the experience level of the "authority." Make certain that the professionals you choose have sufficient expertise in addressing early trauma-aftermath issues using *structured and specific* guidance, counsel, and direction. A credential of educational achievement is not enough; you want someone with a practical, real-world background in prevention who knows how to deal specifically with the issues of injury and trauma recovery *before* they've turned into debilitating psychological disease. There are many practitioners who deal with clients whose problems have blossomed into the classic symptoms of Post-Traumatic Stress Disorder. Relatively few therapists, however, focus on the prevention and limitation of these symptoms.

In the first days and weeks of convalescence, it is critical to ask a lot of questions, *even sensitive, scary, or seemingly stupid ones.* Getting them answered will free up valuable energy and also nourish your mind. Life-changing events consume a great deal of energy, especially in the first few weeks after they occur. Understanding the nature of these events and putting them into perspective is aided significantly by getting answers to questions. The following demonstration will illustrate the nature of life-changing events. Place a dot on a piece of paper; tape it on the wall and walk backwards until the dot isn't visible. When the event first happens attention is focused on it. But, as we move away from it, time provides the buffer of emotional distance, and the experience takes an increasingly lower priority in our lives.

The information-gathering process described above will provide new perspectives that will change your outlook, and the gradual lessons regarding recovery will fill in the other gaps that, when left empty, produce side effects such as intrusive thoughts, focus on losses, and feelings of inadequacy and helplessness.

3. Take notes, document your experience, record what you've been told, and write letters and e-mails. Several years ago, at a behavioral medicine symposium, James W. Pennebaker described his research on the benefits of writing out the experience and feelings of a personal trauma.[2,3] He had studied the lives of college students who were survivors of traumatic events that had occurred up to twenty-five years previously. These people had never even partially recorded their thoughts and feelings about the incident. However, when given the assignment to write about them, they were not only specific in recalling the details, but also expressed the intense emotions associated with the events. For most of the students, the effects of the traumatic events—and the emotional turmoil they experienced at the time of the trauma—had never been resolved. These distressing emotions were only thinly covered over, ready to break through with little provocation. Compared to a matched comparison group of other students who had not experienced trauma, the survivor group had experienced many more physical ailments and other disruptive events in their lives.

What is important about this study is that it shows that a traumatic event can be recorded or "memorialized" even years after the fact. Documenting this information is critical because it demystifies the feelings and helps to place them in perspective. When the "facts" and "feelings" are laid out on paper, they become less threatening because they can be seen for what they are. When left to the subjective imaginings of the mind, they are easily distorted and blown out of proportion; this leads to the

---

[2] Pennebaker, J. W., and Beall, S., Confronting a traumatic event: toward an understanding of inhibition and disease. *Journal of Abnormal Psychology*, Vol. 95, pp. 274–81, 1986.

[3] Pennebaker, J. W., Kiecolt-Glaser, J. K., and Glaser, R., Disclosure of traumas and immune functioning: health implications for psychotherapy. Journal of Consulting and Clinical Psychology, Vol 56, No. 2, pp. 239–45, 1988.

festering that produces disabling psychological illness. Such illnesses are the result of emotional wounds that have been allowed to "abscess" from neglect.

Another compelling reason for writing out details about a personal trauma or recording them on tape is that this documentation serves as a reference point that can be used to measure progress in the healing process. People need to be anchored. They need tangible reminders of events they have experienced and lessons they have learned. Certificates, diplomas, licenses, pictures, documents, and other records establish realities and provide these points of reference in the education process. We need similar points of reference in the process of emotional healing.

During recovery, anything that measures progress is valuable, including the photographs, letters, or keepsakes we receive. In *Man's Search for Meaning*, Viktor Frankl described his experience as a prisoner in the Nazi death camps at Auschwitz and Dachau. Frankl described how he was able to rise above the horror of unspeakable brutality and suffering and focus on those things which are uniquely human—and ultimately the most important aspects of our existence. Among these are love, belief in God, self-respect, and a profound understanding of the sanctity of life. In order to preserve his thoughts and experiences he wrote his "notes" on scraps of paper which he had to hide from the guards at the peril of his life. His writings emphasize his knowledge of the importance of memorializing life events, both for individual benefit and for the benefit of others.

Letter writing or e-mail is another form of recording emotions and experiences. Communicating with others through the written word can be a catharsis through which one is able to express gratitude and report progress. Our written words can keep those who have been most concerned and involved in the recovery efforts up to date and may allow them to feel rewarded for acts of kindness and offers of help. Letter writing or e-mail may also keep the mind focused positively and encourage concentration on rising above and surmounting inevitable daily challenges. Frankl observed: *"Woe to him who saw no more sense in life, no aim, no purpose, and therefore no point to carrying on. He was soon lost."* Sharing thoughts about the things you've learned enables you to lift others and lift yourself. Your perspective as a survivor can validate to others that healing is possible.

Caught in a Crossfire

Applying these fundamentals will help people help themselves. But when additional help is needed for those suffering from prolonged, unresolved emotional distress and psychosomatic physical problems, what can be expected from health care professionals? With rare exception, health care professionals are committed to our recovery and well-being. They do what they can within the constraints of a system which seriously limits the amount of time and attention that can be given to emotionally related problems. But of what value are good intentions if emotional wounds are allowed to fester without adequate attention? What is happening in the health care system?

During the past twenty-five years there has been a cry for increased attention to the development and implementation of disease prevention strategies. Unfortunately unforseen events intervened and the true benefits of prevention have not yet been realized. In the mid-'70s there were bold declarations from experts stating that we had entered a new era, the so-called "second epidemiologic revolution." The first "revolution" was the supposed conquering of infectious diseases through the introduction of powerful antibiotics and improved living conditions. Once-feared diseases such as polio, smallpox, and bubonic plague were either eradicated or brought under control, and the experts believed that the time had come to shift from the treatment of the epidemic killers to the prevention of chronic diseases.

However, a host of new forces came into play that literally turned the health care world upside down. One factor in this upheaval was the emergence of AIDS—along with strains of other, more common infectious diseases against which there were few if any effective treatments. Another and probably more powerful influence was health care financing. The cost of health care had been rising several times faster than any other segment of the economy. It seemed clear that drastic measures would have to be taken or the system would collapse and only the very wealthy would have access to high quality care.

Preventive Services Die at the Hand of Profit

Having set the stage for a catastrophe—largely of their own making—the federal government, along with some major insurance companies, began the wholesale revolution of the system of reimbursements for health related services. The impact that "managed care" would have on the individual patient was understood by very few at that time. On the surface, managed care organizations appeared to be the answer to a whole series of dilemmas threatening the system with destruction. By the end of the century, however, it was clear to most people that managed care is not the panacea hoped for. One of the first victims in this new era of HMOs, PPOs, IPAs, etc., was preventive services. Although prevention saves money in the long run, implementing preventive services generally costs more up front than most health care managers are willing to spend. In today's economy, realizing an immediate profit is the primary concern of most health care managers.

The Way Health Care "Should" Operate

Professional practitioners and the health care systems in which they function, in our opinion, should focus on producing the best results possible regardless of when they are provided and who provides them. The goal should be maximizing the quality of life of the patient, *not* maximizing the profits of the company. If early intervention produces better results in the treatment of trauma survivors, then this early treatment needs to be the standard of care. Simply because more people are trained to deal with the problems that emerge as a result of unattended emotional wounds does not justify waiting until people are seriously debilitated before care is rendered. The sizable and numerous advantages of early intervention must be recognized. Health care options should be available to *all* who are at risk of developing psychological impairment when the severity of their emotional wounds requires rapid and specialized help.

A Call to Arms

Sudden Trauma is a call to arms. If the status quo is to be changed and the benefits of clinical traumatology realized by those who are in need, there must be education. Although some of this will come through word of mouth and Internet access, it is the authors' hope that much will come through the personal application of the information presented in this text. It is our hope that health care providers searching for more effective means of helping their patients will incorporate these materials into their practices. Ideally, professional and public awareness will lead to education on a broad scale and make the health care tutorials of clinical traumatology available to all trauma survivors.

Prevention of Spiraling After-Trauma Problems IS Possible

Clinical traumatology is an effective approach for the prevention of serious and prolonged after-trauma emotional suffering. It offers definitive care for the immediate effects experienced by those who have been subjected to injury or other horrifying events. Clinical traumatology is a discipline whose time has come. Simply because it does not offer the glamour of high technology or the mystique of obscure theories it should not be disregarded. Much can be accomplished through personal study and information gathering, but in acute cases it would be a mistake to assume that any sort of self-help approach will substitute for trained and experienced practitioners.

Clinical traumatology is not mainstream at this point, but the fact that it has, and will continue to, come under fire from the "establishment" does not invalidate it. When it seems there is a conspiracy against progress; when indifference is rampant; when collusion and slander are threatening innovation; when profits, not people, are the top priority, and ambivalence is undermining incentive to bring about change, it is time to consider the power of truth. A commentator has said: *"There is no chance, destiny, or fate that can circumvent, or hinder or control the firm resolve of a determined soul."* Those who dare to introduce new ideas and approaches that threaten the status quo always experience daunting obstacles. However, sufficient determination will bring clinical traumatology to the forefront. Prevention of life-long negative effects in the aftermath of trauma is the only defensible position. Those who have suffered needlessly can be the catalyst to bring about a change, not only for their own good, but also for the well-being of all who want to thrive versus merely survive.

———•———

10

Summing It Up

Survivors Who Follow IRO-STEPS Remain Symptom Free
The survivors, whose stories are recounted in this book received the IRO-STEPS health care tutorials and remain symptom free to this day.[1] However, their "satisfaction" with the services of Barry Richards is *not* the basis of this book. Many pseudo-scientific studies are flawed with the conclusion (overtly or indirectly made) that if someone "feels good" about services that have been rendered, then a satisfactory outcome has been achieved.

The case histories presented in *Sudden Trauma* offer real-life examples and measurable evidence of both qualitative and quantitative benefits resulting from the IRO-STEPS approach—people returning to work in record time, recovering from phobias, saving their marriages, regaining productivity in their jobs, etc. These benefits were derived from appropriate health care information being given at the right time, not simply from charismatic providers or a "good feeling" about services rendered. Where clinical traumatology expertise is not available, the basic principles of the health care tutorials—the key elements that bring about recovery and well-being—can be learned and applied from the stories and the information in the Appendices and Glossary at the end of this book.

---

[1] Symptom-free relative to the impact of their trauma and its immediate or prolonged aftermath. Lifelong personality traits and associated disordering characteristics frequently require traditional methods of treatment, not the focus of clinical traumatology.

Survivors-turned-thrivers Follow Six Basic Steps To Acheive Recovery/Well-Being

1. **Accept and apply IRO-STEPS:**

   Stimulate positive thinking
   Tackle unrealistic fears
   Educate concerning options
   Plan for the future
   Stop unrealistic expectations

2. **Acquire a specific and clear road map from assessment directions.**

   The written assessment is a vital road map survivors can share with all those genuinely concerned with their overall recovery. The assessment, unlike a psychological evaluation, does not diagnose and label. There is no stigma attached and no aspersions cast. The purpose of assessments are to pinpoint the major concerns and feelings of the individuals and *let them know they have been heard*. Assessments clearly separate *pre-trauma* factors from aftermath issues and prescribe specific IRO-STEPS that will deal with both. Voluminous notes are taken by the clinician during the assessment procedure. The full report presented to the survivor afterwards accentuates the secure feeling of being genuinely listened to and understood.

3. **Fully utilize the available support systems.**

   The "three-legged stool" of essential support systems are

   • Emotional support
   • Educational support
   • Encouragement from other survivors

   Family members are usually the best source of emotional support. They are the ones who care the most about us.

   Educational support from a qualified clinician provides the concise and concrete directions needed. The clinician arranges for the encouragement from others who have "been there, done that, and felt what it is like." The support from other survivors is especially valuable because they have been through a similar trauma and healing experience and can validate the benefits of the IRO-STEPS approach.

In order to encourage the most effective emotional support from the family, "prime time interaction" is prescribed. The origin of this term came about as follows:

A local newscaster hosts a popular program called "Prime Time Access." It airs right after the dinner hour when people are well-fed and relaxed and open to interesting insights and timely information. It is doubtful this program would be so well received if it filled an earlier time slot, such as when people were just getting home from work, tired, hungry, and irritable.

Aftermath "prime time" refers to the time we are most receptive, have the energy to give, and the openness to receive. Prime time interaction is what we most need from the ones who care the most about us. Every child needs it from his or her parents, every wife from her husband, and every husband from his wife.

Each person documented in this book was encouraged to engage prime time interaction with those they cared the most about and to wholeheartedly receive any healthy attention offered. This interaction is an irrefutable, basic factor in recovery because of the amazing power of the love on which it is based.

Nurturing—the selfless desire and effort to feed, nourish, educate, train, care about, serve, and rear others—is a demonstration of love. Love that nurtures involves three critical efforts: recognition, acknowledgment, and acceptance (see the summaries of the Basic Necessities and Human Stimulants Tutorial in Appendix 1, pp. 152–58). When these three areas of endeavor are practiced regularly, frequently, predictably, and continually in a caring relationship, emotional and physical healing are facilitated.

4. Frequently use the power of laughter and good humor.

Each person who shared their experience in this book recognized that mental and emotional conditions affected the physical functions of his or her body. Medical specialists have documented with overwhelming evidence the relationship between healthy minds and healthy bodies.

Among the best therapies are laughter and humor—a factor in, though not a focus of, all the stories shared in *Sudden Trauma*. When a person laughs, their aches and pains may be diminished or disappear, even if only for a short time. Muscles relax. Anxieties and tensions lessen, Although it was not possible to reflect it in the text, humor and levity are interjected appropriately throughout the whole tutorial process.

The healthful benefits of laughter have been known for hundreds of years. In Proverbs it is written that "A merry heart doeth good like a medicine: but a broken spirit drieth the bones" (Proverbs 17:22).

A national organization, Nurses for Laughter (NFL), believes so strongly in the healing power of laughter, that it adopted this slogan: "Warning: Humor may be hazardous to your illness."

One of the most amazing case studies demonstrating the benefits of laughter comes from author Norman Cousins, who beat the odds when he was given only a 1-in-500 chance to recover from a painful disease. Cousins documented the amazing benefits of focusing his mind on the positive and humorous. In his book *Anatomy of an Illness*[2] he said, "It has always seemed to me that hearty laughter is a good way to jog internally without having to go outdoors." When we "jog internally" the adrenaline hormone induced by fear is replaced with the health-producing chemicals that enliven the mind. There is a light side to most circumstances, and being able to identify and enjoy it can make a big difference during the recovery process.

5. Accept the key principle: mind over body.

Each of those who contributed their stories to this book accepted the responsibility to memorize and focus their thoughts on selected and uplifting quotes, lyrics, scriptures, poems, etc. (M&Ms—Memorize to Minimize intrusive thoughts and Maximize progress).

They were also given a nonmedicine prescription: "If it is to be, it is up to me." It becomes increasingly clear to survivors that *it is up*

---

[4] Anatomy of an Illness As Perceived by the Patient: Reflections on Healing and Regeneration by Norman Cousins; Bantam, Doubleday, Dell Publishing, 1991

to them to make their survival world into something that will allow them to thrive. No one else can do it for them. Accepting this idea is essential because it forms the foundation for taking responsibility and focusing the mind on future possibilities rather than on losses and limitations. When the survivor is given realistic and encouraging information to ponder and consider (in terms of what future recovery can bring to their unique circumstances), they are led to constructive thought choices that facilitate healing.

6. Experience a change of paradigm.

Stephen R. Covey's "change of paradigm" concept reinforces the idea that simple information can change the way we think, believe, and act. Suffering from a traumatic experience only goes on indefinitely when we don't have the essential information to empower us to stop the emotional upheaval. Each person described in this book was given extensive information concerning the normal side effects and symptoms of their trauma and what they needed to do to overcome them. Those who were given proactive and preventive directions early were spared the "wait until it breaks to fix it" mentality.

The Choice Is Clear

The fates of two men in classic novels clearly illustrate contrasting choices following a time of trauma. Both Jean Valjean in *Les Miserables* and Edmund Dantes in *The Count of Monte Cristo* were unjustly imprisoned for many years. Both were bitter and hardened and desirous of vengeance.

At a pivotal point in Jean Valjean's life, the kindness of a Christian priest started him on a new path. He changed his life, promising to withdraw his mind from "dark thoughts" and to seek no more for vengeance, but to "become an honest man." The rest of the epic story tells about the positive and powerful influence of such "right thinking."

In contrast, Edmund Dantes filled his mind with intrigue and strategies to bring about retribution against all the evil people responsible for his imprisonment. In the end, although he was vindicated and wealthy, the dark nature of his thoughts and actions so jaded his character that he could not acquire the one thing he desired most—the love of the woman to whom he had become engaged just prior to his imprisonment.

The tutorials of clinical traumatology invite all participants to choose the life-enhancing, soul-restoring path of positive thinking and character development. When that choice is made, rapid physical and emotional healing naturally follow. A nurse, who was recently Barry Richards's client, stated, "It is the truth of all these things that set me free from the pain of the past." Her sentiments reflect Biblical wisdom as written in St. John 8:32: "And ye shall know the truth, and the truth shall make you free."

Epilogue
By Barry Richards

From Preface to Appendix it must be clear to the reader that this book came about by a process more controlled than mere serendipity. Indeed, the scholarly, clinical, and technical expertise represented by the various contributors have merged with the experiences survivors share in *Sudden Trauma* in a way that seems nothing short of miraculous. Hence, I felt the need to write this epilogue identifying the behind-the-scenes personalities who from my vantage point have played an invaluable part in making this book possible.

First and foremost I single out the survivors who share their experiences in this book. They know what it takes to become thrivers and are now the message-bearers of hope and encouragement. They epitomize the Latin proverb "Survivors make good witnesses," emphasizing the necessity and urgency of ensuring that essential health care information for trauma survivors is provided in the *early* aftermath of trauma.

The Woolleys' scientific and clinical backgrounds were acquired through many years of research, learning from gifted mentors, and tedious personal study. Similarly, writer, editor, and revisionist Darla Isackson's track record of front-runner publications resulted in part from the guidance of well-trained colleagues and mentors. Her ability with the written word was not developed without abundant and sometimes painful experience.

My own accomplishments did not happen painlessly. Fortunately, I was blessed with parents who instilled in me a spirit of determination that has allowed me to weather the storms of adversity. Diane, my wife of twenty-five years, and our four children (Kathy, Diana, Michael Steven, and Johnathan Morgan) have together provided invaluable love, support, and encouragement when things seemed bleak and futile along the way.

Much wise guidance from a host of individuals combined with fortuitous circumstances have all worked together over the years to enable me in the development of the IRO-STEPS strategies and tutorials of clinical traumatology. Fundamental to this growth was the affirmative response to Larry Bleyl's counsel to "prioritize God and wife" for enduing happiness and success, and the sustaining affection and direction received from Boyd K. Packer, Marion D. Hanks, Vaughn J. Featherstone, Clifton I. Johnson, and Spencer Condie. Each one has played a key role in providing visionary guidance when my feelings of personal limitation and inadequacy would have arrested my progress. Marjan Martin, Eugene Gibbons, and Darnelle Zollinger were invaluable scholastic mentors. Together these personalities and influences have enabled vitally important personal and professional growth.

An awareness and appreciation of the pioneering work and concepts fathered by R Adams Cowley, M.D. (the father and pioneer of Shock Trauma Medicine), brought me into contact with a number of like-minded professionals such as Gerald Caplan, M.D. (the father of Crisis Intervention Practice). The development of the formal IRO-STEPS strategy has attracted the interest and support from an ever-increasing circle of health care professionals, including John Nelson, M.D.; Alan College, M.D.; Daniel Rapp, M.D.; Robert Zamelis, M.D.; Mary Beth Williams, Ph.D.; Carolyn Thomas, MSW; Heber Tippetts, MSW; Jim Whortley, RPT; E. Scott Lee, J.D.; Elliot Morris, J.D.; Stephanie G. Anderson, RN, BSN; and Cynda Nygaard, LPN. All collectively added momentum to the process of introducing the benefits of clinical traumatology.

Added to the above, I am indebted to: Scott Kelley, in the office of Risk Management at Intermountain Health Care, Inc. (IHC); John Mathews, manager of the Utah State Department of Human Resources; John Pingree and David Higbee, formerly with the Utah Transit Authority (UTA); Bruce Blythe at Crisis Management International (CMI); and LaRee Miller at the Utah Citizens Alliance, all forward-minded professionals who understand and promote the benefits of clinical traumatology. Each has understood and endeavored to cultivate the concept of ensuring *early* and appropriate health care direction in the aftermath of trauma.

Appendix 1

Appendix I offers a summary of the career work of Barry M. Richards, pioneering clinical traumatologist. The SPEED Scoring Scale and the tutorials he developed through years of experience with injury and trauma survivors reflect the genius of his work. Separate components of each tutorial can be found in other works—because they are timeless truths. But Richards has brought these principles together in a revolutionary way that has proven to be amazingly effective in expediting recovery.

Appendix 1–A
The Trauma Severity SPEED Scoring Scale

The Trauma Severity SPEED Scoring Scale is a tool that was developed to quickly assess the risk of emotional wounding of a trauma survivor and thereby determine the degree of urgency of responding to their needs with definitive interventions such as the IRO-STEPS strategy. The SPEED Scale is similar in structure to assessment tools used by medical personnel when determining the extent of neurological impairment among trauma victims (Glasgow Score) or the health status of infants immediately following their delivery (Apgar Score).

Delaying the response to nonphysical (emotional) wounds increases the risk of long-term psychological damage, just as delays in implementing definitive treatment for injury-induced shock leads to poor physical outcomes. R Adams Cowley, the father of modern trauma treatment, repeatedly talked of the "golden hour of opportunity." He demonstrated that survival rates improved dramatically by instituting appropriate care, as practiced in Level 1 trauma units, within the first hour following injury. Over the last thirty years, acceptance of Cowley's premise sparked the use of airborne evacuation with specially designed helicopters and led to the development of Level 1 shock-trauma units. Whether treating the physical injuries of major trauma or initiating definitive responses to the associated emotional wounds, time is of the essence. In fact it has been shown that emotional wounds are often more debilitating and produce more long-term problems than bodily injuries.

It is a challenge for busy health care professionals to find the time to determine who is at risk for delayed recovery due to emotional wounds and to initiate appropriate steps. Up to one-third of those involved in serious traumatic events are at high risk for developing emotional wound festering and/or psychological scarring. However, determining who is most likely to need and respond to specific, early educational directives (SEEDs) is best accomplished using a structured format. The purpose of the SPEED Scoring Scale is, therefore, to

a. quickly and accurately determine the severity and impact of trauma on survivors,
b. identify those family and friends associated with the victim who may be at risk and need intervention,
c. determine who should be referred to a clinical traumatologist for additional assessment and education using an approach such as IRO-STEPS tutorials.

No two people respond to a trauma in the same way. Some of these differences can be attributed to pre-trauma events, as well as factors such as the strength of interpersonal relationships and the person's ability to deal with the cumulative stresses of life. Routine implementation of a structured assessment tool instills a higher degree of confidence in health care professionals as they confront the unique challenge of caring for trauma survivors. Also, both the injured survivor and all those seriously impacted by the traumatic event will benefit from the expertise a clinical traumatologist is trained to provide.

Survivors of trauma are rarely alone in their suffering. Individuals who may be viewed as peripheral to a horrifying event may be devastated by their involvement and need intervention more urgently than the person who is physically injured. Unfortunately, they are often overlooked or ignored. Those who should be considered and given (at the very least) a SPEED Score evaluation include family members, close friends, witnesses present at the time of the injury—or shortly thereafter, service personnel such as EMTs, law enforcement officers, fire fighters, search and rescue personnel, and community volunteers. When any of the above come to the emergency room to support or inquire after a trauma survivor, this may be an important cue as to their personal involvement and need for help, i.e., a silent cry for assistance often masked by their concern for the survivor.

The Trauma Severity SPEED Scoring Scale requires less than fifteen minutes to complete. It yields a numerical value predictive of the likelihood that trauma survivors have suffered or will suffer severe emotional wounding. It also predicts their need for expert attention to insure optimal recovery.

The acronym SPEED stands for

S everity of the trauma or threat to security
P erceived impact of the trauma on lifestyle, such as loss of financial well-being
E strangement of family, friends, or other social support
E nvironmental skepticism (a measure of the degree to which the suffering of the survivor may be downplayed by the media or society, especially when the survivor sustained little or no physical injury)
D amaged sense of control

These five factors, or "domains," have been identified by several experts as being critical to emotional well-being. For instance, Fisher and

Ury, two Harvard University researchers, labeled the five areas as Security, Economic Well-being, Sense of Belonging, Recognition, and Control over Circumstances.

The SPEED Scoring Scale (as illustrated in Table 2) is an important tool for emergency department staff or other health care workers. Even though the SPEED Scoring Scale was designed for early intervention, caregivers or a survivor may use this scale throughout the recovery process to assess progress and determine whether further professional help is indicated.

Table 2 Trauma Severity SPEED Scoring Scale©	
Category	**Threat Level** (Circle the number that best describes the level of threat to the trauma survivor in each category.)
	Least Greatest
1. Severity of Trauma: To what degree is, or was, the injury/trauma life-threatening, disabling, disfiguring, or horrifying?	1 2 3 4 5
2. Perceived impact on whole life: To what extent do you believe the injury will have a lifelong impact?	1 2 3 4 5
3. Estranged family/limited social support: To what extent is family support and/or social network limited?	1 2 3 4 5
4. Environmental skepticism: To what extent do you feel the community at large will tend to minimize or downplay the trauma or question the credibility of the survivor?	1 2 3 4 5
5. Degree of lost control: To what extent is a loss of control perceived concerning recovery and future life potential?	1 2 3 4 5

Directions

1. To measure the trauma's threat to the survivor's emotional well-being, answer the question from each category. (Supplementary examples are provided on the following pages for those needing additional guidelines in determining severity of threat.)

2. Circle the number under Threat Level (1= least threat and 5 = greatest threat) which best describes your evaluation of the situation. For instance, when scoring P (the perceived impact on whole life), take into consideration the severity of trauma based on your perception of the effect of the trauma on the survivor's functioning capability. If, for example, the injured person is a concert violinist, even a slight loss of sensation to the fingers will have a significant impact on his or her life, yielding a score of "4" or "5." However, for a brick mason, the same slight loss of sensation would likely yield a "1" or "2" on the P Scale.

3. After circling the Threat Level for each of the five categories, total the score by adding the circled numbers together. The combined score provides a relatively rapid and accurate means of assessing the level of emotional trauma that will impact a person due to a particular event.

The higher the total SPEED score the more urgent the need for obtaining professional direction to avoid or minimize the side effects and symptoms associated with the trauma. Experience has shown that a score of thirteen or higher indicates the need for professional assistance. That does not mean, however, that lower scores should be ignored. Any trauma survivor who feels distressed by the events should avail themselves of help and would benefit from following the guidelines presented in this book.

Supplementary Examples

The following guidelines may help one to more accurately determine the severity of a survivor's Threat Level.

I. Severity of Trauma	
Low Threat	**High Threat**
• Injuries are superficial. • Chances for a complete healing (without lasting affects, either functional or cosmetic) are likely to be 100 percent for all parties involved.	• Injuries are severe and life threatening. • Complete recovery, i.e., restoration to pre-injury level of functioning, is not likely. • Extensive therapy and care are required due to functional and/or cosmetic damage. • No serious or life-threatening injuries; however, survivor witnessed the death and/or dismemberment of individuals in a traumatic event. (Witnessing sudden death resulting from trauma will almost always raise the (S) score to a level 5, especially if the victim is someone known to the patient.) • Perceives themselves as grotesquely disfigured.*

* Disfigurement should be judged according to the situational status of the individual. For example, a teenage girl with a large facial scar will score higher on the severity of threat than an older male with a similar scar, but whose social interactions are limited.

II. Perceived Impact on Their Life

Low Threat	High Threat
• Injuries and nature of the trauma are such that survivor will return to pre-trauma functional status within a matter of days with little to remind them of the incident.	• Survived a particularly heinous crime that will receive wide media attention and also require them to appear as a witness in court. (When a survivor will be highly recognizable, a level 5 is almost always warranted.) • Injuries are not life threatening, yet victim is seen as responsible for the death and/or severe injury of others. • Severity of injury, or the nature of the trauma, makes it virtually certain that the patient will be "marked" for life.*

* The extent to which an injury will preclude a survivor from participating in former essential, valued, or enjoyable activity needs to be considered. When the nature of the injury is such that it will make it impossible for an individual to continue with life in a normal fashion, they may feel "marked" for life. An example of such life-impacting events would be the traumatic amputation of the leg(s) of a professional basketball player, loss of eyesight to an artist, organ failure for a single working parent, or trauma to the reproductive organs resulting in sterility for someone desiring to bear children.

III. Estranged Family/Limited Social Support

Low Threat	High Threat
• Strong, intact social support network of family and/or friends, evidenced by a. members of patient's support network coming to the E.R. or calling to request information on the patient's status. b. individuals from the patient's support network visibly demonstrating their concern/grief over the trauma suffered. c. a large number of calls indicating a willingness to assist the traumatized person, e.g., volunteering to come immediately and donate blood, attend to children or other dependents of the patient. The more specific the offers of assistance, the greater the likelihood that there is a strong and stable support network.	• Limited or no social support, evidenced by a. no visitors (not even family or friends) come to the E.R. or care facility in an effort to support the patient. b. calls that do come in seem perfunctory, indicating that the inquiry was made based on a sense of duty versus a genuine interest in the welfare of the patient. c. family and/or acquaintances who do come or call the E.R. do not seem overly concerned about the patient—even when it has been made clear that the nature of the injuries are serious or the situation which caused the injuries was horrifying and highly distressing to all who were involved.*

*When survivors refuse to permit anyone to be contacted or state "Nobody cares about me" (with the obvious goal to garner attention) a dysfunctional support system is strongly indicated.

IV. Environmental Skepticism

Low Threat	High Threat
• The situation is one the community in general recognizes as stressful—for example injuries that are clearly evident—so that the survivor is likely to get a high degree of sympathy.	• The survivor's statements regarding the trauma are so bizarre as to call into question the legitimacy of the account rendered, or the survivor is highly traumatized by an event that most people would find only mildly upsetting.
• Survivor is known to be a highly credible individual and is likely to be believed regarding statements made about the incident that caused the trauma or severity of injuries incurred.	• The version of events as recounted by the patient differs significantly with accounts reported by other witnesses, especially eyewitnesses who possess a high degree of community credibility.
• Information provided by the patient as to the events surrounding the trauma is highly consistent with information given by other witnesses. Although the patient may add certain details as he or she recalls the event, the added details are internally consistent with previous statements and do not alter the basic information provided.	• Attorneys are taking an exceptional interest in the event. (There may even be evidence of "disinformation" being generated in order to shift the blame for the incident onto the patient.) The very presence of attorneys in the E.R. suggests that the patient may have to deal with a great deal of environmental skepticism.
	• Patient has an unusually high interest in the coverage being given by the media and is anxious to recount his or her version of the event.*

* Even though the patient believes his or her wounds could be or could have been potentially fatal and may wish only to "set the record straight," overenthusiasm for sharing details of a traumatic event may come under suspicion. Society may judge such behavior, albeit sincere, as a ploy for sympathy or possible financial gain.

V. Degree of Control Lost or Perceived as Lost

Low Threat	High Threat
• Patient seems reasonably calm, maintaining appropriate reactions during and after the event. There is little or no evidence of alexithymia, phlegmatic reactions, or other symptoms of denial or lack of emotional response.	• Patient exhibited symptoms of severe post-traumatic stress almost immediately. These would include unreasonable fear of the event or one similar to it recurring and panic attacks in which there may be attempts to flee from the E.R. even though it might exacerbate their physical wounds, e.g., signing out A.M.A.
• Patient can articulate steps that led to the trauma, correctly identifying those factors which could/should have been modified and those which were random events which have a very low probability of recurring.	• Patient is the victim of a crime and will be required to participate in the police investigation. The loss of control will be heightened if the perpetrator was not apprehended and the individual is the only one or one of a very few witnesses who can identify the perpetrator(s).
• Individuals who possess a positive attitude towards the concept of a higher power (or being), divine intervention, or recognize a spiritual dimension to themselves.	• Patient expresses strong doubts as to the degree to which an individual can contribute to their own healing process.
	• Lack of spiritual belief or orientation places patient at high risk.
	• Patients involved in natural disasters are more likely to deny their ability to control life events.
	• Trauma to the patient, others, or both was a deliberate act by another individual.*

*The degree of premeditation, wanton disregard for human life, suffering induced (especially to those least able to defend themselves, e.g., children or the elderly), or the duration of the traumatic event(s) will increase the sense of loss of control.

Appendix 1–B
Assessment

The following information is provided to help you assess progress in the recovery process. This brief summary identifies various reactions that occur following trauma and provides an outline of the stages that a survivor goes through on their journey of recovery.

How Emotions Affect the Body

The emotional reactions to a life-threatening injury may be accompanied by a number of psychosomatic physical symptoms. (The definition of psychosomatic is "resulting from the interaction between mind and body.") They include the following:

- Headaches
- Dizziness
- Nausea or frequent gastrointestinal upset
- Severe abdominal pain
- Loss of energy, drive, or motivation
- Restlessness or periods of irritability (being easily annoyed)
- Severe depression
- Sleep disturbances, including insomnia, nightmares, abrupt awakening, and inability to return to sleep
- Loss of appetite
- Loss of sexual desire
- Memory loss and forgetfulness
- Reduced ability to concentrate
- Sudden unexplainable outbursts of anger and/or hostile behavior
- Periods of uncontrollable crying
- Chronic pain, often in the joints, back, or head
- Pains in chest area, often mistakenly interpreted as symptoms of a heart attack
- Muscle weakness in various parts of the body
- Muscle soreness
- Hot or cold spells
- Numbing or tingling, especially in the hands, feet, and face
- Lump in the throat and occasional difficulty in swallowing
- Hyperventilation, or shortness of breath

In general these disorders are temporary and will resolve themselves as the survivor recovers from the impact of the trauma. However, because some of the symptoms are similar or identical to those associated with potentially life-threatening illnesses, they should never be ignored. Although some of these problems may have had their origin as a purely psychosomatic complaint, if left untreated they can evolve into complicated physical problems that can have lifelong consequences. There are risks posed by such disorders when these problems persist or reoccur at frequent intervals. A medical doctor qualified to diagnose and treat complaints that have a significant emotional component should be seen at once if there is any doubt as to the nature of the complaint. This is definitely a situation where one should err on the side of caution.

Three Stages of Emotional Recovery

Learning about the three stages of emotional recovery allows trauma survivors, their caregivers and family members to anticipate and plan more effectively for the future. The stages described below are typical for most, but not all survivors. Every recovery experience is unique to the individual and there are significant variations. The emotions and behaviors identified within each stage should be used to gauge recovery in general, with the understanding that time frames and experiences vary. The three stages are:

Stage One: Survival Honeymoon —lasting from 4–12 weeks.
During this period, trauma survivors feel a deep sense of gratitude toward doctors, nurses, and paramedics for their lifesaving expertise. They also have a profound appreciation for friends, family, and others who offer help and support. They are strengthened and encouraged by well-wishers, provided with various medications to relieve pain and emotional distress, and are generally protected from outside stresses and demands. They have neither realistically faced the future, nor grasped the full impact of the limitations and lifestyle adjustments that may be imposed by their physical injuries and/or emotional wounds.

Stage Two: Adjustment Shock —lasting from weeks to years.
Recovering survivors experience diminishing attention from family, friends, and medical personnel and as a result often feel isolated and abandoned. They become keenly aware of any physical changes, disfigurements, or limitations resulting from their trauma. Feelings toward God may change from gratitude for having spared their lives to anger that God has seemingly forsaken them and/or is punishing them. Other survivors begin to doubt the existence of God, feeling that no loving God would let such terrible things happen. Faced with the hard, unexpected realities of

life changes, recovering survivors often experience one or more of the following feelings:

- Despondency or ambivalence about life in general
- Loneliness
- Feelings of worthlessness
- Guilt about surviving when others died or experienced more serious injury
- Anger toward rescue workers, medical staff, spouse, family, employers, or others involved in the accident
- Resentment toward those who fared better
- Humiliation over disabilities or dependency on others
- Frustration and desperation that recovery is not progressing quickly enough
- A sense that there is no effective, long-term relief from pain
- Abandonment by those who initially showed interest, love, or care
- Fright or fear about things that are not understood or over which there is little control
- Emotional numbness or insensitivity
- Self-destructive feelings
- Maliciousness
- Belligerence
- Self-deprecation (condemning self)
- Helplessness about the current situation
- Hopelessness about the future

In addition to these common negative emotions, trauma survivors are also likely to ask themselves or others many of the following questions:

- Will I ever be the same as before the accident?
- Will I ever be able to overcome the long-term chronic symptoms and the impairment the accident or trauma caused?
- Will I ever be accepted the way I am?
- Will I lose my job because of my limitations?
- Will I be rejected or abandoned by my spouse, children, or others?
- Will I be able to perform sexually?
- Will I be stared at, talked about, and made fun of?
- Will others take advantage of me?
- Will I lose my home because of the financial burdens?
- Will I ever feel like a capable man (or woman) again?
- When will my unwanted thoughts, ideas, and fears leave my mind?
- When will I overcome my fear of failure in attempting to change or adapt?
- Will I ever stop doing things so slowly to ensure correctness?

- How much should I tell others about my condition?
- Why won't others, such as my doctor, therapist, family, or boss, listen to me?
- How long will my worry, remorse, grief, and other negative feelings go on?

It is also important to recognize four reactions that are common during Stage Two:

1. Grieving: a normal response to injury-imposed limitations and losses, similar to the grief felt at the death of a loved one.

2. Selective Hearing: an instinctive coping mechanism that "protects" the mind by avoiding painful information. Survivors tend to hear only those things that bring comfort and reassurance.

3. Disequilibrium: characterized by disruptions in the normal feedback control mechanisms that maintain homeostasis (physiological stability). Stability is maintained through a series of coordinated mental and physical responses to situations or forces that interfere with normal functioning. When the mind and body are no longer able to react optimally together due to the effects of trauma, life becomes a roller coaster ride of emotional highs and lows.

4. Anniversary Reactions: disruptive emotional upheavals that occur during a period of sustained, successful recovery. They typically happen around the date of the trauma or some other closely associated event. Survivors often lapse into painful recollections of their traumatic experiences and subsequent losses. They may become nervous and hypersensitive about accident-related topics, and they may brood over recovery progress and/or develop unreasonable fears of the event recurring.

Stage Three: Recovery—Again the length of time varies considerably from person to person. This is the point when survivors can become thrivers, the time when trauma survivors regain their original health or well being; or, in the case of disabling or disfiguring injury, are able to establish a different, but meaningful and rewarding, lifestyle.

Recovery heralds a successful adjustment to whatever loss or limitation may have been suffered. People gradually overcome their sense of loss. Feelings of encouragement replace those of helplessness and hopelessness.

One of the first encouraging signs of recovery is when recoverees can talk about their life-changing event comfortably and discuss how they have adapted to their losses or limitations. They experience significantly less tension and anxiety. Self-worth, confidence, and enthusiasm for life increase. They develop new relationships and strengthen old ones.

Appendix 1–C
I. Memory Bank Tutorial

We all have memory banks that store the events of our lives, especially the strong feelings or emotions associated with each event. However, we have to clothe the events in words in order to create a "memory trace" which enables us to relate events even to ourselves. Before the age of two, since we generally do not have the word power to store our experiences in words, we store them only as feelings.

Feelings →Behaviors→Habits→Dispositions

From the time of birth all experiences that produce strong feelings are stored in the memory portion of the brain. These feelings eventually take on a character that we identify as innate beliefs or perceptions; these in turn result in the development of unique and specific behaviors. Our feeling-triggered behaviors are repeated so often that they become habits which crystallize into personality traits or dispositions. The many different personality types result in a wide range of responses to highly emotional situations. Even so, most typically fall within five basic categories of response often referred to as the five "Fs." These five basic responses are fight, flight, fake, fold, and freeze.

Repression and Suppression

Traumatic events that occur before a person develops sufficient language skills to express them in words (generally before age two) are *automatically* repressed. However, even when we are unable to recall the specifics of a previous event, we usually respond to situations that stimulate feelings associated with the event according to one of the five characteristic dispositions. **Suppression**, a *conscious* decision not to deal with the feelings surrounding a particular event, is an option often chosen after age two. Suppression is common in the aftermath of a trauma. Because survivors don't want to be continually reminded of the experience, they may hide their feelings and avoid anything that tends to bring up similar feelings. Or they may even suppress their memory of the whole event and deny, even to themselves, that it really happened.

Programming and Mind Triggers

The Memory Bank Tutorial stimulates awareness of traits and beliefs acquired over the course of a lifetime that may negatively impact successful recovery from injury and trauma. In one way or another, every experience we've ever had affects our judgments and influences our reasoning, comprehension, and reaction or behavior. When a current event triggers memories of a similar event, it connects our current feelings with the feelings we had during the event earlier in our lives. These triggered memories frequently cause us to over- or underreact to a situation we would otherwise handle with a more appropriate response. The information in the Memory Bank tutorial identifies the manner in which early life experiences "program" individuals to engage in impulsive, habitual behaviors.

To Act or To React

Habitual unchallenged perceptions may threaten healing because they contaminate the thought processes and trigger automatic, reactive "victim-creature" behaviors. There are many examples of this level of behavior in childhood. If Jason throws sand at Jimmy, Jimmy automatically throws sand back at Jason, demonstrating his "fight" disposition. On the other hand, when Jason throws sand at Jeff, Jeff automatically runs away and thereby demonstrates his "flight" disposition.

The Memory Bank Tutorial teaches survivors that they can become "creative-achievers" rather than "victim-creatures." Instead of reacting automatically without thinking, they can learn to think things through and act on principles likely to bring them positive consequences. Creative achievers learn to thrive by taking the IRO-STEPS and keeping their eyes on their goals versus focusing on obstacles such as losses, limitations, problems, pain, etc.

II. Psychic Energy Battery Tutorial

All thinking requires energy. When one is fatigued, the ability to reason, analyze, or make decisions is impaired. Motor skills, as well as sensory acuity, diminish when we are tired or sleep deprived. In a similar way, stress provoked by trauma can blunt our ability to perform. The effects of stress are cumulative, so over time an individual's ability to bounce back can be severely impaired. Barry Richards has coined the term "Psychic Energy Battery" to illustrate this principle.

All Systems Are Affected by Psychic Energy

Just as a car battery provides energy for the starter, lights, radio, and accessories of an automobile, the Psychic Energy Battery provides the energy for our psychological functioning, our emotional functioning, *and* our physical functioning—digestive system, cardiovascular system, etc. And as with a car battery, if it is not recharged by the generator/alternator in between uses, its power is soon diminished to the point that the car won't start. Virtually all bodily systems, including the immune system, are affected by how well we are functioning mentally. This is especially true as it relates to our Psychic Energy Battery's charge status. If depleted by stress, especially chronic debilitation brought about by emotional trauma, the toll on our ability to function effectively is heavy, even overwhelming.

Repression and Suppression Drain Psychic Energy

It is a drain on our psychic energy to hold suppressed and repressed feelings (which Richards calls pus pockets) out of our awareness. When our energy is dissipated in this way, it is analogous to trying to operate a large car using a motorcycle battery—there is simply not enough energy available to meet the demands. Consequently, the amount of psychic energy available to reason, analyze, make decisions, and solve problems is greatly reduced.

Relationships Suffer When Psychic Energy Is Low

If we have a lifetime of traumatic experiences combined with attending unresolved feelings, we start each day with "low" psychic energy. Day-to-day problems and stresses tend to put additional drains on our energy. If, in addition, we have a relationship that needs to be nurtured, rejuvenated, and stimulated, we simply don't have the psychic energy to deal with it. Evenings are the only time most of us have available for nurturing relationships during weekdays. If we are exhausted in the evening hours and don't know how to resolve our emotional problems, we are likely to react negatively according to our habits and disposition. All too often, by the end of a series of unsuccessful evenings of trying to improve relations, we become disappointed, disillusioned, and resentful. We may feel that our companion is uncooperative and appears to be expecting things of us for which we simply have no energy. When the above cycle remains uninterrupted, new stresses are added and our psychic energy is drained even further.

Chronic Drain Can Lead to Serious Problems

If such a pattern continues, before long we will not have the energy we need to think and reason at even a minimally acceptable level. The long term result of chronic stress also presents itself in many physical ailments. The most serious of these may have fatal consequences, such as heart disease. There is a growing body of evidence suggesting that some cancers may also have a strong stress component.

How To Slow-Charge the Psychic Energy Battery

The Psychic Energy Battery tutorial focuses on respecting yourself enough to *slow-charge* your psychic battery daily. *Jump-starting* with alcohol, drugs, or overstimulating experiences can, as with any sensitive device, produce more long-term harm than short-term benefit.

So how do we slow-charge our batteries?

1. By getting enough rest, exercise, and nutritious food.
2. By doing things we love to do, such as listen to good music or enjoy nature.
3. Both humor and spirituality may also play an important role in the revitalizing process. Humor that produces a full belly laugh results in remarkable physiologic changes that are highly beneficial.
4. Spirituality is essential. Participating in organized religion is not the only way to increase spirituality. Seeking spiritual solace in books, conversations, and personal meditation is recommended. However we choose to accomplish it, the dimension of spiritual rejuvenation should not be overlooked.
5. Engaging in nurturing relationships that are reciprocal provides an indispensable avenue for charging instead of draining our psychic energy batteries. A nurturing primary relationship has been found to be the most effective source of constant psychic energy.

III. Human Intimacy Tutorial

Human Intimacy is the desire, opportunity, and ability for two people to share their hopes, dreams, and aspirations as well as their worries, concerns, and insecurities. Intimacy is created when two people are able to communicate openly and honestly without fear of retribution. Intimacy requires trust, which is best nurtured by unconditional love. Such love, when allowed to flourish, permits ever deeper and more meaningful levels of communication and understanding. Some degree of unconditional love seems to be the key factor in stable, mutually satisfying relationships.

Intimacy and Basic Needs

Intimacy is encouraged when each partner is devoted to helping the other meet

1. Intellectual needs—awareness vs. confusion
2. Emotional needs—belonging vs. loneliness
3. Spiritual needs—values, morals, direction in life vs. feeling lost and disoriented

   In the aftermath of trauma, those who don't have the guidance of a personal value system based on spirituality, direction, or trust in God tend to become confused and may become susceptible to destructive influences which lead to serious psychological impairments.
4. Physical needs—tactile stimulation vs. stagnation
   a. affection
   b. sexual interaction

Physical stimulation and human touch in a committed, positive relationship lifts people and edifies them, tenderly creating a nurturing interaction. This is in direct contrast with the stagnation and emotional blunting that comes out of selfish and self-serving relationships in which people merely use each other to satisfy physical needs.

In his book *His Needs, Her Needs,* Willard F. Harley Jr. explains that men's and women's needs are prioritized in a completely different order. For example, Harley lists women's most important needs as affection, conversation, honesty, and openness. By contrast, his list of primary needs for men begins with sexual fulfillment, recreational companionship, and an attractive spouse. Harley suggests that identifying and meeting each other's most important needs deepens love and increases the desire to be together.

IV. Basic Necessities and Human Stimulants Tutorial

This tutorial is closely related to the Human Intimacy directions just discussed. However, the goals are directed toward the nurturing relationships among the members of a family and specifically how to apply these principles to parenting.

Although both the Basic Necessities and the Human Stimulants can be defined to include many different attitudes and actions, for our purposes they may be summarized into three domains of necessities and four types of stimulants.

The Basic Necessities are
- Recognition
- Acknowledgment
- Acceptance

The Human Stimulants are
- Touch
- Talk
- Activity
- Material Things

The purpose of the Basic Needs and Human Stimulants tutorial is to cultivate love that will enrich relationships and build solid marriages and families.

Nurturing Love Promotes Emotional and Physical Healing

One of the most important characteristics associated with love is nurturing. This includes the selfless desire and effort to feed, nourish, educate, care about, and serve another. A nurturing love has three important characteristics that set it apart from other forms of affection. These are recognition, acknowledgment, and acceptance. When these three attributes are consistently present in a caring relationship, emotional and physical healing are facilitated.

Because of their fundamental importance in positive relationships, recognition, acknowledgment, and acceptance are referred to as the Basic

Necessities. Below are some of the important ways in which the Basic Necessities can be integrated into a supportive and caring relationship.

1. Recognition: Recognition is sensitive attention to the physical, emotional, spiritual, social, and/or financial needs of others. It occurs when we are alert and responsive to the expressed as well as non-verbal feelings, attitudes, and circumstances of a loved one. This type of insightful recognition does not occur through casual and thoughtless interactions. It takes work to recognize and respond to the messages that are present in another person's body language, verbal inflections, and situational cues. Successful recognition does not demand extraordinary powers of deduction or mind reading. Instead, it requires a selfless love for the person and a willingness to put forth the time and effort to understand what they are saying and to recognize and respond to important nonverbal messages.

Physical as well as mental energy are important determinants of success in achieving the level of recognition that nurtures a loving relationship. Fatigue is the enemy of successful communication and understanding. If we attempt to develop insight and recognition at the end of the day when we are both emotionally and physically drained, the chances of success are minimal. Scheduling time free from distractions, when both individuals are alert and refreshed, is critical to this process. As with any important goal, hard work is required but the rewards can be far greater than imagined.

2. Acknowledgment: Providing consistent and ongoing support of correct decision making through acknowledgment may be one of the most important factors in aiding the recovery process.

Just as children feel good about the outcome of good choices when they receive positive responses from parents, adults respond to positive reinforcement from those whom they love and admire. To some degree or another, most of us make choices that, according to our perceptions, will bring us acceptance and approval and avoid choices that we believe will bring disapproval and rejection. We can acknowledge the challenges, adjustments, and progress of loved ones in many ways, including supportive comments, notes or letters, a caring touch at appropriate moments, etc. It is possible to actively acknowledge and reinforce positive recovery efforts even through small gestures.

In the discussions concerning *recognition* and *acknowledgment*, the importance of paying attention to a person's verbal and nonverbal communication and reinforcing appropriate decision making are emphasized.

As we observe and collect data, we can then act on it to help people to improve. However, not all of the behaviors we observe in a loved one, especially one who has been traumatized, will be positive. Their behaviors or words may be hurtful or frustrating; some may even prompt our anger. When we are hurt, frustrated, or angry with someone, lashing out and hurting back can occur almost automatically. Controlling these impulses can be the key to long-term success and is absolutely critical to meeting the goal of satisfying the Basic Necessities.

Free will or free agency, the freedom to make choices, is a fundamental capacity and desire common to humans. However, the ability to make good choices is often hindered by external influences, especially stressful experiences. Even though the principle of free agency remains an enduring reality, our ability to make truly free decisions may be impaired by any number of factors, including traumatic events. One perception common to almost all survivors of major traumatic events is the loss of control and loss of confidence in their ability to process information accurately and to make wise choices. Survivors tend to rely on others to make decisions for them, which further erodes their sense of control and self-confidence. They may increasingly depend on therapists, friends, attorneys, or any number of other people (reputable or otherwise) who may offer assistance or information.

When we rely on others to make our decisions for us—and in effect give away our free will—we still have to live with the inherent consequences of our choices. It is usually better for survivors to base their decisions on their own deeply held values and beliefs and the best information available to them. When we take responsibility and make our own decisions, we are better able to accept the consequences of our choices regardless of the outcome.

If a loved one is consistently making poor choices, we can show them, using a tender and sincere approach, the link between their choices and the consequences. The critical issue is to acknowledge their right to make decisions. The goal is not to take away their agency, but rather to acknowledge wise decisions and to help them understand the inevitable relationship between the decisions made today and the results experienced tomorrow.

3. Acceptance: The third basic necessity is Acceptance. The word "acceptance" means exactly what it says—to accept people as they are. This does not suggest that we should condone negative character traits or behaviors. It does mean, however, that we accept people as important and loveable. Of course we would like to have those we care for improve, and we will strive to assist them in that goal. Yet we need to remember that people who have been the victims of trauma often see themselves as misfits. Sometimes this is a result of disfiguring injuries; more often, however, it comes as a result of the confusion they experience as a result of their emotional wounds. The best encouragement to accept themselves comes from the acceptance offered by loved ones.

Following the murder-hostage situation, Susan Woolley struggled with PTSD and the emotional trauma inflicted by the criminal justice system. She described herself as "feeling like a freak." Countless times when she was checking out at the grocery store, waiting in line for a ticket, or engaged in casual conversations in public, people would declare in full voice: "Oh, you're the one who was a hostage at Alta View!" At the same time, friends whom she had known for years stopped calling or visiting. She felt that if she had had AIDS, she would have been treated better. At least people would have expressed condolences or given her a hug because those were the politically correct things to do. As it was, one thing was clear—she was no longer "acceptable" to many. Perhaps they were uncomfortable, did not know what to say, or didn't want to intrude. Whatever the reasons, the effect was devastating to her.

Since acceptance is so important in meeting a person's basic necessities, it pays to recognize how we react to loved ones. We can, through recognition, acknowledgment, and acceptance, be a major factor in the healing process that takes place following a traumatic event.

Evidences of Love

Of course when we discuss the elements of basic necessities, we are simultaneously describing ingredients of love. No one can have real love for another without giving respect, regard, and esteem. Love focuses on the positive and tries to uplift and build others. When love governs the interactions with the survivors of trauma, they and their loved ones feel greater security, self-worth, self-esteem, and self-confidence. When this happens, people begin to thrive, not merely survive.

Additional Characteristics of Those Who Show Genuine Love Toward Others:

They are good listeners.
They emphasize and demonstrate courage, hope, and optimism.
They are tolerant and are not quick to judge.
They are forgiving and compassionate.

They admit their own limitations, inadequacies, and mistakes and try to
correct them.

They inspire confidence, calmness, and peace.

They are patient.

They are honest.

They take action and do not avoid being involved.

They are grateful for the positive things in their lives.

Human Stimulants

The Basic Necessities are balanced and enhanced by the Human
Stimulants: Touch, Talk, Activity, and Material Things. The first three are
the most important. "Things" enrich our lives when our relationships are
being nurtured; otherwise they are quite meaningless.

Touch: This is the most basic of the four human stimulants. It is
instinctive and essential to normal growth and development in childhood
and continued happiness as an adult. Early in the development of intensive care units for newborn babies, clinicians noticed that many infants
who were left in their incubators for prolonged periods of time developed
a condition known as "Failure to Thrive." They also noticed that those
who were taken out and held periodically were much less likely to experience this problem. Since this fact is so well understood now, individuals
come to the intensive care units on a regular basis simply to hold and cud-
dle these tiny babies. This has proven to be a lifesaving activity.

Touch continues to be a critically important factor in our lives until
we die. As adults we experience the most intimate touching as we engage
in sexual relations. This touching is considered important by most people
for a normal, well-rounded life. If parents nurture each other and there is
sexual fulfillment, the benefits spill over to the children in affection. As
the title to the popular song states: "My cup runneth over with love."
When the parents' cup runs over, children and others in the home are the
beneficiaries of what spills over. They also know there is something to
look forward to when they are mature. If fathers and mothers are appropriately affectionate with their daughters and sons, there is a healthy balance and emotional malnutrition is avoided. When parents evidence
unconditional love for one another, children tend to thrive and respond
by developing a "we, us, our" attitude instead of the selfish "I, me, mine"
attitude.

Talk: As discussed earlier in describing the Basic Necessity of recognition, talk is more than passively sitting as one might do in a movie or in

front of the television and hearing words. Similarly it is more than speaking as if one were reading from a book or a script without regard to the audience. Talk, if it is to satisfy the needs of human stimulation, must be a two-way interaction. Even when one party may not respond verbally they may communicate awareness of the other's words through expression, intensity of concentration, physical proximity, gestures, and reactions such as laughter or tears. Talk is a form of communication that confirms and reinforces the process of bonding and is reinforced by positive interactions.

Activity: In meeting the characteristics of a Basic Necessity, activity is more than simply engaging in some sort of movement. Movements, of course, range from the basics of breathing and other purely autonomic functions to highly physical and mental activities such as flying an airplane, playing basketball, or singing a song. The *context* of the activity— why you are doing it, with whom you are doing it, what happens as a result, and the costs and benefits—is more important than what is happening. Costs in this context include not only the money spent, but also physical costs such as injuries or health benefits, improved or strained relationships, trust gained or doubts developed, etc. Perhaps there are no more satisfying and beneficial activities than those that are family centered. In such settings we may learn to be more unselfish, considerate, compassionate, tolerant, caring, helpful, and forgiving. Activities teach children cooperative interaction. If positive traits are enhanced through family activities, children take those characteristics with them into the workplace, into their own marriages, and wherever they go. The ability to get along with others and to function well in work and social settings becomes a permanent and lasting legacy. Activities that take a parent away from spouse and children are rarely as beneficial, even to personal growth, as positive family-centered activities.

Material Things: Physical things—clothes, computers, boats, houses, jewelry, cars, toys—are important sources of stimulation. If touch, talk, and nurturing activities are being accomplished within the walls of our own homes, we tend to be motivated to improve our standard of living. All material things are transitory, however, and so have little lasting value. The perishable nature of "things" is best demonstrated in situations where love, self-esteem, and nurturing are not satisfactory. Classic examples are the division of property in post-trauma divorces or the sale of treasured heirlooms to buy a few moments of chemically induced escape from the pain of trauma.

If we disregard the Basic Necessities in our homes (Recognition, Acknowledgment, and Acceptance) as we are acquiring material things, or if our devotion is primarily toward our possessions, they will not contribute to self-worth and self-confidence. However, if we use possessions as a means of bringing those we love together, they can be a very beneficial part of our lives. Often family activities require the purchase of material objects and equipment. Buying things that are mutually enjoyable to the whole family can have great benefits. The issue is not the cost as such; rather, it is the value of the objects as investments in mutual growth and positive experiences.

Preventive Maintenance Prescriptions

Nonmedical prescriptions are assignments written on a prescription pad directing the individual to engage in a specific Preventive Maintenance activity. They are often given in the process of the tutorials. Many are designed to encourage couples to engage together in activities that will enhance the Basic Necessities and Human Stimulants in the relationship. Preventive Maintenance involves regular, frequent, predictable, and continual acknowledgment of the progress and efforts both are making. Clarifying each other's needs and expectations in the relationship takes frequent and effective communication.

Preventive Maintenance keeps a relationship from becoming stagnant. Optimum happiness can be achieved only when family relationships are given a higher priority than work and recreation not shared with one's family members. Focus on relationships makes all tasks and activities more meaningful and rewarding.

Foundation for Life and Trauma Aftermath

If we have been nurtured by the Basic Necessities and Human Stimulants, we will respond with much more confidence when a traumatic event turns our world upside down. We will have more strength to face challenges and afflictions because we will feel emotionally secure. If we come into the aftermath of trauma with deprivation in these areas, in order to thrive rather than merely survive we will need to devote all the more attention to the Basic Necessities and Human Stimulants.

V. Drivers and Fatal Fives Tutorial

Those raised in an environment where Basic Necessities and Human Stimulants were present tend to be more flexible and resilient in their approach to life and their recovery from trauma. They can alter their expectations in regard to task performance and are more likely to be sensitive to their own emotional needs as well as the needs of others.

When Basic Necessities and Human Stimulants have not been provided on a regular, frequent, predictable basis, we tend to get into what is called the "Fatal Fives" as substitutes. This pattern often occurs when a father and mother are not nurturing to one another and so the parents try to use a child as a substitute source for this gratification. They expect the child to give them the sense of worth and accomplishment they are not getting on their own.

Drivers

"Drivers" are directions that we subconsciously carry around in our heads that move us away from spontaneous interactions in our relationships. They drive us to become like machines performing to meet the expectations of others.

The concept of and the term "drivers" has been used for many years by psychologists and other mental health professionals in the behavioral approach known as Transactional Analysis. The person generally credited with developing the "drivers" theory is Taibai Kahler.[1] Kahler suggests five drivers:

1. Be Perfect	*(These drivers are not inherently bad; they*
2. Try Hard	*become problematic when they are used*
3. Hurry Up	*excessively and at the expense of solid, nur-*
4. Please Me	*turing relationships.)*
5. Be Strong	

Clinical traumatology adds a sixth driver: "Be Busy." Transactional Analysis (TA) suggests that the drivers originate in commands of parents or other strong adult authority figures who place demands on children to perform in certain ways. These demands are not made to benefit the child, but to satisfy some need of the adult, e.g., to be socially acceptable, etc.

---

[1] Kahler, T., Drivers: the key to the process of scripts, *Transactional Analysis Journal*, Vol. 5, No. 3, pp. 280–84, July 1975.

Children who grow up relying primarily upon habitual and mechanistic "drivers" are likely to be highly task oriented. While they may accomplish a great deal in terms of achieving external goals, they will generally not have a great deal of success in building and maintaining close, nurturing relationships.

The concept of drivers adapted from TA has been shown to have great utility when applied in conjunction with the IRO-STEPS tutorials.

"Be Perfect" Driver

The first driver is called "Be Perfect." Barry Richards recounts the case of a young fellow whose parents grounded him for a month because one A minus marred his straight A report card. They wanted the recognition that goes with having a child with a straight A's—and this was in elementary school! What did this kind of expectation do to this child? It caused him to become preoccupied and obsessed with perfectionism. He was not able to develop a normal spontaneous, interactive relationship with his parents or peers. Instead, his "performance" became the focus of his life. Unless he learns to see things differently, he will carry that driver around in his head for the rest of his life. He will continue to direct his efforts at receiving praise from others that is often not forthcoming, especially when the expectations of others are unrealistic or ambiguous. People who are self-critical, flaw-conscious perfectionists are not likely to attend to relationships as they need to. They are more focused on "getting something done and getting it done right." They are unlikely to be integrated into social interactions effectively. Not because they don't want to be, but because they don't have the skills and the self-confidence to risk rejection. They believe others are going to judge and punish them as their parents did whenever they don't live up to some vague set of expectations.

"Try Hard"

The second driver is "Try Hard." It is linked to the "Be Perfect" driver. It is based on the false belief that if you just try hard enough you can become perfect. It sets people up for failure since they are trying to accomplish the impossible. No one reaches a state of perfection or full development in this life. No one can "leap tall buildings in a single bound" or become a cardiac surgeon by taking a correspondence course.

Keep in mind that these driving mechanisms accelerate in the aftermath of a trauma and people find their drivers mentality a huge handicap to their recovery from emotional turmoil. The tutorials help survivors learn how to use the Basic Necessities and Human Stimulants as their

160

focus as they function and interact with others, rather than focusing on completion of tasks.

"Hurry Up"

The third driver is "Hurry Up." A constant refrain heard in many homes is, "Hurry up!" Unfortunately, getting children off to school or preparing for important events is not the only time the drive to hurry is felt. We live in a society that seems to thrive on speed and the need to do things "right now." To a large degree we have created an attitude that life must be lived by the clock and that *our* clock is most accurate and most important. This selfish view of the world leads to strained relationships between spouses and children. Family arguments concerning amount of time spent on the telephone or a computer are all too frequent. The pleasure of events, such as family outings, can be clouded by anger and contention that can occur just getting ready to leave. Once on the road, traffic jams, impolite drivers, getting lost, and/or lack of parking can add to the stress. Many children grow up dreading family outings simply because of the anguish involved in getting to the location where they occur.

Much of the problem stems from the common belief that people should run on a precise schedule and that faster is better than slower. After trauma, this pattern may be converted to an expectation that healing should occur according to a timetable that works for everyone. People become frustrated when they are told that the healing process is best accomplished through slow, steady progress. If they have been raised to obey the "Hurry Up" driver, there is also a strong tendency to resist working through the tutorial process thoroughly and completely. These people want an instant cure. Until they learn to overcome the "Hurry Up" driver they will have a difficult time, because *you can't hurry healing*.

"Please Me"

The fourth driver is "Please Me." If children are doing everything to please a parent, they are not learning to make decisions on their own and will have a difficult time understanding the relationship between choice and accountability. As they grow into adults, if they are not given the agency to choose their own music or clothes and are not encouraged to express their religious feelings or political outlooks, they will likely fail to develop a strong sense of self. Convictions that will stand the test of time are developed over years of learning what truly pleases the inner self, rather than what pleases others.

Freedom of choice does not mean the absence of guidance.

Children are more likely to learn to make good choices if there are a variety of acceptable options. For example, in the matter of choosing what clothes to wear, children can be allowed to choose from among styles, colors, and fabrics appropriate for their age, reasonably priced, and suitable for the places they are to be worn. There is a big difference between a parent purchasing an item and saying, "use it or go without," versus letting children select among several acceptable alternatives. When one grows up never having made any real decisions because they are making only those choices certain to please a parent, the pattern of making choices to please another person tends to continue into adulthood.

"Be Strong"

The fifth driver is called "Be Strong." Little boys are commonly taught to hold back their feelings. If they are called cowards when they cry, they may become inhibited in their expressions—tough guys who don't talk about feelings or show emotions. Confronted with frustrations, difficulties, disappointments, and disillusionments, the "Be Strong" person will inhibit the natural expression of emotions. In playing the role of the strong stoic, unaffected by anything, including their own trauma, these "Be Strong" people will actually compound the effects of the wounding. Suppressed emotions increase the risk of long-term stress-induced problems. The artificial barrier created by the "Be Strong" driver needs to be dealt with and overcome; otherwise the healing process will be severely slowed and those burdened with the "Be Strong" driver may not respond to even the best of interventions.

"Be Busy"

The last driver is "Be Busy." Being busy can keep our minds off many things in our lives, including the emotional pain that follows trauma. Although this may seem to be an acceptable way to deal with grief and distress, it is a false diversion. Ignoring problems because we are too "busy" to deal with them doesn't make them go away; it only buries them and allows them to fester and grow until the facade of keeping busy can no longer block them out.

To demonstrate that they don't need help, survivors may engage in activities that keep them busy and their minds off the problems which, as noted, leads to bigger problems. Just as the primary trauma survivor can be caught up in a false sense of security (believing that a busy schedule will block out the pain), this "Be Busy" driver can also affect caretakers who wish to help their loved ones recover. A caretaker may stay busy to avoid problems they don't comprehend and/or don't know how to deal with. They too are victims, although of a different sort; they are caught up in a vicious cycle of their own. They may attempt to help by trying to give directions and/or make plans for the trauma survivor. Too often, however, the survivor is not able to deal with the reality of the feelings they are experiencing and may become resentful of intrusion into their lives. As a result, the caregiver may feel slighted and embarrassed by the rebuff and respond by becoming even busier in their own diversionary activities. When there is any discussion of the issues, the sense of frustration mounts because it feels like "the blind leading the blind." When neither survivor nor caretaker knows what to do, they bury their feelings once more in "Being Busy." Staying busy can keep us from being sensitive or attentive and from tuning in to our own and/or others' feelings and behaviors.

Being involved in all kinds of time-consuming activities can lead us away from relationships that are important in the healing process. It can also lead us toward destructive relationships that will compound the already unaddressed problems arising from the traumatic event.

People carrying this driver around in their heads are usually so busy that they don't take care of their primary relationship. Soon they are faced with resentment, disillusionment, and anger from the malnutrition in the relationship. Among married couples one of the most common and tragic outcomes of trauma is divorce. Although divorce has become a routine event in our society, it always comes at a high cost to both partners—to say nothing of the cost to children who may be involved.

Successful healing requires time and attention, ideally not only on the part of the survivor, but also from their caregiver. Spouses, children, parents, or others who are in this role need to learn what they can do to truly help. This learning cannot occur while masquerading as the world's most occupied human. The victim who is denying the existence of the problem by covering it over with an appointment calendar that has no time available for the next six months needs help. Demonstrating that you are willing to take the time to learn how to help and that you will continue to do what needs to be done for as long as necessary can strongly motivate the survivor to reassess their own time priorities.

The Fatal Fives

The six drivers discussed above fuel a group of behaviors known as the Fatal Fives. In their most abstract form they may be labeled

1. Academics
2. Athletics

3. Aesthetics
4. Theatrics
5. Religiosity

The tutorial dealing with the Fatal Fives identifies the most common task-driven behaviors that threaten progressive recovery from injury and trauma. These are often magnified by unrealistic expectations acquired early in life that equate success to subordinating nurturing relationships to wealth, fame, power, and control. Each of the five areas of activity are legitimate and vital to our well-being when they are kept in balance. However, when we choose to focus attention on any one of these fatal five behaviors to the exclusion of other essentials, the results can impede recovery.

In the absence of the Basic Necessities and Human Stimulants, people usually find ways to get in the spotlight and gain accolades that they are not receiving in their primary relationships at home. When they focus on any one of the Fatal Fives, they may create an ambience of power, wealth, or position, but often become shallow in their relationships and forget how to give and receive emotional support. Focus on the Fatal Fives usually drives us to win at all costs—and one of the costs is forfeiting tender, loving interaction.

Briefly, the Fatal Fives may be defined as follows:

Academics: The pursuit of knowledge whereby one can claim "expertise" and be regarded as an expert in a particular field. In the context of using academics as one of the Fatal Fives, the importance of the knowledge is secondary to the accolades that accompany the achievements. The area of study is not important. It may be the study of computer science or beekeeping. What is important is the recognition and the ability to continually play a superior role while interacting with others. Often the knowledge is thin and lacks any applied value; the person simply has a vast amount of information and expertise for which he or she is recognized.

Athletics: People commonly participate in athletics to excess. Interestingly, the degree of skill is secondary to the intensity with which the person engages in the sport. The possibilities are as varied as those who participate in them. Some are able to join teams which require large blocks of time for play and practice. If one is truly good at the sport, of course there will be praise. Winning trophies, ribbons, or certificates along with "team pictures" that can be prominently displayed can become all-important.

Even if one doesn't have any particular ability, there are sports that can be played alone or among friends. The issue is the time it takes and the supposed demonstration of great knowledge and involvement in the activity. There seem to be countless opportunities to plan and participate in charity sports events or other peripheral activities that consume great amounts of time and provide access to public acclaim.

Aesthetics: There are an almost unbelievable number of aesthetic activities that can engage someone seeking a socially acceptable outlet. Painting, model making, musical activities, and home decorating are among the common aesthetic outlets available to almost anyone. With a desire to become heavily involved, one can become immersed in these activities in a remarkably short amount of time. Participants are not only those who produce the works, but also those who view, listen to, or purchase them. Because of their subjective nature, the arts can accommodate virtually anyone as a creator, critic, or consumer. The amount of time and money that can be spent is limitless, but does not equate with healing or thriving. The sheer number of ways to engage in aesthetic activities makes it an "ideal" category in which anyone can find a way to hide from reality and the issues at hand.

Theatrics: Theatrics is not the same as being an actor in a theater. It is the purposeful activity of "playing to an audience" for personal gain with a hidden agenda. The topics are varied, but often trauma survivors become professional reporters or storytellers, using their own experience as the text. In other cases where the subject is too painful they will dwell on other aspects of themselves or others which can hold an audience. The primary goal is the same as with the previously discussed fatal five behaviors—*attention*. Bringing people into the story and eliciting some sort of reaction is the primary goal of the person who engages in theatrics. Often there is an effort to gain sympathy or to get the listeners to spread the story so that there will be additional opportunities for the person to act out in whatever way brings about the desired responses. This is neither a healthy healing process nor a good way to establish relationships. When one is using theatrics as a way of avoiding the necessary steps to bring about healing, it is almost certain to have a bad outcome. Eventually people will be angered or put off by the theatrics or histrionics of the performer. Unfortunately these activities often result in fabrications, half-truths, or outright lies being told in order for the stories to have sufficient impact. For a while one may gain great notoriety, but eventually the unhealed wounds will emerge. The destructive nature of the theatrics themselves will take their toll and the healing process becomes an even greater challenge than it was before the diversion into theatrics.

Religiosity: All of the comments regarding the destructive nature of the previous four activities apply to the fifth of the Fatal Fives, religiosity. Ordinarily, participation in religious activities is a healthy and important part of the healing process. However, the person who submerges themselves in religiosity can do greater harm to themselves than in any of the other areas. Religiosity is not mere scripture study or attendance at religious meetings; religiosity is becoming a zealot. Some individuals within religious organizations may assure the trauma survivor that this zealous behavior is the best means of healing. But when one turns his or her attention to any activity to the exclusion of family, friends, employment, personal health, or recovery from emotional wounds, the consequences can be destructive. Balance is important in maintaining a healthy mind and body. To think that a steady diet of any activity (no matter how noble or worthy the cause) will bring about recovery from emotional trauma is to be sadly misinformed.

There are ways to keep the Drivers and the Fatal Fives from hindering recovery. The key is to know what the pitfalls are, recognize them for what they are, and avoid them. This can be accomplished by working with a loving caregiver and by seeking help from competent professionals when necessary.

VI. Fear Wheel Tutorial

This tutorial addresses the most common fears that survivors experience subsequent to a life-changing event. It also explains the long-term consequences of not dealing with them promptly. The Fear Wheel is an especially effective tool because it teaches the survivor how to change the way he/she perceives life-changing events, including the traumatic event itself. It has often been said that truth or reality is what we perceive it to be. Consequently, what one perceives as a catastrophic event, another may perceive as an important opportunity for growth. (It has been pointed out that the character for "crisis" in written Chinese also means "opportunity.") The directions that accompany the Fear Wheel tutorial are similar in emphasis and specificity to those discussed in the best-selling book *The 7 Habits of Highly Effective People*, authored by Stephen R. Covey.

The Fear Wheel diagram on page 169 is used in this tutorial to illustrate the negative behaviors associated with fears. There are a series of behaviors grouped under various headings that attempt to help the trauma survivor understand how fixating on fears will eventually become so emotionally painful that a means of escape is necessary. These escapes or diversions are usually destructive and may ultimately lead to serious consequences including criminal acts and/or death. Unless these fears and their associated harmful behaviors are conquered, survivors remain at high risk for problems they could not have imagined prior to their traumas. There are many stories of individuals, once recognized as being at the top of their profession, whose lives plummeted into an unbelievable morass of sexual deviancy, substance abuse, and antisocial behaviors following traumatic incidents. There is a natural tendency for people to avoid things that are painful—and fear is painful. If the fears arising from trauma are not addressed promptly and appropriately, the fallout can be catastrophic. The efforts required to attack these fears head on, and beat them, are well repaid in long-term benefits, including lives that are saved and transformed.

Fear and the Sense of Abandonment

Although fear is a common emotion, among trauma survivors, *exaggerated* fears may become a dominant part of everyday life. A multiplicity of fears are felt by most victims, but the predominant fear is fear of abandonment. When a person is traumatized, there is a feeling that the normal "support" factors failed and left them vulnerable to whatever it was that caused the trauma. Both external and internal support can diminish our fears. External support comes from others: family, friends, colleagues, or trained professionals. For example, parents provide support as they guide and nurture their children and provide them with the physical necessities of food and shelter. The internal supports are generated mentally to provide a "reasonable" level of personal security. One such internal or mental support factor is the law of averages. In a world filled with potentially traumatic events most people can allay their fears of potential disaster by using the logical rationale that statistically, most disasters will probably not happen to them.

For example, if an airplane crashes, the risk of death or serious injury is very high. However, the probability that any given airplane is going to crash is very low. So it is not unreasonable to protect yourself with an imaginary support which allows you to feel that "it will never happen to me." The odds are that an airplane crash *won't* happen to you, especially if you only fly in commercial airplanes. When something *does* happen that destroys the illusion of invulnerability, trauma survivors, even those physically uninjured, feel abandoned by external or internal supports.

Because abandonment has already been experienced to some degree by virtually every trauma survivor, it is already an issue. Fears of further abandonment by family, friends, or society are greatly heightened by involvement in a traumatic event.

Most Common Fears

Several other fears are commonly experienced following a trauma; unfortunately some of these fears may have a basis in reality. But, attended to promptly and appropriately, they can be prevented from escalating to the level where self-destructive behaviors result. When fears become too threatening, the "natural" reaction is to try and hide from them. Attempts to run away from fear leads to destructive behaviors.

Most commonly seen among trauma survivors are the fears of

1. Abandonment
2. Failure
3. Rejection
4. Loneliness
5. Exploitation
6. Physical Pain
7. The Unknown

The Fear Wheel diagram illustrates techniques for overcoming ruinous behaviors that are linked to fear. A critical step to healing is understanding that, in one way or another, all of these negative activities are efforts to "hide" from reality.

The three key elements of openness are shown at the left of the diagram: recognition, acknowledgment, and acceptance. When these elementary needs are fulfilled, an individual becomes accessible; they are not closed down from fears of rejection or humiliation. When a person feels stripped of recognition, acknowledgment, and acceptance (a condition often experienced by victims of trauma), fears are generated. Accessibility is an essential step in the development of an individual's sense of identity. The basic elements of a positive sense of identity are self-worth, self-esteem, self-confidence, self-respect, and security.

Understanding the Fear Wheel and recognizing the importance of maintaining openness and accessibility are of inestimable value in helping to protect against the downward spiral brought about through fear.

Ambitious
- Driven
- Win at all costs
- Inadequate
- Inferior
- Ruthless
- Manipulative
- Lonely
- Shallow

Chemical and Other Dependence
- Alcohol
- Prescribed drugs
- Illicit drugs
- Deep emotional pain

Suicidal
- Ideation
- Distortion
- Threats
- Gestures
- Attempts

Psychotic
- Paranoia
- Delusions
- Hallucinations

Deviancies
- Pedophilia (child molesting)
- Rape
- Exhibitionism
- Prostitution
- Pornography
- Voyeurism
- Promiscuity

Medical Problems
- Dizziness
- Headaches
- Stomach disorders
- Heart Disease
- Cancer
- Kidney Disease

Non-conformist
- Antisocial
- Withdrawn
- Loner
- Aberrant
- Eccentric
- Kinky

FEAR

Accident Prone
- Preoccupied and distracted
- Transfer of psychological problems to physical incidents

Neurotic
- Phobias
- Eating disorders
- Fanaticism
- Obsessions
- High anxiety
- Sleep disturbances
- Hyperactivity

Criminal Tendencies
- Hostility
- Passivity
- Compulsive
- Ritualism
- Obsessive
- Manipulative
- Controlling

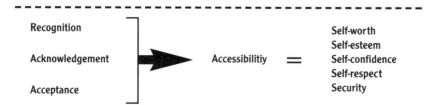

Recognition

Acknowledgement

Acceptance

Accessibilitiy =

Self-worth
Self-esteem
Self-confidence
Self-respect
Security

Appendix 1–D
Synopsis of Auxiliary IRO-STEPS Tutorials

The twenty-three auxiliary tutorials are presented, as needed, either along with or subsequent to the Six Basic IRO-STEPS Tutorials. The amount of time and depth of study and discussion devoted to them is tailored to the needs of the individual survivor. Simply because they may not apply equally to all survivors, the auxiliary tutorials should not be considered to be less important than the primary six. For someone who needs the specific information contained in an auxiliary tutorial, one of these may, in fact, be the most important tutorial they receive. A brief summary of each is presented below.

"Wait Until It Breaks To Fix It" Land Mine: This tutorial cautions survivors, their caregivers, friends, family, and other interested persons against assuming that "everything is fine" because the physical injuries were either minimal or have been stabilized. In general, trauma survivors and/or those impacted by horrifying events can neither accurately assess the degree of emotional damage caused by the event, nor determine the long-range consequences of neglecting emotional wounds. A key aspect of this tutorial is helping the survivor understand the importance of obtaining early professional direction to deal with emotional wounds. They learn that if prompt, appropriate attention is received, there should be no need for extensive psychotherapy. The "wait until it breaks to fix it" attitude so prevalent among most employers, insurance adjusters, benefits specialists, and uninformed health care providers makes it imperative that the survivors themselves understand the necessity of proactively seeking appropriate intervention and the value of prompt response to their frequently unrecognized needs.

Physical Injuries, Emotional Wounds Distinction Tutorial: The goal is to help survivors realize that complete recovery includes healing of both physical injuries and emotional wounds. They learn that prompt attention to both types of pain is critical if complete healing is to take place. Also, they learn to distinguish between physical problems that are precipitated by emotional distress versus those that are purely organic in origin. The tutorial helps all involved to recognize that early, professional attention that specifically addresses trauma-induced emotional wounding will minimize the probability of developing serious psychological problems.

Integrative/Holistic Health Care Tutorial: Instructions focus on the need to acquire health care directions and information from all of the appropriate providers available. There is an emphasis on the need to coordinate and combine the efforts of medical and health care professionals from a variety of disciplines. The survivor learns that **all** of the answers to health care are not the sole domain of any one health care specialty. They are warned about possible turf-protection by some individuals who seek to control their care and limit their access to other resources that could be extremely beneficial. The survivor learns to place more emphasis on good outcomes than on the impressive credentials of any one provider or discipline.

Dignity Destroyers, Survival Exploitation, and Psychological Baggage Tutorial: These instructions help the survivor to look at the risks imposed by generic "crisis intervention" counseling and therapy that is not specific to healing emotional wounds arising from traumatic events. They learn about procedures that create dependencies on medications, nonspecific procedures, and individual providers. Care is taken to clearly separate the survivor's pre-trauma lifestyle and level of functioning from those factors that are a result of the aftermath of the trauma, since different solutions may be indicated for each. Survivors are encouraged to set goals and focus on specific activities that will help them and their caregivers to *thrive* rather than merely survive and tolerate losses and limitations.

Educational Empowerment Tutorial: The goal is to help the survivor and their caregivers, family, and other loved ones understand the benefits of education regarding their emotional wounds. They learn that the correct information will aid them in making correct choices that are critical to their recovery. Further, they learn that without this information they will very likely continue to experience progressive feelings of helplessness and a loss of control over their lives.

***In Vivo* Desensitization:** In this activity the survivor goes back to the scene of their injury/horrifying event with the clinical traumatologist as soon as possible after they are medically stable. This process helps them gain self-mastery over the experience and brings closure to the event. The principle is similar to getting back on the horse after falling off. The process tends to restore self-confidence and a feeling of personal control.

Pain Versus Suffering Tutorial: In this tutorial the differences between physical pain and unnecessary emotional suffering are explained.

The survivor learns that emotional wounds that have not been attended to promptly and properly result in prolonged suffering that is independent of and may extend beyond physical pain from the injury.

Symptom Magnification: The subconscious process of developing chronic and ever-increasing pain as a means of gaining attention is discussed in this tutorial. When emotional wounds have been overlooked or inappropriately treated, survivors experience residual problems they are unable to correctly address. The result is the development of pains and symptoms which are subconscious devices used to gain attention (referred to as "secondary gain"). Until the primary emotional wound is dealt with, these problems are likely to continue.

Origin of pain-prone delayed recovery: This tutorial is related to the Symptom Magnification Tutorial in that it helps the survivor to understand the factors that lead to prolonged symptoms of pain. If allowed to continue untreated these factors undermine the healing process. The four primary factors are

1. Masked depression over disruptive and destructive experiences/behaviors that either occurred in the past and/or continue in the present.
2. Inadequate support and understanding or inappropriate comments from caregivers, friends, family, or others.
3. Secondary gain behaviors as explained in Symptom Magnification above.
4. Medications and/or treatments that are substituted for or interfere with the learning process necessary to achieve emotional wound healing through the IRO-STEPS tutorials.

The "M&Ms" of Thought Empowerment: The survivor is taught to appreciate the power and benefits of learning and filling the mind with uplifting material, including quotations, lyrics to inspiring songs, scripture verses, and positive stories and experiences of others that edify and encourage. By doing this, the survivor can **Minimize** the frequency and impact of unwanted and intrusive thoughts and **Maximize** their own personal potential for recovery.

Spirituality and Healing: The goal of this tutorial is to help the survivor understand the importance of bringing the "whole person" into the healing process. This is done when there is attention to the body (physical), mind (emotional), and spirit (spiritual—relationship with God). Attending to all three areas is critical to complete healing. The survivor learns how tragedy and adversity can be overcome by bringing behaviors and thoughts into harmony with the spirit and with the higher values of spirituality.

Rescuer-Victim Complications: The survivor is warned about the consequences of allowing good-intentioned but uninformed or inappropriate individuals to provide directions or become intimately involved in the recovery process. Deanna Edwards refers to these people as "Surrogate Sufferers" in her book *Grieving: the Pain and the Promise.*[2] These people may be professionals, such as traditional psychotherapists, well-meaning friends, family, or acquaintances who try to "spare" the survivor from doing their own "grief-work." In so doing they retard emotional growth and healing and interfere with the assistance provided by the IRO-STEPS tutorials.

Key Terminologies: This tutorial teaches the survivor about four terms that are used extensively by psychologists and other mental health providers. These terms are more fully described in the glossary at the end of the book. They are

- Transference
- Displacement
- Projection
- Secondary gain

These terms all refer to negative reactions or defense mechanisms that survivors may experience following their trauma. They are all unconscious behaviors or mechanisms that are linked to the past and brought into the present as a result of the emotional turmoil associated with the survivor's trauma. They must be understood and dealt with expeditiously or they will prolong recovery by shifting the survivor's focus to losses, disabilities, financial issues and/or disruptions to normal living.

Impairment, Apportionment, and Disability Ratings: In order to avoid surprises and disappointments, these three assessment techniques (used to establish eligibility for compensation from various sources) are discussed with the survivor. This proactive step offers a realistic understanding

---

[2] *Grieving: The Pain and the Promise,* by Deanna Edwards, Covenant Communications, American Fork, Utah, 1989.

of what the potential compensation will be and dispels the unrealistic expectation that the compensation will "make it all better." It also helps the survivor to avoid the turmoil that results from disillusionment over the failure of the "system" to recognize and appropriately compensate the survivor.

Worker's Compensation and Independent Medical Evaluations (IME): As a part of the healing process, and to help survivors understand the laws and procedures associated with workplace injuries, this tutorial provides critical insight often overlooked in current care procedures. The tutorial gives the survivor reassurance that they are protected, but clarifies possible limitations and exclusions that may apply in their situation. The nature and purpose of the IME is explained. The IME is an evaluation (made by a physician who has not been involved in the survivor's care) of the combined treatment and recovery assistance that has been given and determines the individual's disability or impairment. It also attempts to identify any other services or actions that should have been or could still be provided to benefit the survivor.

Legalities and Secondary Gain: In this tutorial the goal is to warn about the liabilities associated with seeking large settlements through legal remedies. Because of the adversarial nature of the legal system, court battles, hostile depositions, prolonged litigation and a host of other negative factors may significantly hinder recovery from emotional wounds. The possibility of "winning the battle while losing the war" is discussed and the alternatives, such as reconciliation and forgiveness, are explained.

Investigations, Surveillance, and Pandora's Box: Individuals receiving worker's compensation are frequently given this tutorial. In it they are informed about the possibility of private investigators and surveillance procedures that may negatively impact the process of recovery. These procedures are almost always a result of the suspicion that the recipient is attempting to "beat the system," or in other words, commit fraud. In a related but different vein, the Pandora's Box phenomenon occurs when, in the process of dealing with the emotional wounds associated with a worker's compensation matter, other matters related to past problems are discovered. Worker's compensation administrators are reluctant to pay to treat "preexisting" conditions. Therefore, it is critical to assess the nature of the emotional wound and separate the new issues from those that existed previously so that fair and appropriate compensation can be given to deal with the injury-related matters.

Pseudo-Recovery and Delayed Healing: Occasionally the survivor will obtain a small amount of information regarding emotional wounding and assume that they can handle everything independently from then on. This is referred to as a "flight to life" in that the survivor is fleeing the situation where they are required to put forth effort to learn how to aid themselves in their recovery through the process of the IRO-STEPS tutorials. In fleeing what they perceive as hard and perhaps unnecessary work, they create a situation where they will likely fail and have a significantly delayed healing process. This is analogous to trying to fly across the ocean with too little fuel. The takeoff and cruise may all go well, but when the fuel runs out, a crash is inevitable.

Spiral Effect and Re-traumatization: The survivor learns straightforward scientific principles. These explain why unattended emotional wounds may delay physical healing and cause a downward spiral with additional trauma, injuries, and exploitation worse than those experienced with the original incident. This tutorial teaches the survivor how to avoid this pitfall and encourages them to continue to acquire the information that will lead to emotional wound recovery.

Nonchemical Prescriptions: The clinical traumatologist will often write a prescription for activities that will aid in the recovery process. These prescriptions are written on a standard prescription pad so that the client understands their significance. These prescriptions are as important to recovery as is a prescription written for an antibiotic to treat an infection. A typical prescription would identify a specific activity such as reading from the book *Man's Search for Meaning*, specifying how long to read each day and for how many days to read. Other common prescriptions are for meditation, exercise, and writing.

Illustration by Rob Wells

Writing the Details of a Traumatic Experience: This tutorial focuses on the healing benefits of writing down the factual events **and** the feelings (emotions) associated with a traumatic experience. The relationship of this activity to the overall philosophy and procedures of the IRO-STEPS tutorials is explained. Memorializing (recording on tape or in writing) has been found to be a key element in the recovery process.

The Hour of Power: This tutorial emphasizes the benefits of creating the habit (ritual) of setting aside one hour per day divided into three equal activity periods (twenty minutes each). The three suggested activities are

- Inspirational reading
- Physical exercise
- Meditation/prayer, planning and prioritizing

Time Structuring: This tutorial is derived from a psychological technique called "Transactional Analysis" (TA). It explains that there are different categories for structuring and prioritizing our relationships with others. These are

- Withdrawing to be alone and contemplate.
- Rituals that serve to connect individuals that have a common purpose.
- Pastime communication activities (communications that can either strengthen or weaken the survivor). Weakening communications include gossip and prolonged discussions of negative events. Strengthening communications include sharing new ideas or perspectives and pointing out strengths and virtues in others.
- Activities and work that help to improve and enrich lives.
- Games and deceitful behaviors in which one gets ahead at the expense of others. These should be replaced by activities in which both parties are benefitted so that the activity becomes a win/win proposition.
- Intimacy where there is physical, emotional, and spiritual closeness. This occurs with loved ones and family usually within the confines of the home.

Appendix 1—E
Tips for Caregivers
Twelve Techniques to Stimulate Thriving after Surviving

1. Appropriate touch and physical closeness provide the survivor with a sense of security. From early infancy through old age, physical contact is an essential means of giving comfort.

2. Let the survivor know that the time and effort you spend in helping them to recover brings you happiness and are not a nuisance or a bother. Communicate the message, "You're not heavy, you're my brother," by interacting with the survivor physically, emotionally, and spiritually. Listen to them patiently and with interest and try to identify their major concerns. Such support will enable them to deal more effectively with the upheaval caused by their traumatic experience.

3. Openly express and demonstrate your emotions (such as crying or laughter). Do not postpone or inhibit tender loving care.

4. Focus on "tying the heartstrings" versus "pulling up the bootstraps." Tune into the survivor's major concerns and respond candidly and truthfully to their fears.

5. Trigger positive, stimulating, uplifting, and humorous thoughts while the survivor is undergoing physical treatment, especially treatment that is painful or frightening. Provide things that will help them see, feel, and think of something other than doom, gloom, and despair.

6. Connect the survivor, as soon as possible, with those individuals who care the most about them. These are family, friends, or other loved ones who fill the role of caregiver. This is the single most important factor, in addition to technically sophisticated medical attention, for saving the life of the trauma survivor.

7. Communicate the message, "You and your feelings matter most." Survivors need attention to their feelings as much as they do to their damaged bodies. When feelings are addressed with love and sensitivity, the survivor will more positively be able to deal with fear and uncertainty.

8. In the upheaval associated with trauma, priorities are often put in the wrong order. Get them straight—**the person comes first!** Billing issues, insurance problems, finances, work replacements, and other such issues are secondary concerns.

9. Give frequent, ongoing attention to the survivor's priorities and concerns.

10. Prioritize and provide important information only as fast as the sur-

vivor is able to assimilate it.

11. Combine and coordinate efforts to optimize the survivor's recovery. Everyone needs to work together: the survivor, their family and friends, and all medical and health care personnel.

12. Provide guidance and stimulate hope and optimism with realistic encouragement. Use specific directions such as those listed in the Dos and Don'ts section of this book.

Appendix 1–F
Dos for the Survivor

- Follow medical directions and treatment recommendations. If you have questions, write them down and ask the doctor, nurse, or other health care professional directly. If you are not satisfied, don't hesitate to ask for additional opinions.
- Be patient with yourself and with those trying to help you. Allow yourself and others to make mistakes and admit to limitations. Recognize that your support group of family and friends are not usually trained professionals. Don't expect them to do what traumatologists, physicians, nurses, therapists, and psychotherapists do.
- During early recovery/convalescence have a family member designated as a spokesperson to give progress reports and updates to friends, neighbors, co-workers, members of church congregations, etc.
- Expect periods of wide mood swings when you seem to be on an emotional roller coaster. During these periods, find trusted family members and friends who will listen as you express your mixed thoughts and feelings.
- Believe in yourself and in your ability to "turn stumbling blocks into stepping stones." Rely on the remarkable strength that the body and mind have to significantly heal themselves and adapt to difficult circumstances.
- Be positive and optimistic. Immerse yourself in uplifting and inspiring music, books, magazines, and movies. Associate with optimistic people who will encourage you and can recognize your successful recovery efforts.
- Learn to draw on your inner spiritual strength. Resume and maintain your spiritual and religious activities.
- Resume and maintain physical activities as soon as medically recommended. Do things you enjoy doing. Try new things. Focus on realistic ways to compensate for any temporary or permanent limitations.
- Look to the future. Become a forward thinker and concentrate on plans for future success. Remember that "attitude determines altitude," by connecting positive perspectives with positive actions.
- Set challenging goals. Make the most of your talents, skills, and intelligence. Push yourself to grow and develop in all aspects of your life. Visualize in your mind doing something that is important to you. See yourself doing it over and over. Make it a goal to actually do it.
- Be flexible. Learn to adapt. Be a creator of circumstances rather than a "victim-creature" of circumstances.
- Keep a daily journal that includes your thoughts, feelings, and concerns. Identify your aspirations. Record any indication of progress, no matter how small it may seem.

179

- Express verbal and written appreciation to others for their interest and concern. Keep copies of all correspondence sent. Save all written encouragements you receive and reread them from time to time, especially when you are feeling discouraged, uncertain, etc.
- Socialize. Get out as often as possible (but follow the advice of your doctors and therapists).
- Establish a network of people to help guide and direct you. This support network could include family, friends, work associates, spiritual leaders, people who have recovered from similar injuries, and professional people such as your medical doctors, nurses, clinical traumatologist, physical therapists, and attorneys.
- Seek understanding and direction regarding your recovery from emotional wounds early. The sooner you receive the care you need, the sooner you will recover.
- Expect the unexpected in the reactions you get from others. Some people may say or do things that are offensive to you because they are unfamiliar with your circumstances or are unaware of what they should say or do. Try to put them at ease. Be more understanding than they are. Be forgiving.
- Love and serve others. Look beyond yourself into the lives of people around you. Share in their happiness and pain, their laughter and sorrow, progress and setbacks. Learn to love people just the way they are. Look for ways to help them, even if that means doing nothing more than listening.
- Learn how to graciously accept reasonable assistance from others. When it is obviously very important to them, for their sake, let them do their "good deed for the day."
- Make up your mind to get well.
- Cultivate a positive sense of humor. Laugh out loud and look for the humorous aspect of everyday situations.
- Keep a humor file.
- Make a list of services or gifts that you would appreciate. Share the list with those who ask what they can do to help. The sense of being unable to "do" something for you may cause frustration or sadness for many who want to help, but don't know what to do.

Appendix 1

Don'ts for the Survivor

There are a number of common mistakes made by almost all survivors during their recovery. Hopefully, the following suggestions will help you and your loved ones to avoid them.

- Don't make hasty assumptions about limitations for progress.
- Don't assume "everything is going to be fine" concerning the future.
- Don't expect life to be exactly the same as it was before the traumatic experience.
- Don't expect your doctors and therapists to do more than they are capable of doing. Remember that physical healing will progress more rapidly if your emotional wounds are also getting appropriate attention.
- Don't make sudden changes or quick decisions on significant matters such as marital status, residence, employment, or financial transactions without the help of a qualified and experienced financial advisor.
- Don't rush into legal matters or business transactions without qualified counsel.
- Don't focus on negatives, limitations, or losses.
- Don't avoid thinking about or planning for your future, as well as the adjustments that could enhance it.
- Don't reject family, friends, or other people who are genuinely trying to help.
- Don't hold grudges, brood on the negative, try to get even, or resist the earliest possible reconciliation with all who may have been involved in the incident that resulted in your trauma.
- Don't isolate yourself physically or emotionally.
- Don't feel you have to be a "Captain Courageous" who never shows fear, weakness, or discouragement.
- Don't keep your feelings "bricked up" inside you.
- Don't be embarrassed about things that are out of your control or about issues that you have not yet been able to deal with.
- Don't hesitate to ask questions and obtain accurate information from credible sources.
- Don't be surprised when you are confronted with situations you never expected.
- Don't replace reality with fantasy. Don't make assumptions or draw conclusions without getting the facts and discussing your expectations with your health care providers.
- Don't be too hard on yourself or others by expecting more than is realistic or by blaming yourself for what has happened.
- Don't try to shortcut the overall (emotional and physical) recovery

process. Don't artificially prolong recovery with the expectation of get-ting more insurance benefits or winning a lawsuit.

- Don't give up hope.
- Don't be afraid to get well. Don't ignore the Fear Wheel diagram and other concepts in the Fear Wheel Tutorial.
- Don't turn to alcohol, medications, or illicit drugs for solace or to escape emotional pain.
- Don't avoid personal recovery by hiding behind such things as crutch-es, braces, and wheelchairs in order to prolong the attention, affection, or sympathy you get from others.
- Don't try to make others, especially relatives and friends, feel guilty because they are able to do things you cannot do.

Review these lists often and apply the suggestions liberally. They could make the difference between a thriving, productive, meaningful life and merely surviving. But don't be overwhelmed; work only as many points as you can effectively deal with at a time. Then when you feel com-fortable with those, systematically work through the others.

Appendix 1–G
Dos for Caregivers and Loved Ones

- Be patient. Plan for a steady, gradual healing of physical injuries and emotional wounds. Although both processes will occur simultaneously, the rate of recovery is rarely the same for both physical and emotional wounds.
- Encourage the survivor's recovery by recognizing and acknowledging daily progress, even in things that may seem small or insignificant to you.
- Expect sudden changes in moods and temperament.
- Listen attentively when the recovering survivor wants to express feelings and frustrations. Listen without being judgmental, and allow yourself to show positive, natural, sympathetic emotions (including crying, remorse, grieving, or laughing).
- Cultivate a positive, warm, and uplifting sense of humor.
- Encourage and support the survivor in developing higher levels of independence and self-sufficiency through learning and applying the information in the IRO-STEPS tutorials.
- Respect the survivor's need for privacy. Plan your visits. Call ahead (if you don't live in the same house) and ask if it's all right to visit at that time and discuss how long you will stay, even if the survivor is your spouse or other family member.
- Ask about and show genuine interest in any plans, progress, activities, and/or ongoing interests they may have.
- Share yourself in natural, appropriate ways, including touching, joking, laughing, and crying.
- Accept the survivor as completely as possible. Give love as unconditionally as you can; show that love through consistent acts of support, the tone of your voice, and expressions of concern.
- Encourage the trauma survivor to follow the directions and suggestions of traumatologists, doctors, nurses, and therapists.
- Take time for yourself. Eat, sleep, and exercise. If you are the primary caregiver, periodically arrange for others to care for the trauma survivor so you can have a break. You can't be effective in helping someone else if you allow yourself to become drained physically and emotionally.

Don'ts for Caregivers and Loved Ones

- Don't underestimate the positive power of your loving concern and your example, even if they do not seem to be well received by the trauma survivor.
- Don't be overly helpful by doing for the survivor what they really could or should do for themselves. This tends to convey the impression that

the person is helpless, inadequate, or worthless.

- Don't assume trauma survivors are fine just because they look that way or say they are.
- Don't expect that everything will be returning to normal. For the trauma survivor and many of those around them, life may never be exactly the same.
- Don't expect complete recovery to occur by a specific date.
- Don't discourage natural expressions of emotion, such as laughing, crying, remorse, and grieving.
- Don't be overprotective by limiting acceptable activities, responsibilities, or obligations.
- Don't compare the trauma survivor's progress with what you think should be "normal" or with the progress of others who have experienced similar events or injuries.
- Don't drop in unexpectedly, leave abruptly, or overstay your welcome.
- Don't become so involved in conversations with other visitors that you exclude the trauma survivor.
- Don't ask for vivid details of what happened or who was at fault.
- Don't hide information, keep secrets, or try to make things look better or worse than they really are.
- Never give up hope.

Recovering from a traumatic experience is often a difficult and complex process. Your influence can make a significant difference in the survivor's life. If nothing else, just being there shows how much you really care.

Deanna Edwards, in her book *Grieving: The Pain and the Promise*, offers examples of comments that hurt or heal in the aftermath of tragedy.

Examples of hurtful comments	Examples of helpful comments
"I understand exactly how you feel." "Something a lot worse than that happened to me." "It's God's will." "Aren't you over it yet?" "God gave you this trial to make you stronger."	"I love you." "You're not alone. I am with you." "What are your needs right now?" **To a person who has lost a loved one:** "He/she made a difference in my life because…" "I remember when…" "We love them and will not forget them."

Appendix 2

Suggested Reading*

1. *As a Man Thinketh*, by James Allen, DeVorss & Company, Marina Del Rey, California, 1983.
2. *As a Man Thinketh, Volume 2*, by James Allen, compiled by James H. Fedor, Mind Art Publishing, Bountiful, Utah, 1988.
3. *Family Secrets*, by John Bradshaw, Bantam Books, New York, 1995.
4. *Games People Play*, by Eric Berne, Ballentine Books, New York, 1964.
5. *Grieving: The Pain and the Promise*, by Deanna Edwards, Covenant Communications, American Fork, Utah, 1989.
6. *Healing Troubled Relationships*, by Victor L. Brown Jr., Bookcraft Publishing, Salt Lake City, Utah, 1989.
7. *His Needs, Her Needs*, by Willard Harley, Fleming H. Revel Co., Old Tappan, New Jersey, 1988.
8. *Human Intimacy*, by Victor L. Brown Jr., Deseret Book, Salt Lake City, Utah.
9. *I'm OK, You're OK*, by Thomas Harris, Avon Books, New York, 1967.
10. *Life after Trauma*, by Dena Rosenbloom, Mary Beth Williams and Barbara Watkins (contributor), Guilford Press, New York, 1999.
11. *Love, Medicine, and Miracles*, by Bernie Siegel, Harper Row, New York, 1986.
12. *Man's Search for Meaning*, by Victor E. Frankl, with Gordon Allport, Mass Market Paperback, Washington Square Press, New York, 1998.
13. *Manufacturing Victims: What the Psychology Industry Is Doing to People, 2nd Edition*, by Tana Dineen, Robert Davies Publishing, Montreal, 1998.

* Note: Some of the books on this list are out of print. However, all of them had wide circulation, so copies should be available from libraries, used bookstores, or book dealers on the Internet. A number of Internet book dealers specialize in out-of-print publications.

14. *Men Are from Mars, Women Are from Venus,* by John Gray, Harper Collins, New York, 1992.

15. *Minding the Body, Mending the Mind,* by Joan Borysenko, Bantam Books, New York, 1988.

16. *People of the Lie: Hope for Healing Human Evil,* by M. Scott Peck, M.D., Simon and Schuster, 1987.

17. *Staying OK,* by Amy and Thomas Harris, Harper and Row, New York, 1985.

18. *The Road Less Traveled,* by M. Scott Peck, M.D., Simon and Schuster; Touchstone Books, 1983.

19. *The Road Less Traveled and Beyond,* by M. Scott Peck, M.D., Simon and Schuster, 1998.

20. *The 7 Habits of Highly Effective People: Powerful Lessons in Personal Change,* Stephen R. Covey, Fireside, 1990.

21. *Thriving after Surviving: How To Overcome the Devastating Emotional Wounds Caused by Accidental Injuries,* by Barry M. Richards, Hartley Communications, Murray, Utah, 1990.

22. *Trauma and Recovery,* by Judith L. Herman, Basic Books, Harper Collins, New York, 1992.

23. *Unlocking the Powers of Faith,* by Garth Allred, Covenant Communications, American Fork, Utah, 1998.

24. *When Bad Things Happen to Good People,* by Harold S. Kushner, Avon Books, New York, 1981.

25. *You Can Choose Christmas,* by Clyde Reid, Word Books Publishers, Waco, Texas, 1976.

Ethical Considerations and Code of Conduct for Clinical Traumatologists

The Code of Ethics for clinical traumatology informs all people of the professional conduct expected of all its practitioners. The following information outlines the general areas of ethical concern in the practice of clinical traumatology.

Competence

Clinical traumatologists aspire to the highest levels of professional competence. They recognize that they function within a specific area of expertise and endeavor to carefully integrate their discipline with other health care providers while respecting their particular professional limitations. As such, they provide only those services and use only those procedures for which they are qualified by virtue of their education, training, and experience.

When providing services to individuals or groups whose cultural mores and values differ from their own, great attention is given to meeting and accommodating unique needs. Further careful judgment is used in an effort to protect people from potential harm in areas of practice where recognized professional standards are insufficient to meet the unique needs of groups or individuals. Clinical traumatologists constantly strive to increase their professional knowledge and skills, while simultaneously contributing to the knowledge base of the profession. Expanding the knowledge base of the profession is accomplished through conducting scientifically valid research, publishing research results, and participating in the development of innovative approaches to problem solving through the application of sound research findings and well-substantiated clinical data.

Proactivity

The hallmark of clinical traumatology is initiating—as soon as physically possible and medically advisable—definitive, ongoing care to those who have suffered emotional wounds as a result of trauma or exposure to some horrifying event. This is referred to as "providing the right care at the right time" to survivors of injury and trauma. Therefore, clinical traumatologists must be constantly vigilant, attentive, and responsive to survivors even though the survivors may, at the time, not recognize the importance of early intervention through the application of specific health care directions. Clinical traumatologists recognize and respond to the *golden hours* that immediately follow injury and trauma by both collecting and providing critical information that will optimize the benefits of the health care directions they provide. Thereafter, they prompt survivors to learn as much as possible about the specific information that will promote their self-help recovery. They foster cooperative interactions with other health care professionals rendering care to survivors. Clinical traumatologists respond to and resolve to the best of their ability the specific and most urgent concerns of survivors (and their caregivers) so that reactive demands to emerging post-trauma problems are minimized and potentially stigmatizing treatment for disease is prevented. Ideally, this means initiating intervention with survivors within twenty-four hours of the traumatic incident and no later than thirty days after the event.

Precision

The use of precise, uniform, educationally-therapeutic procedures characterize the practice of clinical traumatology. In timely response to the upheaval and uncertainties caused by injury and trauma, clinical traumatologists utilize specific interventions and instructions that are designed to immediately alleviate fear and confusion. This is accomplished through the stimulation of positive thoughts and providing critical information that prepares the survivor to deal with anxiety-provoking situations and emotions. There are no generic "remedies" that are applied to every survivor. Instead, the individual's specific needs and circumstances are rapidly assessed and then addressed using a systematic, time-limited, and defined strategy. In doing so, clinical traumatologists confer, consult, and cooperate with other professionals and institutions to the extent necessary to serve the best interests of their clients (survivors). Ideally, every educational therapeutic procedure provided by the clinical traumatologist reinforces and enhances the overall treatment the survivors receive from professional providers and their individual environmental support systems.

Diligence

The clinical traumatologist must be available and accessible to rapidly and professionally respond to the usual as well as unexpected side effects and symptoms associated with injury and trauma. Consequently, clinical traumatologists rapidly engage survivors as well as their caregivers (family, friends, or other loved ones) in those procedures determined through assessment that will promote their health and well-being. This includes initiating follow-up contacts with survivors; actively collaborating with health care professionals; communicating as necessary with the survivor's employer(s); locating and communicating with individuals who are key members of the survivor's primary support system and engaging them in the educational procedures; and earnestly pursuing appropriate community resources. These actions are all taken in order to obtain the optimal benefit for the survivor from their participation in the IRO-STEPS procedures. Ideally, this is accomplished through a written assessment of survivor needs and professional recommendations that are approved and agreed to by the survivor, which can then be disseminated, by the survivor, to those persons who are involved with promoting rapid recovery.

Integrity

The clinical traumatologist must be committed to the honest and forthright application of the highest values, ideals, principles, and standards of practice. Because integrity lies at the very core of their practice, clinical traumatologists are highly values-laden when teaching the correct principles of healing and recovery from traumatic injuries or other horrifying events. They seek to promote integrity in the science, teaching, and practice of the profession in every aspect of their conduct. Clinical traumatologists champion the survivor's rights and need for candor of expression and their right to be fully informed, never compromising or subordinating these rights for personal gain or favor, the preferences of other professionals, employers, agencies, or affiliations, or any theories or philosophies that subordinate truth and scientifically substantiated facts. Clinical traumatologists strive to be aware of their own belief systems, values, needs, and limitations and their effect on the recovery process of survivors. Clinical traumatologists must clarify their role—which is to educate and empower survivors with knowledge, not identifying and treating pathologies that preexisted the injury and trauma. Ideally, this education begins during the initial contact with the victim-survivor and their caregiver(s). At the time of this first contact, preliminary information is provided and assessment procedures conducted that emphasize the value and worth of the survivor and their capability to *thrive* versus merely survive following a traumatic event.

Dedication

The discipline of clinical traumatology is dedicated to promoting public awareness of those effective interventions that will prevent many of the psychological impairments stemming from and to aid in the physical recovery associated with the aftermath of injury and exposure to traumatic events. Clinical traumatologists are dedicated to enhancing the well-being of the individual and society as a whole. This is done, in part, by promoting the public's awareness of and sensitivity to the plight of trauma survivors who are typically underinformed and ill-prepared to cope with the effects of their emotional wounds when given only rudimentary or haphazard information. This purpose is reinforced by educating society about clinical traumatology's professional role and the practitioner's responsibilities and ability to alleviate human suffering stemming from traumatic injuries. To the extent possible, clinical traumatologists emphasize their unique expertise and oppose dilution of their effectiveness, the misuse for commercial purposes, or subordinate assimilation by any other profession of the IRO-STEPS strategy. As members of the health care team, clinical traumatologists look for opportunities to voluntarily contribute their time and professional expertise to the community, pro bono. Ideally, the dedicated efforts of clinical traumatologists are recognized, acknowledged, and accepted through referrals from medical and health care professionals seeking to enhance the recovery of survivors following injury and trauma.

Whenever and wherever clinical traumatology is put into action, its practitioners must adhere to the highest ideals of professional and ethical conduct. These standards of excellence should be readily apparent to any individual or group who monitors compliance with the above stated Ethical Considerations and Code of Conduct for Clinical Traumatologists.

Glossary
of Clinical Traumatology Terms

Aftermath of Trauma: That period of time immediately following a serious injury, an actual or *perceived* threat to one's own life, or damaging or destructive threats to other people's lives, property, or circumstances.

Aftermath Reactions: Impulsive thoughts and behaviors that frequently interfere with either lifesaving technical procedures and/or interventions to deal with the emotional effects of trauma.

Aftermath Stress Dysfunction: A negative consequence of aftermath stress reactions that often results from the manipulation and exploitation of survivors by those seeking to benefit from prolonging their suffering.

After Trauma Assessment: Written report by a clinical traumatologist that details a person's experience in survival, their major concerns, and personal support systems. Also includes the clinical traumatologist's health care recommendations for the person's optimal recovery.

Aftermath Prime Time: Time a survivor spends with those who are caring and committed to assisting them in their recovery. These people include spouses and other caregivers whose knowledge and compassion permit open expression of and meaningful responses to feelings.

Aftermath Symptom-free: Condition of recovery following injury and trauma that is without the distress associated with the horrifying event or injuries.

Against Health Care Advice: A term used to describe the decision to decline the prescribed IRO-STEPS health care tutorials after an assessment has shown the need and benefit from such help. Similar to the "AMA" (Against medical advice) disengagement from recommended medical services.

Alexithymia: Inability, difficulty or reluctance to express or discuss feelings about sudden-impact injury and/or traumatic events.

Anecdotal Validation: Reports of successful treatment, often associated with "satisfied patient" surveys that confuse biased accounts of good recovery based upon patients having a "good feeling" about a clinician or facility with scientifically valid, independent measures of a positive outcome.

Attending Trauma Physician: The qualified physician who directs the *initial* medical treatment in a designated trauma care facility.

Aversion: Generally a negative psychological reaction to a person or situation. Specifically, when a trauma victim refuses or avoids appropriate help in dealing with emotional wounds, often due to the perception or inference that he or she may be psychologically impaired.

Basic Necessities: The Basic Necessities for emotional trauma recovery are: Recognition, Acknowledgment, and Acceptance. These include the essential elements of nurturing interactions between survivors and those who care the most about them. (See Appendix 1, pp. 152–58.)

BDF Factor: Encouragement from someone who has "**B**een there, **D**one that, **F**elt what it is like." Someone who has experienced a similar trauma can *most effectively* empathize and encourage a survivor's recovery.

Bedrock Principles: Clinical traumatology's precise health care guidelines for responding to the emotional wounds of trauma survivors. They are (1) Survival is only the beginning; (2) Learning means less suffering; (3) The sooner knowledge is acquired, the more quickly complete recovery can be anticipated.

Brain Atrophy (Shrinking Brain): There is mounting evidence that there are physical changes to the brain in addition to the neurochemicals that are associated with the emotional reactions to trauma. Using Magnetic Resonance Imaging (MRI) it has been noted that the area of the brain known as the hippocampus in people who develop Post-Traumatic Stress Disorder has atrophied (shrunk). This area of the brain serves as a temporary storage place for long-term memory for a period of days or weeks until the memories are finally localized elsewhere. The evidence suggests that the physical changes in the brain itself are related to the problems survivors experience with retaining the memory of events following their trauma.

Bounce-back Resiliency: The ability of trauma survivors to resume pre-injury activities and life satisfaction following significant traumatic upheaval.

"Call-girl" Syndrome: A common reaction of third-party payers toward remunerating the services of clinical traumatology, i.e., "The value of the services is rapidly diminished once they are delivered."

Case Managers: Nurses or other health care professionals (usually assigned by insurance claims adjusters, carriers, or workers' compensation officers) who are responsible for ensuring patient compliance and follow-through with medical and health care procedures. (Often function in conflict-of-interest roles.) Seldom with clinical traumatology expertise.

Catastrophic Events: Fatal, irreversible, or disastrous events that impact survivors personally or situationally.

Clinical Procedures: Activities that are carried out to deal with a specific problem. These are not tutorials, but are procedures in which the survivor and the clinical traumatologist work together in a methodical but "unscripted" manner. One of the most common clinical procedures is *in vivo* desensitization, which can be used to deal with phobias or to overcome some fear associated with the traumatic incident. (See *In Vivo* Desensitization.)

Clinical Traumatologist: A relatively recent addition to the health care professional team. The clinical traumatologist has certified expertise gained through advanced accredited education, an internship within a hospital emergency department and shock-trauma intensive care setting, and a specified amount of clinical practice under the guidance of a qualified mentor. Uses state-of-the-art assessment procedures for determining the magnitude of emotional wounds, then provides sequential, structured, and specific health care tutorials to reduce their impact, while simultaneously promoting steady and progressive recovery from the physical and emotional aftermath of horrifying events.

Clinical Traumatology Intervention: A therapeutic modality ideally implemented within seventy-two hours of an accident or other traumatic event. This strategy was developed to prevent emotional wounds from remaining unattended which often results in their mushrooming into major psychological problems that debilitate the victim(s). Originally pioneered in the 1980s by hospital trauma teams, it provides essential health care information and direction during the initial aftermath of a life-threatening, disabling, or disfiguring injury or other horrifying event. Its emergence from the work of trauma teams is similar to the development of physical therapy emerging from the nursing profession. Clinical traumatology patients participate in carefully structured, sequential health care tutorials that minimize the complications often associated with delayed treatment of the emotional wounds of trauma. Clinical traumatology empowers and enables survivors to optimize their recovery potential.

Conventional Crisis Counseling: Generic procedures most often provided to trauma survivors in response to the intense emotional upheaval associated with horrifying events; too often nonstructured and nonspecific.

192

Critical Incident Stress Debriefing (CISD): CISD was developed for talking through the reactions and emotional stress experience among emergency personnel following particularly stressful situations. Now the technique is widely used to "debrief" victims of trauma in the general public. This procedure has become increasingly controversial in regard to its use and effectiveness among trauma *survivors*.

Crisis Intervention: The first professional response specifically addressing the emotional aftermath immediately following a horrifying event or traumatic injury.

Critical Medical/Technical Procedures: Initial emergency lifesaving response to a physical injury that is life threatening, disabling, or disfiguring.

Cross-gender Therapy (work): A clinical procedure in which a therapist of the opposite gender from the survivor is deliberately selected. The theoretical advantage to this approach is a higher probability for overcoming resistant transference issues. (See Transference.)

Crossroads: The short time period following injury or other horrifying events for survivors and their loved ones to obtain the maximum benefits from the implementation of concrete, specific health care directions to avoid delayed recovery and other preventable problems.

Cumulative Trauma Stress Dysfunction (CTSD): Long-term unresolved emotional wounds that provoke a pronounced increase in after-injury disability. When these preexisting problems are added to a new traumatic wound, extreme overreactions are typically observed.

Cutting-edge Strategies: The newest or most advanced approach that can be applied in a given situation. Cutting-edge strategies are a substantial improvement over the previously used methods.

Debriefing (post-trauma): Typically an unstructured process of "talking out" concerns and feelings associated with a traumatic event. This practice has become increasingly controversial as applied to survivors of violent and terror-induced trauma.

Displacement: The psychological process of transferring emotions from their original point of attention to another thing, person, or circumstance.

Dos and Don'ts: List of specific directions for survivors and personal caregivers to enhance recovery from injury and trauma. (See Appendix 1, pp.179–84.)

Educational Tutorials (IRO-STEPS®): A set of structured instructional packages providing precise guidance for trauma survivors and their loved ones to inform them about the normal signs, symptoms, and side effects of emotional wounds. The tutorials prepare them for the predictable stages of trauma recovery and teach them how to prevent unnecessary problems and setbacks.

Emotional Shock Absorbers: Those factors that permit survivors to tolerate the emotional chaos and stress associated with traumatic events. Among the key determinants of such resiliency are a strong support system (family, friends, co-workers, etc.), mental stamina, sound nutrition, good physical health, humor, and spirituality.

Emotional Wound: The changes in perceptions, beliefs, and feelings associated with a physical injury or horrifying event. Frequently people with emotional wounds develop the perception that the world has changed and that the people in it have become threatening and unreliable. This perception gives rise to uncertainty and apprehension and a decreased ability to function normally.

Emotional Roller Coaster: Chaotic mood swings and confused thought patterns characteristic of the emotional wounds associated with traumatic events. These feelings of anxiety and uncertainty may come and go unexpectedly and suddenly following a horrifying event whether or not the person has physical injuries.

Emotional Wound Resuscitation: Proactive attention to the intense feelings of helplessness and hopelessness that follow an injury and/or horrifying events. Similar to Structured Early Education Directions (SEEDs) but initiated at a later time, i.e., generally between three and thirty days after the trauma occurred.

Family Support: Involved participation and ongoing supportive interaction by the trauma survivor's immediate family/loved ones (caregivers) during the recovery process. Also participation in the assessment process and health care tutorials of clinical traumatology.

Fears—The Most Common: Fears impacting injury and trauma recovery that most often impede progress. They are fear of abandonment, failure, rejection, exploitation (by practitioners or other opportunists), loneliness, prolonged physical pain, and the unknown.

Fear Wheel Tutorial: A basic IRO-STEPS tutorial explaining how the side effects of basic fears that are common among trauma survivors manifest themselves in the form of physical symptoms and behavioral dysfunctions. (See Appendix 1, pp. 166–69.)

First Do No Harm: This maxim comes from the Latin *primum non nocere*, dating back to approximately 500 B.C. Translated as either "first do no harm" or "above all do no harm," the meaning is clear—before one engages in any sort of treatment, therapy, or intervention as a health care practitioner, you should have strong evidence that what you are doing will not cause harm. In terms of today's ethics, the potential benefits *must* significantly outweigh the risks. This phrase is consistent with concepts found in the Hippocratic oath.

Flashbacks: A distressingly vivid recollection of the original traumatic event generally triggered by a stimulus associated with the original trauma. Common stimuli are noises, smells, voices, or places. Flashbacks are often accompanied by physical reactions including rapid pulse and/or respiration, profuse sweating, cold damp hands, difficulty focusing, and disorientation. There is frequently a sense of immediate danger although none is present.

"Flight to Life" Syndrome: A situation where an emotionally wounded survivor acquires one or two IRO-STEPS tutorials (and/or the assessment services) and abruptly discontinues further services, assuming they are then fully capable of recovering from the emotional wounds of injury without specific directions.

Gallows Grin or Sardonic Smile: A tendency to inappropriately or incongruously smile when discussing the details of one's trauma or when reporting that "everything is just fine" when it is apparent that things are not "fine."

Guilt (Survivor and/or Real): Feelings of guilt held by survivors of traumatic events. Often the guilt is unrealistic, as in the case of an unarmed victim who could not "save" another person who is injured or killed by an armed assailant. Real guilt may be associated with a situation where a victim knows they were the cause of trauma to themselves and/or others, as in the case of a drunk driver. Guilt may be transient or prolonged depending on the nature and severity of the injuries.

Hippocratic Oath: An oath taken by most physicians at the time they graduate from medical school. The origins of this code of ethics are obscure, but are linked to the ancient Greek physician Hippocrates who lived approximately 400 B.C. The oaths that are administered today have been modified significantly, but essentially contain a commitment to patients and an avoidance of immoral and corrupt behavior.

Hour of Power: A part of the clinical traumatology strategy. The patient is assigned to spend one hour a day in a set of focused exercises each morning. The sixty minutes of assigned exercises are to be done upon rising, before other daily activities, in time increments as follows: twenty minutes for the body, twenty for the mind, and twenty for the spirit.

Hospital Based Traumatologist: A designated member of the hospital "trauma team" specifically assigned to assess the emotional wounds of the patient who has been admitted for medical treatment. If indicated by the assessment, the traumatologist prepares survivors and their caregivers to begin the IRO-STEPS Health Care Tutorials as soon as it is practical.

Human Intimacy Tutorial: An IRO-STEPS tutorial providing an understanding of how to initiate improvement in each of four areas of personal interaction and communication to develop a more nurturing primary relationship. The four areas of need are intellectual, emotional, spiritual, and physical. Balanced participation in all four areas is necessary to a healthy, affectionate bond. (See Appendix 1, p. 151.)

Human Stimulants: Four different types of stimulus as discussed in conjunction with the Basic Necessities in the tutorial designed to foster human intimacy. The four are Touch, Talk, Activity, and Things. *Touch* is tactile stimulation; *Talk* includes all types of communication; *Activity* is release of physical energy; and *Things* are the material objects that facilitate touch, talk, and activity. Learning to use these stimulants to facilitate a nurturing relationship between the victim/survivor and their caregiver is a critical part of the recovery process.

Iatrogenic: Iatrogenic illness is that which is induced unintentionally by a health care provider. For example, in treating a victim of emotional trauma, a therapist can induce specific symptoms consistent with a diagnosis of post-traumatic stress disorder even though the clinical data needed to support such a diagnosis may be absent.

Injury Adjustment Assessment: A written report by a clinical traumatologist that details a patient's adjustment to physical injuries. The assessment records objective data, personal concerns, individual support systems, and health care recommendations to serve as a guide through the course of gradual healing and recovery. It is not a psychological evaluation and the assessment is generally shared with family and health care providers to optimize the recovery process. The Injury Adjustment is similar to the After Trauma Assessment and the two are often used together.

Impoverished Thinking: Behaviors resulting from an inadequate understanding of the facts regarding trauma recovery and having insufficient information needed to appropriately deal with its aftermath side effects and symptoms. The results include impractical expectations, unrealistic fears, and impulsive behaviors that prolong recovery and interfere with ongoing medical procedures and the ability to follow sound health care directions.

In Vivo **Desensitization:** The process of desensitization is based upon the observation that psychological reactions (sensitivities) can be reduced or eliminated by repeatedly exposing a person to a stimulus that causes the unwanted reaction. This technique is commonly used in the treatment of phobias. If, for example, a person is excessively afraid of spiders, the process might begin by having the person look at pictures of spiders, then look at preserved dead spiders and perhaps handle them, etc. Gradually when the external stimulus (the spider pictures, dead specimens, etc.) no longer produce a fear reaction, the person would be considered desensitized to a greater or lesser extent. (This process may also be referred to as progressive desensitization.) As used in clinical traumatology, *in vivo* desensitization returns the survivor to the scene of the event (as soon as the survivor is medically stable) in order to diminish the intensity of their feelings and fears associated with that location. By spending time at the place, supported by caregivers and a clinical traumatologist, the sense of vulnerability and helplessness that the location once provoked can be significantly reduced.

IRO-STEPS: These initials stand for *Injury Recovery Orientation-STEPS*. These are the specific health care tutorials of clinical traumatology. There are six basic tutorials and approximately twenty-three auxiliary guided learning programs (tutorials) that can be used to meet the specific needs of individual survivors. STEPS is an acronym standing for **S**timulate positive thinking; **T**ackle unrealistic fears; **E**ducate about stages of recovery; **P**lan effectively for the future; and **S**top impractical expectations.

Joint Commission on Accreditation of Health Care Organizations: An independent, not-for-profit organization with a stated mission "to improve the quality of health care for the public by providing accreditation and related services." The Joint Commission evaluates and accredits more than 18,000 health care organizations in the United States, including hospitals, health care networks, managed care organizations, and health care organizations that provide home care, long-term care, behavioral health care, laboratory services, and ambulatory care services.

Laser Learning: A descriptive designation for the rapid acquisition of therapeutic principles using the precise, structured tutorials of clinical traumatology.

Lethargy: The slow, sluggish, unmotivated functioning often present in victims of emotional trauma. Lethargy occurs as a result of feelings of powerlessness in the aftermath of tragedy and the inadequate stimulation of thought processes that are necessary for optimal recovery.

"M&Ms": Clinical traumatology shorthand for the mental exercises of *memorizing* uplifting and encouraging thoughts about recovery options and potentials, *minimizing* the negative impact of intrusive (unwanted) thoughts, and *maximizing* the ongoing gradual recovery process.

Managed Health Care: A somewhat ambiguous concept to describe a system of health care delivery that tries to manage the cost of that care, its quality, and access to that care. The common denominators include a group of contracted health care providers (that never includes all available providers), limits or economic penalties to subscribers who use "nongroup" providers, and an authorizing system, commonly referred to as a "gatekeeper." Gatekeepers are generally primary care physicians (family physicians, general internists, pediatricians, and in some cases obstetrician/gynecologists.)

Memory Bank Tutorial: The initial clinical traumatology (IRO-STEPS) health care tutorial that emphasizes learning as the key process for changing the negative behaviors of so called "*victim-creature* circumstances" into positive and productive "*creative-achievement* outcomes." (See Appendix 1, pp. 147–48 for summary.)

"Nonmedicine" Prescription: A nonmedicine prescription written using the same format commonly used to prescribe medications filled by a pharmacist. The nonmedicine prescription assigns injury/trauma survivors specific cognitive health care exercises that are tools for recovery. For example: "Rx: Read in *Road Less Traveled* one hour a day this week" or "Rx: Implement 'Hour of Power' every day for twenty-one days."

Pain Prone Patients: Those trauma and injury survivors who have preexisting emotional/psychic pain that interferes with the usual healing process following new injury. Such leftover problems result in a compounding of the pain and suffering. Prospects of an optimal outcome are seriously impaired unless immediate attention is given.

Pain Vis-a-Vis Suffering Syndrome: An intensification of the physiological pain arising from a trauma because the associated emotional wounds have been neglected and/or have not responded to the therapeutic interventions attempted. This development is similar to the effects seen with cumulative trauma stress dysfunction (CTSD).

Paradigm Shifts of Clinical Traumatology: Changes in perspective occurring in people progressing through the IRO-STEPS Tutorials. These "shifts" are brought about by the dynamics of knowledge gained from the tutorials interacting with the emotional effects of increased control of one's personal environment. For example: The passive "Fix me" mentality is changed to the energized "If it is to be, it's up to me."

Para-Traumatologists: Specially trained registered nurses and other licensed health care professional certified in the use of the Trauma Severity SPEED Scoring Scale who perform initial assessments of trauma victims to determine the presence or risk of emotional wounding. These assessments provide attending physicians with objective information in order for them to recommend and/or prescribe clinical traumatology assessment services and Injury Recovery Orientation-STEPS tutorials.

Phlegmatic: An unusual or atypical emotional reaction to circumstances that ordinarily stir or provoke strong emotions. The phlegmatic person remains nonchalant or seemingly indifferent. This behavior is a characteristic among those who want to appear as unflappable "strong men" or "rock of Gibraltar" people. Their demeanor is uninviting and insulating versus engaging and sensitive. These attributes tend to create feelings of indignation and/or fear of rejection in those around them and blunt efforts to offer help or to express compassion.

Phobia: An obsessive, persistent, unrealistic intense fear of an object, activity, or situation that results in an overwhelming urge to avoid the subject of the fear. Common phobias seen in survivors of trauma include: acrophobia, a morbid fear of heights; agoraphobia, a fear of open places; algophobia, fear of pain; claustrophobia, a fear of closed places; panphobia, a vague and persistent fear of the unknown; xenophobia, fear of strangers; thanatophobia, an exaggerated fear of death.

Physical Symptoms and Side Effects: Predictable physical reactions and disturbances to thought processes that result from injury and horrifying events.

Post-Traumatic Stress Disorder (PTSD): A diagnosis describing an anxiety disorder produced by experiencing a life-threatening, disabling,

disfiguring, or other horrifying event characterized by (1) persistent recollections of the event, (2) emotional numbing or withdrawal, (3) hypersensitivity to various stimuli and/or other symptoms of generalized anxiety. The diagnosis can only be made after *all three* categories of symptoms
have persisted for at least thirty days.

Preventive Maintenance: A clinical traumatology term used to describe
the necessity of having sufficient Prime Time Interaction between survivors and their loved ones who provide emotional support to them.
Prime Time can be defined as time set aside, without interruptions, when
both parties are rested and able to interact effectively. Preventive
Maintenance can lead to the avoidance of disillusionment, disappointment, resentment, and the diminished psychic energy that usually accom-
panies deteriorating or impaired relationships.

Prime Time Interaction: See: "Preventive Maintenance" above, and the
Basic Necessities and Human Stimulants Tutorial. (See Appendix 1, pp.
152–59.)

Principle of Equivalency: The concept that people of similar dispositions
tend to be attracted to one another when forming primary relationships,
such as marriage. The old adage; "birds of a feather flock together"
describes the equivalence of capacities and liabilities that enhance or
diminish nurturing often found in partners.

Proactive Approach: A proactive intervention, such as clinical traumatology, serves to prepare for an expected occurrence and thereby control
the outcome. By providing care when it is most effective, as soon as possible following a traumatic event, clinical traumatology adheres to the principles of "the right care at the right time for the right reason." The proactive approach optimizes recovery potential.

Projection: A mental mechanism by which something emotionally unac-
ceptable to a person is thrust into their unconscious and is subsequently
attributed to the external world or other people. For example: someone
who is overly critical, will often accuse others of being highly critical, but
deny their own criticizing behavior. Another form of projection occurs
when people overreact to objects. For example: a person who has inappropriate sexual urges may condemn a nude statue, e.g., Michelangelo's *David*
or the *Venus de Milo*, recognized by most as great art and not sexual objects.

Psychiatry, Psychology, and Psychotherapy: Psychiatry is a medical specialty concerned with the diagnosis and treatment of mental illnesses/

disorders. A psychiatrist is a medical doctor who has completed an accredited psychiatric residency program. Both psychiatrists and clinical psychologists diagnose illness through interviews, psychological tests, and the patient's history. Both treat illnesses through many forms of psychotherapy which involves discussions between the therapist and the patient. Therapy can be either in an office or hospital setting, depending on the nature of the illness. These therapy discussions may continue for years, depending on the particular training and beliefs of the therapist. Only psychiatrists can prescribe drugs or use invasive procedures such as shock therapy, also known as Electroconvulsive Therapy (ECT).

Psychic Energy: The essential power that permits the mind to function effectively. Energy is required for thought, reasoning or problem solving, learning, etc. Although not strictly an electrical force, psychic energy is diminished when the body is tired and/or has been stressed, just as a battery is drained or a circuit is overloaded by too many appliances. Stress competes for energy that is needed for other purposes. The combination of emotional turmoil and fatigue from sleep deprivation can reduce the amount of energy available for thought processes so that a person can become mentally dysfunctional. Another drain on psychic energy is unresolved emotional wounds, sometimes called pus pockets or brain boils.

Psychic Energy Battery Tutorial: One of the six basic clinical traumatology educational tutorials. This tutorial enables recipients to understand the basis for delayed recovery from injury and trauma. (See Appendix 1, pp. 149–50 1 for summary.)

Psychological Abscess: A clinical traumatology term used to describe the psychological scarring and impairments that are consequences of emotional wounds being allowed to fester following trauma. See: "Pus Pockets" below.

Psychological Impairment: Thought disorders are disruptions in normal mental functioning that are demonstrated by changes in such diverse areas as reasoning ability, perception, behavior, and control over impulsive acts.

Psychoneuroimmunology (PNI): The study of the relationship between the mind and the immune system. It is well known that stress affects peripheral immune function. The goal of PNI is to use the body's natural healing abilities by modifying the communication that occurs between the nervous system, brain, and the body's immune system.

Psychotherapy: See "Psychiatry, Psychology, and Psychotherapy" above.

PTSD: A psychiatric illness resulting from an injury or other form of horrifying or emotionally traumatic experience. See "Post-Traumatic Stress Disorder" above.

Pus Pockets (Brain Boils): A metaphorical clinical traumatology term that describes the consequences of leaving emotional wounds unresolved. The destructive results include thought disturbances, dysfunctional behavior, and defective personal relationships. See "Psychological Abscess" above.

Red-Alert: A term used in clinical traumatology to describe instinctive "fight or flight" responses that result when a person is exposed to a stimulus that is perceived to be threatening or dangerous. Because the body reacts to such situations by producing large amounts of chemicals (such as adrenaline and noradrenaline) that affect the brain, the ability to reason and function normally may be impaired. Because these chemicals remain active for hours or days after the event has passed, they continue to alter mental activity. This prolonged period is also referred to as a Red-Alert.

Re-Traumatization or Secondary Wounding: Psychologically reliving a traumatic event through exposure to environmental triggers and/or intrusive thoughts. Interactions with those who invade personal privacy or blame the victim for not overcoming feelings of guilt or anxiety are a common source of Secondary Wounding. Unintentional comments and innuendoes will often trigger intense emotional reactions resulting in complications or recovery setbacks.

Repressed Trauma: Distressing, traumatic experiences that occur early in life (usually within the first two years) that are normally beyond conscious recollection. These troubling emotions may result in decreased psychic energy and-less-than-optimal mental performance capacity.

Rule of Thumb: Precautionary maxim used in clinical traumatology cautioning trauma survivors *against* changing their employment, residence, marital status, or making any major financial transactions within one year following a traumatic experience without obtaining objective (professional) guidance.

Satisfied Patient Data: Information obtained from patients, generally using unscientifically sound questionnaires. The ratings given tend to be biased by patient's positive feelings toward the practitioner and are not a valid measure of the quality of the care given or its efficacy. Personal endorsements are not a scientifically acceptable means of determining the merits of any particular therapy or institution.

Secondary Gain: Using their status as "victims," some people will attempt to acquire attention, status, undeserved monetary compensation, or other benefits. Rather than accepting the responsibility needed on their part to work toward healing, these beneficiaries of secondary gain will prolong their "sickness" in order to increase the compensations. Excessive secondary gain behavior may be an indication of significant mental illness that existed prior to the injury/trauma.

Secondary Trauma Victim: Family members or loved ones who are emotionally tied to the trauma survivor are at greatest risk of becoming secondary trauma victims. As these individuals attempt to support and provide care for the survivor, they are so sensitive to their feelings, that they begin to experience the terror themselves.

Secondary Wounding: See "Re-Traumatization and Secondary Wounding" (above).

SEEDs: An acronym that stands for **S**pecific **E**arly **E**ducational **D**irections. The SEEDs approach provides rapid (within twenty-four to seventy-two hours), definitive, educational interventions to those suffering emotional wounds following a traumatic event. SEEDs differs from traditional crisis intervention and other "debriefing" practices because it is specific, is structured to meet individual needs, and provides continuity in the survivor's healing process until trauma-related issues are resolved. It also includes the family and/or others who are identified as caregivers for the victim.

Selective Hearing: The tendency to filter out portions of a conversation. The "hearing loss"is not physical, rather it is produced by mental filters. Commonly a survivor will selectively hear only those things that will bring comfort and reassurances—especially during the earliest stages of trauma aftermath recovery.

Shrinking Brain: See "Brain Atrophy" (above).

Sleep Deprivation: Sleep deprivation is a physical state reached following a period during which a person has been unable to sleep in a normal fashion. The disruptions in sleep are caused by such factors as insomnia, nightmares, startle responses, and psychological turmoil. The sleep-deprived person is generally lethargic, has slowed bodily functions, and a reduced state of consciousness. They may show a decreased sensitivity to external stimuli.

Sources of Support: In clinical traumatology there is a concept of a "three-legged stool" referring to three sources of support vital for optimal trauma recovery. These are emotional strengthening, education, and encouragement.

Stages of Recovery: Survival Honeymoon, Adjustment Shock, Recovery. (See Appendix 1, pp. 144–46.)

Structured Settlement: Monetary settlements are frequently made to survivors of trauma through insurance claims, worker's compensation, or awards from lawsuits. Rather than paying the total amount of the award in one lump sum, it is common to have a structured settlement, which means that the payments are made over time. This is actually a positive thing in many situations, especially when it involves a minor or there is a need to pay ongoing medical or other rehabilitation expenses. Because trauma survivors often experience difficulty in making decisions and are prone to spend large sums on items they would ordinarily not consider appropriate, a structured settlement may benefit them by reducing the risk of making unwise investments.

Sugarcoated Information: Medical or health care information that is incomplete, overly optimistic, vague, or nonspecific and creates unrealistic expectations about recovery potential.

Surveillance (Claimant): A process initiated by insurance company claims adjusters or worker's compensation officers when a survivor's recovery process is delayed beyond normal time frames for similar cases, or there is an indication that benefits are being obtained through fraud.

Survival Realities: The survival realities taught in clinical traumatology are (1) Life will never be the same. (2) Complete recovery is both a physical and an emotional process. (3) Early response to emotional wounds is as important as immediate attention (emergency care) is to physical injuries. (4) Just because a person looks fine or even says they are fine doesn't mean that they *are* fine. (5) No two people recover in the same way. (6) You cannot predict with any degree of certainty how long complete recovery will take.

Survivors-Turned-Thrivers: A description of the emotional "status" of those who successfully complete the clinical traumatology IRO-STEPS tutorials or other effective health care interventions. The common components of effective interventions include a high level of personal commitment to recovery, a substantial spiritual approach, and sustained supportive attention beginning in the early stages of recovery from injury and trauma.

Symptom Magnification Syndrome: When emotional wounds do not receive prompt and appropriate attention, the number of physical symptoms increase both in number and intensity until they become seriously limiting or debilitating.

Therapeutic: Having a beneficial or curative effect on diseases or disorders, either mental or physical.

Therapeutic Hug: An *appropriate, nonsexual*, physical demonstration of affection between a clinician and a patient.

Technical Procedures: In clinical traumatology this refers to medical procedures such as blood pressure monitoring, urinary or heart catheterization, X-rays and other imaging techniques, blood transfusions, and intravenous therapies.

Thriving after Surviving: The name of a self-help handbook authored by Barry M. Richards that briefly explains to survivors how to overcome the devastating emotional wounds caused by accident, injury, or other horrifying events. See also "Survivors-Turned-Thrivers" (above).

Transference: An unconscious shift of emotions, particularly those from childhood, from one person to another. For example, it is not uncommon for patients to shift feelings they had for a parent to a therapist, traumatologist, nurse, physician, etc.

Traumatic Incident Reduction (TIR): A controversial short-term crisis intervention technique used by various professionals to aid in the immediate reduction of post-injury stress symptoms/side effects.

Trauma Severity SPEED Scoring Scale: A simple evaluation device used immediately following a traumatic incident to determine a survivor's risk of developing significant emotional problems and their need for a clinical assessment and/or the provision of the IRO-STEPS educational tutorials. (See Appendix 1, pp. 134–42.)

Trauma Team: A multidisciplinary, hospital-based group of health care professionals specially trained and qualified in managing virtually all aspects of traumatic injuries.

Vital Signs: A set of physical measurements that are routinely made on injured or ill patients to determine their health and/or changes in well-being. Typically the most basic three measures taken are blood pressure, pulse rate, and respiratory rate. Additional vital sign measures can be assessed depending on the technical sophistication of the setting and the needs of patient.

"Wait Until It Breaks To Fix It" Mentality: Delaying the response to emotional wounds until pronounced symptoms become apparent. The common problems that finally *demand* attention include prolonged inability to heal from physical injuries, behavioral disturbances, work absenteeism, deteriorating relationships, chronic medical problems, and psychological turmoil.

Wound and Injury Recovery Center (WIRC/America): Center located in Salt Lake City, Utah, where the majority of the pioneering work by Barry M. Richards on the clinical traumatology IRO-STEPS program was developed. Notable accomplishments include the IRO-STEPS Tutorials, the clinical traumatology Assessment Procedure, the Trauma Severity SPEED Scoring Scale, and the published handbook *Thriving After Surviving*.

"You Matter Most" Principle: A critically important attitude embraced by those who are successful in assisting in the recovery of a trauma survivor. This attitude should be apparent to the survivor in their interactions with family, friends, clinicians of all disciplines, and others who are engaged in supporting the recovery process.

Index

Biographical Sketches
Ross and Susan Woolley

Since completing his Ph.D. at Brigham Young University, Ross has spent over twenty years working and teaching in the fields of public health and preventive medicine. As a Professor and Division Chair in the Department of Family and Preventive Medicine at the University of Utah School of Medicine and as a Department Chair and Interim Dean of the School of Public Health at the University of Hawaii, he labored to expand the horizons of public health. He is known as an outstanding teacher and mentor and has achieved an exceptional record of scientific research encompassing a broad area of health-related topics. His research projects have included one of the largest comprehensive cancer screening studies undertaken in the United States; development of primary health care programs for rural populations in the western U.S., West Africa, and numerous islands in the Pacific; studies of infant mortality among different socio-economic groups; and several studies dealing with health care among Native Americans.

For many years he served with the Council on Education for Public Health (CEPH), the accrediting body for schools of public health and for graduate programs in public health in the U.S. He served as president of the Utah Public Health Association and was chairman of the Special Interest Group on Bio-ethics and member of the Governing Council of the American Public Health Association. In addition to his academic positions, Ross also served as a Special Officer with the University of Utah Police Department and received two special commendations from the Utah Chiefs of Police for developing strategic plans for law enforcement in the State of Utah.

Prior to *Sudden Trauma*, Ross co-authored numerous medical and nursing texts. He was the principle author of *Problem-Oriented Nursing* which was translated into three languages and used as a resource around the world. His scientific writing includes forty-five peer-reviewed articles that have appeared in major scientific journals. He has been an invited speaker at over fifty national scientific conferences and a visiting professor at universities in Scotland and Australia.

Ross is currently an in-house epidemiology consultant on evaluation and surveillance for the Utah Department of Health and continues to maintain a small consulting practice.

Susan has spent over thirty years in the field of perinatal (obstetrical and newborn) care as a registered nurse and a nursing director. At five hospitals she has served as the Director/Manager of Maternal and Child Health, Labor and Delivery, or the Director of Perinatal Services. In addition to her management roles, she has also been a Clinical Nurse Specialist, Nurse Researcher, and Clinical Educator.

Her clinical as well as management skills are highly regarded by nursing and physician groups at the regional and national level. She has served as a consulting instructor of fetal monitoring for Hewlett Packard Corporation, has been an advisor to several law firms, and has served as an expert witness on issues related to standards of care in malpractice litigations. Her certifications include NCC-Inpatient Obstetrical Nursing, Basic and Advanced Fetal Monitoring, Basic Life Support-Provider, Advanced Cardiac Life Support, and Newborn Resuscitation.

Susan has served as a clinical faculty member for several university nursing programs where she provided supervision and hands-on training of nursing students in the hospital setting. She has developed and participated in numerous management workshops and training seminars including completion of the *Interaction Management* certification program and the *Managing Differences and Leader Training Course*.

The opportunity to work with new families and to share the thrill of the birth experience is both a privilege and a responsibility that Susan takes very seriously. At the present time, she is serving as the Director of Perinatal Services for the Encino-Tarzana Regional Medical Center in Tarzana, California.

While functioning as Charge Nurse at Alta View Women's Center in Sandy, Utah, in September of 1991, Susan was witness to the murder of her colleague and was taken hostage by a crazed gunman for over eighteen hours. Some details of her experience are recounted in the Preface.

Since this devastating experience, both Susan and Ross have devoted much time and effort to studying the emotional effects of traumatic experiences. They have both presented numerous lectures and workshops on Post-Traumatic Stress Disorder, considering both its medical and psychological aspects. Prior to contributing their expertise to *Sudden Trauma*, the Woolleys developed educational materials for health care providers to increase awareness of the consequences of inappropriately managed emotional wounds.

Susan and Ross consider their greatest accomplishments to be their marriage of over thirty-six years and being parents to five children and grandparents to seven. Of their five children, four are in health care professions (two are nurses and two are medical students); the other is a computer information systems specialist. When discussing the advantages and disadvantages of a career in nursing with a determined daughter, Susan was challenged to "Just tell me that you haven't enjoyed it." This is an admission she could never make.

Darla Isackson

Darla Isackson brings a unique perspective to *Sudden Trauma*. She has collaborated in this project, contributing both professional talents as writer and editor and personal experience with the emotional wounds of trauma.

She graduated as a valedictorian from Utah State University. Soon after her marriage she lived in Spain, then Algeria, and began writing professionally. Her writing abilities were recognized quickly; she began publishing in the late 1960s and has an impressive list of credits. While raising five sons, she continued her work, writing for church and family magazines and coauthoring a book, *To Parents, with Love*, and a newspaper column, *Parent Patter*, with her sister, Arlene Bascom. The unique contribution of *To Parents, with Love* was evidenced by eleven years of sales by select booksellers throughout the country. The success of her book and wide appeal of her columns led to many speaking engagements, including Brigham Young University's Continuing Education lecture circuit.

Beginning in 1984, Darla gained firsthand knowledge of the effects of trauma. Without the right help at the right time in the emotional aftermath of a serious accident, problems of a lifetime mushroomed and her twenty-two-year marriage ended.

In the years between the accident and the divorce, Darla attempted to reach out to other women who had challenges. She became the Managing Editor of *Latter-day Woman* magazine, which she co-founded and to which she contributed original articles and poetry. The magazine focused on helping women overcome discouragement and cope more effectively with the trials, pressures, and demands of today's fast-paced life. She also co-founded an organization called Coping Network which provided resource referrals and support groups for women suffering emotional pain.

Darla also gave inspirational lectures, workshops, and seminars. Covenant Communications produced six of her inspirational talks. Two of the titles reflect her personal struggles: *How to Slay Your Dragons of Discouragement* and *Stress and Depression*.

After her divorce Darla began a five-year stint as Managing Editor for Covenant Communications, a company specializing in religious and motivational products. She pioneered their successful book division, bringing in titles such as *Grieving, the Pain and the Promise*, by Deanna Edwards.

In 1989 the well-known name "Darla Hanks" changed to "Darla Isackson" when she married Douglas L. Isackson. Doug's two sons contributed spice to their newly blended family of seven young men!

In 1993 Darla joined Aspen Books and Gold Leaf Press and was Aspen's Managing Editor for three years. Her work continued to give her more insight into the problems faced by victims of trauma. Working on many books such as *The Burning Within*, Rannelle Wallace's story of the aftermath of a fiery plane crash, and *Nobody Don't Love Nobody*, describing the plight of homeless children, gave Darla a graduate course in the problems and needs of trauma survivors. She made the decision to coauthor *Sudden Trauma* after her discovery that clinical traumatology masterfully addressed those problems and needs. She was thrilled to learn that there were solutions—that a process had been developed for healing the emotional wounds that she had suffered and become acutely aware of.

Darla's most recent publication is entitled *To Be a Mother, the Agonies and the Ecstasies*, which she coauthored with Emma Lou Thayne—a prolific and high-profile writer and poet. Darla's contribution to the booklet chronicles her experiences of raising children to adulthood and the spiritual support that helped her keep her balance.

Darla has worked out of her home for the past few years as a freelance editor, allowing her to care for her elderly mother, who passed away as this book was going to press.

The two hundred-plus books she has guided from manuscript to bookstore shelves are evidence of her energy and productivity. Her drive comes primarily from a passionate belief in the power of the written word to inspire and change lives for the better.

Barry M. Richards, Clinical Traumatologist

Sudden Trauma! When Life Will Never Be the Same Again. . . Revolutionary Principles for Healing Emotional Wounds . . . Featuring Real-Life Accounts of Trauma Recovery from the files of Pioneer Clinical Traumatologist Barry M. Richards. The title page of this book appropriately describes both the man and his work. His formal and informal training and experience have come together in the development of the IRO-STEPS strategy of clinical traumatology which is revolutionizing the attention being given to the emotional wounds of the survivors of trauma and other horrifying events.

Richards's understanding of trauma and its aftermath includes not only his graduate school expertise and nearly encyclopedic knowledge of the relevant trauma literature, but also a wealth of practical experience gained from observing and attending to the needs of thousands of trauma survivors in a variety of settings.

Richards is a decorated Vietnam veteran, where he was injured while serving in the United States Marine Corps. He has also been a police officer in California and an Emergency Medical Technician in Salt Lake City.

His master's degree from Arizona State University qualified him to practice medical social work. This first step toward fulfilling his career aspirations was followed by his membership on the pioneering Trauma Team of the LDS Hospital in Salt Lake City. This hospital is home to one of only two Level I shock trauma units in the vast Intermountain area, caring for the most severely injured patients. There he immediately began to identify the need for early and diligent attention to the emotional wounds always present with trauma. It was in this setting that Richards conceived of the foundation principles of his specific approach—clinical traumatology. These principles have since proven to be of incomparable value to survivors of traumatic injury and horrifying experiences.

As he began to consistently and precisely address the patients' nonphysical recovery needs, superior outcomes became readily apparent. This success led to opportunities for him to speak at numerous conferences and also to conduct training seminars at hospitals around the country. Of greater significance for the thousands whose lives have since benefitted from Richards's expertise as a clinical traumatologist, were the insights he gained about the long-term consequences of neglected emotional wounds. The revolutionary techniques he developed were aimed at staving off the downward spiral seen in trauma survivors whose emotional turmoil did not receive prompt, appropriate attention. Prior to the introduction of Richards's innovative strategies, patients' emotional wounds were generally neglected. Typically they were addressed only when a myriad of problems mushroomed to disrupt overall recovery. Richards's approach is proactive and preventive. It dramatically reduces the need for psychiatric treatment of neglected emotional wounds that frequently escalate into complicated psychological problems.

Recognizing the unmet needs and expectations of trauma survivors and those who care for them following a hospital discharge, Richards left LDS Hospital. He established an outpatient facility known as the After Trauma Adjustment Center, closely interacting with three physiatrists (physician-specialists in rehabilitation medicine) and a physical therapist. In this setting, he refined the educational strategies that enable survivors to become thrivers. Subsequently, Richards founded the National Institute for the Prevention of Post-Traumatic Stress Disorder, later renamed the

Wound and Injury Recovery Centers of America (WIRC/America).

The key to Richards's success has been his steadfast devotion to principle. The values-laden educational tutorials (the foundation of his copyrighted Injury Recovery Orientation-STEPS© strategy) provide guidance, but ultimately hold individuals accountable for their own success. Using their own God-given talents to expand their thinking, survivors are enabled to thrive. They become thrivers because they are taught the principles necessary to regain the control over their lives that they temporarily lost as a result of traumatic events. The strong bonds of trust needed to apply the principles correctly are built between survivors and clinician. However, dependency, common to many therapeutic techniques is minimal. The need for love and nurturing by family and close friends is emphasized in most of the educational tutorials. Richards's "Prescriptions for Healing" mirror his own lifestyle and his deeply held spiritual belief system.

Richards's credits include past membership on the Presidential Task Force of the International Society of Stress Studies, and faculty membership with the International Worker's Compensation College. His publications, especially the book *Thriving After Surviving: How to Overcome the Devastating Emotional Wounds Caused by Accidental Injuries* have helped thousands in their progress toward successful recovery.

Currently, Richards applies his Clinical Traumatology expertise both in a private practice and as a part-time LCSW Child Protective Service Investigator for the Utah Department of Human Services. He and his wife are the parents of four children and they reside in Salt Lake City, Utah, near the WIRC/America Office.

Quotes Validating the Need for Clinical Traumatology

"The earlier a person (a trauma survivor) receives information about Post Traumatic Stress (PTS) the more stabilizing it will be. When you explain the dynamics of PTS it is very relieving to the person who is suffering. It gives them an intellectual hook to hang on; because they can begin to understand what they are going through… It is very helpful and beneficial."

John P. Wilson, Ph.D., American Red Cross

"The United States is missing opportunities for a healthier population by not putting more emphasis on *preventive* care."

Jocelyn Elders, Former U.S. Surgeon General

"A system that provides only for disease, and that fails to *prevent* it, does not deserve to be called a "health care" system. Only by restructuring how health care is delivered can we … have a system that really provides health care rather than just disease treatment."

Utah Nurses Association

"No public official should be allowed to get away with a proposal that does not first address the problems of waste, greed, and fraud. Nor should they be permitted to bypass the issue of prevention, an area of health care that is too often neglected and where more is always better. Simply put, health care is not health, and no health care … proposal will—or should succeed if it does not encourage and reward *prevention*."

C. Everett Koop, M.D., Former U.S. Surgeon General

"Prevention of ALL work related hazards to safety and HEALTH is the goal of its ergonomics directives."

OSHA Bulletin 3123, 1990

"It has been our experience that the real culprit [for rehabilitation failure] is time. If rehabilitation is [begun] early, the patient usually does well. "

R Adams Cowley, Father of Shock-Trauma Medicine

"Ecclesiastes stresses the fact that for everything there is a season; a time for every purpose and for every work; a time to keep silent and a time to speak. We are convinced that the time has come to speak and to work for the rights of the victim, with the aim of mobilizing public opinion in benefit of this excessively neglected subject."

Israel Drapkin, Emil Viano, *Victimology: A New Focus*

"Why would any physician who took the Oath of Hippocrates to 'first do no harm' withhold important medical information from his patient or the patient of another physician, especially when withholding that information can harm the patient? One of the principal reasons appears to be fear, especially fear of litigation. Fear drives irrational behavior and can cause some physicians and administrators, among others, to become confused about their duty to the patient."

> Norwood Hill, M.D., Physician Scientist, House Sub
> Comm. Hearing, May, 1991

"Crime and victimization, generally considered major problems in metropolitan areas, are most frequently addressed by law enforcement officers, court officials, sociologists and criminologists. However, we believe that another professional group—nurses and physicians and mental health clinicians have an important role to assume with this problem, specifically in helping to reduce the trauma experienced after a crime."

> A. Burgess, Dr. of Nursing Science

"I have previously observed the importance of "immediacy" (SPICE Model) in responding to the needs of the workplace disabled patient. Now there is the STEPS strategy. Its application is clearly apparent to all sorts of workplace injury, but vitally more important when there is major traumatic upheaval.

"The STEPS strategy [fully explained in *Sudden Trauma*] is simple and concise. It is positive, stimulating and proactive. It responds sensitively to many very important expectations about the nonphysical side of healing—without the stigma of 'psychological problems.'

"When the STEPS strategy is implemented early, patients get crucial perspectives that will enable them to be actively involved in their overall healing process. Passive dependence on treatment and prolonged disability will thus be minimized. With understanding and clear directions about future functioning, optimal health and wellness can be achieved sooner than later—and at much less cost and consequence. Whenever and wherever STEPS can be implemented, it should be."

> Alan Colledge, M.D., ACOEM, Occupational
> Medical Advisor, Utah State Industrial Commission

"Clearly a paradigm shift is required ... that traumatology constitutes a veritable scientific field ... The public is clearly ready to accept the field of traumatology, for trauma is increasingly recognized as ubiquitous in our every day world. The potential contribution of traumatology to good critical thinking ... is incalculable."

> Denis M. Donovan, M.D., *Journal of Traumatic Stress Studies*, Vol. 4, No. 3, 1991